ABOUT THE COVER

Cover design often incorporates specific geometric shapes. In this particular instance, a circle was chosen. Colonel Randall found that many of his earlier life experiences had a way of completing themselves in later life. Full-circle if you will. Thus, we have utilized the Enso Circle, a symbol of deep meaning—strength, determination, focus, and harmony. A fitting motif.

Legacy of Valor

Colonel James E. P. Randall
An American Patriot

Legacy of Valor

Colonel James E. P. Randall
An American Patriot

Kathleen F. Esmiol

East of the Mountains and West of the Sun™

RHYOLITE PRESS LLC
Colorado Springs, Colorado

Copyright © 2025 Kathleen F. Esmiol

All Rights Reserved. No portion of this book may be reproduced in any form or by any electronic or mechanical means, including information storage and retrieval systems, without permission from the publisher, except by a reviewer who may quote brief passages in a review.

Published in the United States of America by Rhyolite Press, LLC
P.O. Box 60144
Colorado Springs, Colorado 80960
www.rhyolitepress.com

Esmiol, Kathleen F.

Legacy of Valor

Colonel James E.P. Randall—An American Patriot

August 1, 2025

ISBN: 978-1-943829-73-6

Library of Congress Control Number: 2025915278

Publisher's Cataloging-in-Publication Data

Names: Esmiol, Kathleen F., Author.

Title: Legacy of Valor : Colonel James E. P. Randall, An American Patriot / Kathleen F. Esmiol.

Description: Colorado Springs, CO; Rhyolite Press, LLC, 2025.

Identifiers: LCCN: 2025915278 | ISBN: 978-1-943829-73-6
Subjects: LCSH Randall, James E. P. | United States. Air Force--Biography. | Air pilots--Biography. | Fighter pilots--United States--Biography. | African-Americans--Biography. | BISAC BIOGRAPHY & AUTOBIOGRAPHY / Military | BIOGRAPHY & AUTOBIOGRAPHY / Aviation & Nautical | BIOGRAPHY & AUTOBIOGRAPHY / African American & Black
Classification: LCC UG633 .R36 E76 2025 | DDC 926.2913--dc23

Book design and layout: Suzanne Schorsch. Cover design: Don Kallaus.
All photographs are from the Randall family collection unless otherwise noted.

for Essie

CONTENTS

Pre-Flight Briefing: A Prologue i

1. All in Due Time 1
2. Wheels Before Wings 7
3. A Big Surprise in a Small Package 11
4. A Few Broken Arms 17
5. How the Other Half Lives 21
6. Decisions and Consequences 25
7. Nothing But the Truth 31
8. Living Life to the Fullest 35
9. Reversing Roles 39
10. The Sound of Silence 43
11. Picking Up the Pieces 47
12. Starting Anew 53
13. Whirlwind 57
14. Riding the Rails to Flight School 61
15. Wings and a Wedding 67
16. Logistics 71
17. International Students in the Deep South 77
18. From Combat in Korea to Diapers in Dover 81
19. Icarus 89
20. The Pull of Gravity 97
21. A New Start in the West 105
22. Life in Post-World War II Europe 109
23. Showdown in South Carolina 123
24. On a Wing and a Prayer 133
25. Encore at Nellis 151
26. Return to Thailand 169
27. The Librarian 175
28. Crossroads At Nakhon Phanom 183
29. Honoring a Leap of Faith 189

30. Taking Command	199
31. Piecing Together the Puzzle	207
32. The Rest of the Story	215
33. The Colors of Patriotism	221
34. Righteous Resolutions	233
De-Briefing: An Epilogue	*239*
Notes	*243*
About the Author	*265*

PRE-FLIGHT BRIEFING: A PROLOGUE

Who could imagine that the privilege of a lifetime would begin with an innocent phone call and the request of a favor? That is how it unfolded, though, when Candice McKnight, president of the African American Historical and Genealogical Society of Colorado Springs, contacted me late one afternoon. She asked if I would help a young artist named Charles Harrington find a new direction in his career. A few days later Charles sat in my living room and answered questions about the dramatic samples of art in his portfolio. He trended toward a young audience, so I suggested he appeal to the older generation, too. It might be gratifying and perhaps even lucrative.

Charles was the caretaker for his elderly father, Alvin Harrington, and the artist was a devoted son who was proud of his dad's 24 years of military service, so a project focused on painting individual portraits of Tuskegee Airmen seemed the perfect fit. The city was fortunate to have quite a few of the remarkable World War II veterans in our midst. Intrigued by the idea, Charles decided to pursue that goal.

The project was well underway when Charles and I headed out to the windy plains east of the city to visit his next subject, Colonel (ret.) James "Jim" Randall. As we reached the Randalls' lovely home, the smiling couple greeted us warmly and seated us at a kitchen table where Jim had placed an open box of photos. Charles slowly reviewed each historic picture that documented Jim's awesome career. He studied Jim with an artist's eye, considering how to portray his subject. Meanwhile I engaged the 91-year-old fighter pilot in conversation about some of his experiences.

By the end of the visit, Jim handed Charles a photo he had requested, and we left feeling fortunate to have met such a remarkable man. Charles was inspired. I was amazed. During our visit, I learned that Jim was assigned to Nellis AFB as an F-111 test pilot and Base Operations Officer the same years that my former husband Doyle Ruff was Right Wing of the Thunderbirds, the USAF aerobatic team. I was on the Nellis AFB flight line with our three young children—Rebecca, Eric, and Ramelle—every time the team took off to perform a show and each time they returned. It was stunning to think that Jim and I were probably out on that flight line together more than once. Yet, we never met.

In ensuing visits, Jim and I reflected on the dramatic events we experienced at Nellis, the exhilaration of the star-spangled high points and the ebony-edged despair over the losses. Jim empathized with my painful recollections of Jack Thurman, a bachelor who was thrilled to be a Thunderbird…only to be killed on a solo training flight in 1969. Then Jerry Bolt and Joe Howard, both proud young fathers of baby boys, were lost in 1972. It was heartbreaking. Jim commiserated. As an F-111 test pilot, he provided vital information to General Dynamics about their aircraft's performance. His commander often asked for his analysis of an accident, so Jim had sometimes stood on crash sites where a friend had died…sacred soil.

Things were progressing as planned with the Tuskegee Airmen portrait project until Charles' father became so ill that he was unable to complete Jim's portrait. Jim was understanding, but I knew it was a disappointment so I offered an alternative. With Jim's permission, I took his historic photos to the Pikes Peak Library District's Special Collections so that his photos could be digitized for the public. Returning the original photos to Jim, I anticipated that I might not see the Randalls again so I thanked both Jim and his wife Essie for welcoming Charles and me into their lives. As I turned to leave, Jim asked me to stay a moment longer. He pointed out that I had asked him a lot questions, and now he had a big one for me. Would I write his biography? I was surprised but truly honored.

James Randall was a patriot, and I fully understood what a patriot was. In my father's family—the E.E. Huffords—there were six brothers and one sister. They lived on a verdant Indiana farm that benefited from the alluvial soil of the Ohio River near a village named Patriot. Five of the brothers—Ray, Gayle, Fletcher, Griffith, and my father Mike, fought in World War I. In 1941, after the heinous attack on Pearl Harbor—where the youngest brother Johnny was stationed—all the brothers, except Ray, were reactivated and scattered across the warring world once again.

Although humbled by the prospect of penning a biography about an American patriot who had served in three wars, I agreed to Jim's request. Having experienced military life as a child as well as a wife and mother myself, I embraced the chance to write a fighter pilot's story and add insights about the unspoken challenges military members and their families face. Flying, like life itself, presents both roadblocks and rewards that precipitate the gamut of emotions, sometimes all in one flight.

Since I was project manager for the creation of a sculpture to be placed in the heart of the city honoring historic local businesswoman Fannie Mae Duncan, time was of the essence. Taping weekly interviews with Jim seemed the best way to lay the groundwork for writing his story. It worked. Jim was excited and committed to helping me establish an accurate timeline, but he soon became frustrated by what he considered a lot of extraneous questions. He felt his answers were explicit and we were wasting time on minutiae. "Why do you need to know that?" he asked.

"Descriptions will help readers envision your dramatic experiences. If we don't describe situations vividly, only pilots will read your book," I said, "and they all have their own stories to tell." He pondered the concept until I added, "You want to motivate youngsters with your story, right?" Remembering his own lust for flight as a boy, Jim instantly viewed our conversations with a new perspective. As a fighter pilot, he was razor-focused on miniscule details to fulfill a mission, but writing a book about his life was an alien experience. Nonetheless, he was a team player as well as a tease, so he responded to my first question in our next Tuesday afternoon interview with, "It was a beautiful day. The sky was blue. Not a cloud in sight." We both had a good laugh and then got down to business.

From that point on, when I asked Jim to be more descriptive, he would fold his hands and begin with an explanation of the weather and the appearance of the sky, two elements of utmost importance to a pilot. It was a standing joke between us.

James Randall had a wry sense of humor, and he loved catching me off guard when I was trying to connect all the dots of his complex life.

As autumn's spectacular golden palette faded to winter white, Jim's health began failing rapidly. Concerned, I blocked out his book into chapters. Knowing which ones would mean the most to him, I worked to capture those powerful moments in his life. Late one Tuesday afternoon I arrived without my tape recorder or voluminous book of scribbled notes and maps. As we sat down at his dining room table, I pulled out a sheaf of papers from my tote bag and said, "I have a surprise for you today. I have finished writing a chapter for your book, and I am going to read it to you."

Delighted, Jim leaned back in his chair, closed his eyes and listened intently. When I reached the harrowing climax of the story, he nodded his head slightly. He had re-lived every moment. He knew his story would be told with sensitivity and dignity.

A year later, the bronze sculpture of Fannie Mae Duncan was gleaming in front of the Pikes Peak Center, and the large granite tablet with her story etched in stone was standing tall. I had hoped that both Essie and Jim would join the celebration, but it was not to be. Jim was so ill that he had entered the Veterans' Center at Fitzsimons in Denver. Essie arrived, though, and she was wearing the biggest smile in the crowd.

Visiting Jim in Denver was a poignant time, reminiscent of when my dad Mike Hufford lay dying in a veterans' hospital in Florida while my former husband Doyle Ruff was a

27-year-old fighter pilot flying A1-E Skyraiders out of Bien Hoa Air Base in Vietnam… the very same year that Jim nearly lost his life during a combat flight over North Vietnam. Conflicting memories and emotions flooded my mind as Essie Randall and I sat on black granite donor walls and watched a huge crowd of people admire a beautiful new sculpture. Within weeks, Colonel James Randall was gone.

Enlightenment, like light itself, falls in a spectrum as we move along the arc of life, and it often reveals pathways we might have otherwise overlooked. Jim Randall and I missed crossing paths at Nellis AFB, but we seemed destined to meet. I am thankful that I eventually found my way to the Randalls' door. It is an honor to preserve the story of a true patriot so that future generations can learn exactly what that means. Colonel James E.P. Randall was an American patriot.

Humility must always be the portion of any man who receives acclaim earned in the blood of his followers and the sacrifices of his friends.

– Dwight David Eisenhower

Essie Randall and Kathleen Esmiol reflect on Colonel Randall's illustrious career following the dedication of the newly installed sculpture of Fannie Mae Duncan in front of the Pikes Peak Center for the Performing Arts in the heart of downtown Colorado Springs.

Samuel Edward Randall standing in front of his home at 126 Rutherford Avenue NW in the Gainsboro neighborhood of Roanoke, Virginia.

CHAPTER 1

ALL IN DUE TIME

Ora Evangeline Flood worked as a teacher in the Gainsboro neighborhood of Roanoke, Virginia, in the 1920s. She was an intelligent young woman—tall, lithe, and reasonably attractive—but she was approaching her 27th birthday and still unmarried. A "maiden lady," some people called her circumstances while others were far less tactful. Ora had met someone, though, and her more socially adroit friends were encouraging the couple.

Samuel Edward Randall, a strong and capable but somewhat reserved man, was 17 years older than Ora and totally focused on his hazardous job at Norfolk & Western Railroad's Machine Workshop in Roanoke. He was in charge of repairing and cleaning the company's huge iron behemoths. As a long-time employee, Sam was accustomed to spending the day in the midst of chemicals sprayed through the air, and being covered with grease and cleansing agents. He was inured to the ear-splitting noise in the machine shop that minimized the ability to convey anything more than an occasional comment or the necessity to give directions to the all-male crew. As a result, he was not adept at having polite conversations with an attractive young woman. Still, he was beginning to realize that the chance at family life was passing him by, and Ora, though much younger than he, was organized and independent—qualities Sam fully appreciated.

Although Sam was a man of few words, one of his redeeming graces was that as soon as he left the machine shop, he hurried home; showered off the greasy traces of a day's work; meticulously scrubbed his hands and fingernails; and donned a clean shirt and tie before dinner. It had become his daily ritual, and once he was presentable, he cut a handsome figure. Sam was fearless at work even though injuries for railway workers were seldom minor, but approaching the confident young Ora about marriage terrified him. After weeks of practicing before a mirror, he somehow managed to stumble through a proposal and much to his relief Ora accepted. In May 1925, Ora became Mrs. Samuel Randall. Little did Sam and Ora realize when they welcomed their first child, James Edward Preston

Randall, on November 30, 1926, that little Edward would eventually become a figure in American history. They were just grateful to have a healthy baby.

Sam Randall and Ora Flood enjoying a Sunday afternoon with friends after attending services at the St. Paul's United Methodist Church in Gainsboro. Romance is in the air, and friends are encouraging it as Sam finally summons the courage to ask Ora for her hand in marriage.

Although Ora always referred to Sam as "Mr. Randall" out of respect, she began to understand and appreciate him as a person. His biological mother Anna was only nineteen years old when Sam, her third child, was born, but she died a few years later, and so Sam's father, James Daniel Randall, married Julia, a widow. Losing his mother Anna when he was only a few years old was traumatic for the youngster. Suddenly he had not only his own brother and sister—Charles and Lily—but he also gained Julia's brood as siblings—John, Lucian, and Addie. Sam finally adjusted to being one of six children, but he also became more subdued and faded into the background of the active family. His stepmother Julia was well aware of the change in him, but she had her hands full. Once Ora became a new mother herself, she could empathize with the losses Sam experienced as a child and it made a difference in their relationship.

Having a son of his own gave Sam great satisfaction and even more purpose in life. Edward became Sam's shadow and tried to imitate his father in every way, including the little boy's penchant for wearing a shirt and tie. The youngster's admiration and love for his father slowly healed the empty spaces in Sam. The Randalls proudly maintained their home at 126 Rutherford Avenue NW and even though it was a rambling, two-story edifice, young Edward seemed to fill it with his exuberant curiosity and imaginative adventures. Being older parents compared to many of their neighbors, Sam and Ora were set in their ways. He continued to work endless hours at Norfolk & Western's Roanoke Machine Shop, and she returned to her job as a teacher.

**Left: James Daniel Randall and Anna Chandler Randall, Sam's mother and father.
Right: After Anna's death, James marries Julia, Sam's stepmother who is pictured in her later years. The Randall family nearly doubled overnight.**

Fortunately, Ora's mother Martha Flood lived nearby on the corner of Rutherford Avenue and Third Street. Since she was within walking distance, she was readily available to take care of young Edward while Ora was at school. In fact, she was delighted to help out the family whenever they asked. Soon Edward had almost as many of his toys nestled in the nooks and crannies of Grandma Flood's house as he did at home.

Ora's mother and father, Martha Ellen Johnson Flood and Pleasant Preston Flood

By the late 1920s, the Randalls were pillars of the community. They contributed to Gainsboro's reputation for being a wonderful neighborhood where Black families were self-sufficient and able to live without being dependent on downtown Roanoke where they were not welcome after 6 p.m. In Gainsboro the residents were physicians, small business owners, dentists, educators, and medical personnel as well as grocers, entertainers, laborers, repairmen, and railway workers. There was always someone available, competent, and willing to accommodate every need.

Norfolk & Western Railroad was positioned in the heart of the community, and it was one of the major railway systems in America at the time. Travelers, from cities up and down the Atlantic coast and beyond, could disembark and within minutes head up the hill to the illustrious Hotel Roanoke for accommodations. In addition to maintaining a bustling commerce and providing for the education of its citizens, Gainsboro also took pride in its cultural center. St. Andrew's Catholic Church, completed in 1902, offered spiritual support; the Gainsboro Library stimulated intellectual development; and two local theatres provided entertainment.

When famous Black artists such as Louis Armstrong, Count Basie, Lena Horne, Dizzy Gillespie, Ella Fitzgerald, Duke Ellington and Cab Callaway came to town to perform at the Hotel Roanoke, they were welcome as performers but not overnight guests. On the other hand, the Hotel Dumas in Gainsboro was delighted to treat such dignitaries with the respect they deserved. As a result, local residents were sometimes treated to an impromptu night of jazz, and they hobnobbed with the finest Black musicians of the day. Other than the fact that medical facilities needed to be expanded for the increasing population, residents lived almost completely independent of the rest of Roanoke. Still, the indignity of segregation was undeniable, and the Norfolk & Western Railroad tracks represented the line of demarcation between Blacks and Whites.

In spite of roadblocks to progress, Gainsboro's thriving community was a tribute to its industrious residents. Many of the adults were the grandchildren of slaves, and they took pride in what they were achieving rather than dwelling on the injustices of the past, but they did not forget the stories that had been passed down to them. Ora, like many of her friends and colleagues, was well aware of her roots.

Ora's maternal grandmother, Madora, was born in 1845 on the Thaxton plantation which was only about 20 miles northeast of Roanoke. Madora's mother Pauline was the Black housemaid in servitude to the Thaxton family. The original wording on Madora's birth certificate—Madora Thaxton—led to speculation about her mixed parentage especially when, according to records, she was later adopted by Wesley and Pauline Campbell and was always listed as Mulatto in future census records. When Madora grew up and married Pleasant Flood, her new last name clouded old issues. Then Madora's son Pleasant Preston Flood married Martha Ellen Johnson, and they became Ora's parents. After several generations, the Thaxton name was buried in Madora's records, but Ora saved the information in her heart. Like other Black families striving for success in Roanoke's Gainsboro neighborhood, Ora tucked away the family secrets, but the truth lay waiting to be exposed…some day.

Ora's maternal grandmother, Madora Thaxton Campbell

Meanwhile, Sam and Ora fell into a rhythm and worked as a team pursuing their careers while planning for young Edward's future. With the neon lights of the Ebony Club beckoning patrons downtown at night; the steeples of the magnificent Saint Andrew's Catholic Church marking its location for parishioners on Sundays; and paperboys tossing the latest news on front porches as the dew settled on lawns early each morning, both Sam and Ora stayed focused on their dreams. Proud of what they were accomplishing, they hoped for even more opportunities for their son. Consequently, Edward, like many of his peers, lived unaware of segregation's slights….until he grew older.

For Edward, the biggest disruption in his life at that point was the arrival of his sister Martha on February 4th in 1928. Suddenly he had to be much more creative to gain the attention of his parents.

Young James Edward Preston Randall becomes a big brother to Martha Evangeline who is always happy and smiling and innocently stealing the spotlight.

CHAPTER 2

WHEELS BEFORE WINGS

Bright warm rays of sunlight penetrated the curtains in young James Edward Preston Randall's bedroom, and his big brown eyes popped open with excitement as he threw off the covers. Jumping out of bed, he ran to the window. Rutherford Avenue was still quiet in Roanoke, Virginia, but he had big plans for the day. As the enticing aroma of bacon and eggs traced its way upstairs, Edward hurried to put on his shirt and shorts. He was on a mission.

It was a lazy summer Saturday and Edward's father was home for the weekend. Five days a week Sam spent endless hours at Norfolk & Western Railroad repairing, restoring, and rebuilding the massive engines of the trains that kept America on the move. Monday through Friday Edward's middle-aged father often left before his young son awakened, and usually he returned home too late for the youngster to tell him about the discoveries of the day. But Saturday was different. On Saturday Edward had his father's undivided attention, and today he intended to make the most of it.

Bounding down the steps, he hurried into the kitchen, and tugged on his mother's checkered apron to steal a quick hug before taking his place at the table beside his father. Edward's baby sister Martha was already seated in her high chair, but she reached out her chubby arms and kicked her feet up and down at the sight of her brother, so he stopped for a minute to tickle her toes and make her laugh. Edward was only 1½ years older than Martha, but he was officially a big brother. Father made it clear that was an important responsibility, and Edward took it seriously.

Once his mother Ora served the plates and was seated, Edward awaited with curiosity to learn the words of wisdom for the day. Sam picked up the family Bible that always lay on the oilcloth beside his knife and spoon. Opening the cherished book, he thumbed through the delicate pages until he found one of his favorite passages. He began reading. Edward didn't always understand the meaning of the strange sounding language, but he loved listening to his father's deep baritone voice.

When Sam closed the leather-bound Bible, Edward and Ora bowed their heads on cue as Sam began the family blessing. Edward knew part of it by heart, but he was keeping that a secret for now. Sneaking a peek at his assembled family, the young boy felt gratitude that everyone was together once again. During the week Edward and his little sister were shuttled off to their Grandma Flood's house while Ora and Sam were at work. The children actually spent more time with their grandmother than their parents. But today was Saturday!

Eating quickly, Edward squirmed in his chair as he listened to his parents discussing a problem called the Depression. The look of concern on their faces and the lowered tones of their voices revealed that something was amiss, but the youngster was too young to understand. Instead, he was filled with anticipation and delight about his plans.

He sat as patiently as possible, but once Ora began clearing the dishes, Edward hopped out of his chair, took his father's huge hand and urged Sam to follow him out the front door and down the sidewalk to Grandma Flood's house. Still holding Sam's hand tightly until Grandma Flood answered the doorbell, Edward ran through the hall to the screen door in the kitchen that opened onto the fenced-in back yard. It was still there…sitting in the freshly mown grass, exactly where he had left it…his brand-new red tricycle.

Each day when Ora picked up the children from Grandma Flood's big two-story home, Edward skipped down the sidewalk while Ora followed behind, cuddling Martha in one arm and carrying her briefcase full of school papers in the other. It had been Ora's custom to give the children a snack in the afternoon…a peanut butter sandwich or a homemade oatmeal cookie served with a glass of chilled milk from the ice box. However, that ritual had changed with the arrival of the tricycle.

Edward was obsessed with mastering his new form of transportation. When they reached Grandma Flood's house each morning, he made a beeline for the kitchen, raced out the screen door, and mounted his 3-wheeled trike. Each day he practiced how to maneuver it, only stopping for lunch at noon and reluctantly leaving it parked in Grandma Flood's back yard when Ora insisted they had to go home in the afternoons. Peanut butter sandwiches and oatmeal cookies were no longer as effective an enticement to leave Grandma Flood's house. His parents had taught him that "practice makes perfect," though, and Edward had learned that lesson well. He had big plans to surprise his father over the weekend.

The long-awaited Saturday had finally arrived, and as his father watched him, young Edward proudly mounted his red tricycle, placed his bare feet on the rubber-covered pedals, and grasped the handlebars with confidence. Looking back over his shoulder and smiling at his father for only a moment, Edward leaned forward with a look of determination and took off across the path he had worn in the grass during a week full of practice sessions.

Focusing on the picket fence that stretched across the back of the yard, he pumped the pedals furiously, his little bare legs moving in rhythm like pistons. Almost airborne and making a precariously tilted two-wheel turn, he raced back to his surprised father in record time. Samuel Randall beamed with pride as Edward slipped off the tricycle's seat and reaching around the pant legs of his lanky father, he hugged him. Bending over, Sam patted the youngster on the back in recognition of his derring-do feat. The experience of mastering a vehicle and feeling the thrill of pushing his red tricycle to the limit remained etched in Edward's memory. It was his first test flight, a prelude to his future.

Young Edward, speeding across his Grandma Flood's back yard on his tricycle.

Young James Edward Preston Randall, whom the family called Edward, with his mother Ora, on the left, his father Sam, and his Aunt Thelma, his mother's sister on the right. They're standing in front of the Randalls' home on Rutledge Avenue in the Gainsboro community of Roanoke, Virginia.

CHAPTER 3

A BIG SURPRISE IN A SMALL PACKAGE

By the spring of 1931, Ora was pregnant again, and Edward was hoping for a baby brother this time. Thinking he could persuade his mother to have a boy—in the event she was planning to have another girl—Edward would question her almost daily, "Is it a boy?" He always got the same answer. "It's a surprise," Ora would tease. Little did she realize the accuracy of her response.

One late afternoon in April, long before her due date, Ora instinctively cried out as she experienced a staggering pain that brought her to her knees. Right away she feared the worst. She was almost 33 years old, and the odds were against her. With only enough time to call her mother, put a pot of water on the stove to boil, and grab some towels, Ora headed to the bedroom. Through pain-minced words, she instructed a wide-eyed Edward to wait at the front door. Then she lay down and steeled herself against whatever was to be.

Meanwhile, Martha Flood grabbed the first aid kit she had assembled to handle emergencies in the veritable child care center she provided for her grandchildren, and she raced down the street to her daughter's house. Caught up in the unexpected maelstrom of emotion, Edward opened the door and was relieved to see his wise and comforting grandmother. Quickly securing her namesake in a high chair and leaving Edward in charge of entertaining the toddler, Martha headed for the bedroom to be Ora's mid-wife.

By the time Sam arrived home, Ora had given birth, but the family dynamics had changed dramatically while he was wrangling the enormous engines in Norfolk & Western's Machine Shop. Cleaning up before checking out the latest addition to the family, he was startled at first glance. Then a wide grin spread across his face, and he said, "Well, look at you. You're just a little fella." The newborn baby, a girl, was so tiny that Sam could hold her in the palm of his hand.

The chance for survival of a premature baby born at home in 1931 was poor, but the tiny infant had two very determined parents and an insightful grandmother who had grown up on a farm where she had seen many births. Martha instinctively knew what to do. She emptied the sturdy top drawer of the oak dresser, lined it with a doubled-over wool blanket, and then headed into the kitchen to warm towels in the oven. It would be critical to keep the tiny miracle warm.

The contrived incubator was no match for the equipment available in a medical facility, but that was no longer an option. Besides, the hospital in Gainsboro would not accept a newborn now that she had arrived. It would be too risky for the babies who had been born in sterile conditions. Counting every miniature finger and toe, Sam was alarmed when he discovered that the delicate skin on the baby's tiny back had stretched to the breaking point and had slightly torn during the delivery. He asked his mother-in-law how to heal the wound and dozens of other questions about how to care for his baby daughter, all the while stroking the "Little Fella" and gently rocking her in his hand.

Once Martha retrieved the warm towels and lined the drawer with them, she diapered the infant with one of Sam's fresh cotton handkerchiefs, swathed the newborn in a small but warm hand towel, and placed the infant in the top dresser drawer. Three adults stood fixated and watched every breath the baby took for quite some time, even after she closed her eyes. During the night Sam and Ora got up separately to tend to the baby. Ora awakened at the slightest whimper and lifting the little one to her breast, she cooed and encouraged her to nurse. When Sam startled awake, he walked over in the dark to the dresser drawer and touched the "Little Fella's" chest with two fingers to make sure her heart was still beating. *She's like a little hummingbird,* he thought as he crawled back in bed. Both he and Ora beamed with happiness when they awakened to the baby's cries the next morning.

Even though her parents officially named their daughter Bernice, Sam called her "Little Fella" for years.

Thankful that her child was not a stillbirth, as she had feared, Ora was razor-focused on Bernice's care. She knew the child's first year of life would be critical, and so Bernice was seldom out of Ora's sight. Of course, Martha was still young enough that she was tied to her mother's apron strings, so Ora and her two daughters became a triumvirate, and Edward unintentionally became "odd man out."

As Bernice began to thrive, Ora accepted afternoon visits by curious neighbors who were fascinated and doted on the miracle baby. Everything that Bernice learned to do for the first time—smile, coo, roll over, kick her tiny feet—was greeted with amazement by her parents, relatives, and occasional visitors. Edward watched in dismay as the spotlight shifted away from him. Even his 3-year-old sister Martha seemed to have bonded with Bernice, perhaps because they were sisters. Martha acted like Bernice was her baby doll and truly the little one was about the size of a toy. Edward tried every way he could imagine to gain attention but instead of receiving praise for being creative, he was usually admonished to act his age.

Edward, in a shirt and tie, stands behind his Aunt Thelma who is holding his sister Bernice. Martha is seated next to Thelma's younger brother Larry.

When Grandma Flood appeared to be joining the new baby's fan club, that was the last straw for Edward. The situation had become intolerable. After considering his limited options, he decided to leave home in protest. There were no brightly-colored, ergonomic backpacks in those days, but children had rucksacks, so Edward packed up his favorite toys, marched downstairs with the heavy load on his back, and tracked down his mother who was preparing dinner while Bernice was napping. Standing resolutely by Ora's side he announced his intentions to his mother.

"I am going to run away."

Ora didn't look up. She just continued peeling potatoes at the sink as though she were deep in thought and hadn't heard her son's pronouncement.

"I said, 'I am going to run away,'" he repeated with a bit more urgency.

Edward was shocked when Ora made no effort to stand in her son's way. Instead, she asked him to go out and cut some wood for her before he left. Confused and outwitted, Edward pulled off his heavily loaded rucksack and made as much noise as possible as he plopped it down on the kitchen table. Ora never flinched or looked up. She just kept peeling potatoes at the sink and muttered something about what they would be having for dinner.

Frustrated but obedient, Edward opened the screen door and broke his mother's cardinal rule by slamming it shut so hard that it almost popped off its hinges. He stomped down the back steps and headed to the old stump where his father had embedded a small hatchet next to the big axe. Soon Ora heard the sound of the hatchet splintering logs from the woodpile near the heavily laden cherry tree in the back yard. Pulling out a Mason jar full of cherries that she had canned during the previous season, she prepared dough and pressed it into a pie tin. After spreading the sweetened red cherries across the crust, she cut lattice strips of dough, and arranged them artfully across the top of the pie before placing it in the oven.

Soon the enticing aroma of the dinner menu reached a tired young boy as he finished splitting wood. He began to realize he had not thought out all the important details of his decision carefully enough, and the aroma of cherry pie indicated the consequences of those omissions. He was hot, sweaty, and exhausted, not to mention hungry.

Without looking up when Edward pushed open the screen door, Ora smiled to herself when he announced, "I decided not to go."

Nothing was said at dinner about Edward's cancelled agenda, and he was relieved, but Sam commented on his surprise that Ora had prepared such a feast when it wasn't even a holiday. After dinner when Edward asked to go to bed early, Sam worried that his son might be ill and started to say something about it until he glanced over at Ora. Her smug look as she placed a warning finger to her lips was not what he had expected. Later in the evening when Sam and Ora sat on the front porch, watching fireflies flitting through the night sky, she revealed the events of the day. Lying in bed and listening to the ebb and flow of his parents' conversation, Edward felt secure. He soon drifted off to sleep, only waking up once to the sound of his father's hearty laugh.

For several weeks thereafter, Sam thought about his own childhood and how lost he had felt when his beautiful young mother died and his father remarried a widow with 3 children. Suddenly, he had to compete for his own father's attention. He remembered the feelings of loneliness. Sensitive to Edward's dilemma, Sam promised himself to make every moment with his son as special as possible.

On Saturdays, Sam added a new event to the family's busy schedule, and Edward accompanied his father to the barbershop, a magical place traditionally designated for men only. The minute Edward walked through the door with Sam, the father-son duo was welcomed by many of Sam's friends, including several of their neighbors who also worked for Norfolk & Western. The atmosphere was noisy and alive with so many interesting conversations floating through the barbershop that Edward was exposed to every subject imaginable—from the country's entire train system to politics to even a few subjects that were discussed in such hushed voices that he couldn't quite make out what they were saying. When the men punctuated those conversations with raucous laughter, Edward figured maybe they were telling jokes.

Sam understood the importance of having father and son time with Edward. It was a privilege Sam had rarely experienced as a child, and he wanted Edward to grow up to be a mature and honorable man. Sam strived to set the example for his son. He was a man of few words, but he chose them carefully.

Sam made a practice of giving his son a shiny quarter before they entered the shop so the boy could pay for his own haircut. Once it was Edward's turn, he scrambled into the barber's chair and sat straight and still while the chatty barber went about snipping and trimming here and there. There was a cadence to his technique as he moved the boy's head to reach the back of his neck and behind his ears. The best part of the ritual was when the barber was satisfied with his work, and he would whirl Edward's chair so that he could check out his fresh haircut in the mirror. As soon as Edward gave his approval and pulled out his quarter in payment, the barber would whisk off his young customer's protective "bib" so that he could jump down from the padded leather chair. Edward's feet still dangled above the shiny steel foot rest, but the barber usually commented on how much the young boy had grown each week so Edward gained confidence that some day he would grow up to be just like his hero, his father.

Customers sitting in the wooden chairs by the window awaited their turn in the barber's chair, and Edward learned that he could sit there among them and watch the party-like tonsorial procedure, as long as it didn't leave a customer standing. There were magazines and newspapers carelessly stacked on low tables, that were free for anyone to pick up and read, too. The place was like a library except that there was no lady in the barbershop reminding you to be quiet.

The wonderful smells of shaving lotion permeated the air and the rhythmic *Snip, Snip, Snip* of the barber's scissors as he cut hair added a beat to the experience. But the most exciting moment to the youngster was watching how masterfully the barber would lather up his customer before pulling out his long-edge razor to methodically glide down a customer's cheek, removing shaving lotion and beard in one fell swoop. Edward couldn't wait until he was old enough to get a shave. A visit to the barbershop was better than going to the movies.

CHAPTER 4

A FEW BROKEN ARMS

Bernice slowly gained a little weight and grew stronger, and Ora lost the edgy tone in her voice…except when Edward would forget it was Bernice's naptime and jump over every other step as he raced downstairs from his bedroom. Invariably, that was the end of Ora's few minutes of rest for the day. Since Edward didn't have to get up multiple times through the night to feed a fragile newborn, he didn't understand sleep deprivation. He slept without stirring throughout the night and bounded out of bed at the break of dawn each morning ready for the day's adventures.

As usual, Vacation Bible School started again in June and once it was over, Edward had great fun playing in the sprinkler with Martha; climbing up in the highest branches of the cherry tree to spy on the neighborhood; and playing hide and seek with his Uncle Lawrence, his Grandma Flood's late-in-life baby. Although Lawrence was not much older than Edward, he was Edward's uncle, nonetheless. Sam had once tried to explain the circumstances. It was because Lawrence was Edward's mother Ora's younger brother. Edward couldn't begin to figure that one out. He just accepted it. Lawrence never insisted on his rightful title anyway.

As summer began winding down, and the custodians in Gainsboro's schools were frantically working to prepare every room in each building for the onslaught of youngsters, Edward became increasingly obsessed with two unrelated things—starting school and getting a bike. Since Edward's sixth birthday was November 30th, he was not eligible to start school until second semester in February. He had to wait a little longer, and he was distraught. Ora explained it would be to his advantage because he would be more mature in a few more months, but he was not convinced. Then Ora found the winning approach. She agreed to give him private lessons each day so that by February, he would be ahead of everyone in his class. Edward liked that idea.

Since Ora had left teaching to rear her children once Bernice was born, she looked forward to the daily lessons with Edward, and he loved the extra attention. Ora kept him busy with exciting educational activities, and soon he knew his numbers and the alphabet. He could even read short sentences. He had also become a loyal visitor to the public library, which featured a children's story hour and special events on holidays. The librarian always took photographs of the children on these occasions, and Edward was delighted to see himself in the pictures when the librarian posted them on a display board.

There was also a globe in the library, and Edward wished he could take it home so that he could memorize all the countries. He was fascinated by their irregular shapes and different sizes and the bright colors that helped to differentiate one from another. He wondered how people made globes and maps before they could go up in airplanes to get an aerial view. His heart's desire was to become a pilot when he grew up, and if he could make his dream come true, he just might get to fly to one of those countries on the globe. Meanwhile, he had to be satisfied with looking at every book in the library about every topic even remotely connected with flying.

Each evening when Sam returned home, Edward chattered non-stop about what he had learned that day, and just as Ora had promised, the months flew by until suddenly it was November 30th, Edward's long-awaited 6th birthday. With all the excitement of the Christmas holidays and the New Year, Edward realized that it was almost time for him to begin school. He was still frustrated that he had long ago outgrown his tricycle, but there was a more immediate issue, a situation that had not previously occurred to him—school clothes!

Edward felt he looked his best, and more like his father, when he wore his white cotton shirt with a tie. He was still stuck with short pants because Ora said he wasn't old enough for trousers like Lawrence wore, but he had not given up on that debate yet. His problem was that he had only one white shirt so if he planned to wear it every day, Ora said he was going to have to learn how to wash and iron it every night. If that was what it would take to look his best, Edward was up for the challenge. Thinking he wouldn't be interested, Ora offered to teach her son how to iron, and much to her surprise Edward mastered the process by the end of the week. He was ready.

On opening day, as previously agreed upon with Ora, the school principal walked over to the Randalls to escort the young pupil to school. Edward had been waiting for her, and he knew it had been worth all his effort when the stately woman, who was dressed in a suit herself, told him how "spiffy" he looked in his brand, new clothes. He didn't correct her as she took his hand. He never noticed Ora peeking out the window as her first born disappeared around the corner. He was too busy asking endless questions, while the principal attempted to answer each one before he blurted out another. A school bus transporting youngsters to another school passed them midway on their 8-block journey, but Edward was still bursting with energy and a new self-confidence as he made his grand entrance at school, walking hand in hand with the principal herself.

School was not what he anticipated. He liked his teacher, but the class moved at a much slower pace than he expected, and there were lots of rules, even more than he had at home. Since there were so many students in the class, he had to wait his turn to have all his questions answered. When he complained about it to Ora, she simply explained the virtue of patience and that was the end of the discussion.

After the first weeks of school, young James Edward Preston Randall settled into the new rhythm of his life. He had learned a lot, some of it unexpected. The characters in the books they were beginning to learn to read did not have children that reflected the people in his Gainsboro neighborhood, and they didn't talk like them either. Thanks to Ora's focus on Edward's learning to read before he entered school, he was considerably more advanced than his contemporaries and sitting through the class's initial attempt at oral reading seemed to take forever. When Edward would try to read ahead to see how a story ended, the teacher would lean over him and turn the page back to the class's place in the story.

Whereas Edward was accustomed to going outside whenever he pleased, once he entered school everything was scheduled by the hour. There were set rules that everyone was expected to follow, and there were consequences if you didn't. Well, at least he understood that. His mother was the ultimate taskmaster. She was known to correct the grammar in letters of adults who wrote her. She even sent the corrected version back to them, so he felt certain he could handle his teacher's expectations.

Knowing his numbers was a big help, too. He was surprised to learn all the things you could do with numbers in arithmetic. Soon that was his favorite subject, except for recess. Edward was grateful to have the chance to go outside and run and play until he dropped, at least for one period during the school day. Even though the teacher organized games and activities outdoors, he was mostly free to enjoy new friends and the fresh air.

Edward's initial grade reports pleased his parents, and so he was motivated to keep up the standard he had set, but secretly, he had already begun to make big plans for the upcoming summer. He had mentioned wanting a bicycle to his parents, and Sam had said, "Not now," but when he added, "Maybe later," Edward held out hope for a while . . . until the night he overheard snatches of his parents' conversation after his sisters were asleep.

The recurring word was "finances," and Edward figured that meant not having enough money to pay bills. Reluctant to ask for a bicycle more than once, Edward decided to build one of his own, based on his original design. Once school was out for the summer, and

Vacation Bible School classes ended in mid-June, Edward was in hot pursuit of building a bicycle. He tracked down a discarded 2' x 4' scrap of lumber and also a roller skate that he dismembered in order to pirate the wheels. Then he attached the well-worn metal wheels to the underneath side of the wood. Hammering a narrow and upright piece of wood at the front of the rustic contraption, he used an ice pick to hollow out a hole near the top and threaded a metal rod through the opening to create handlebars.

The vehicle was primitive and turned out to be more of a scooter than a bicycle because he had to use his left foot to start and stop, and he couldn't make sharp turns . . . but other than that, it was a functional vehicle . . . unless he needed to come to a gentle stop at the end of a hill. That's when he realized his invention was missing an important feature—brakes! As long as he was on even ground, he could move at a fast clip, but he learned about velocity, momentum, and crash landings when it came to stopping, even on modest inclines.

Entranced by Edward's idea, some of his friends copied his design, but none of their "bicycles" had brakes either. The only option was to drag your foot to impede your speed long enough to stop or else use something like a curbside garbage can as a barrier. Soon there was a rash of broken arms among Edward's group of friends! Parents faced the reality that a broken arm and the ensuing visit to the doctor cost more than a bicycle. A few boys lucked out when their parents caved in and bought one, but for Edward, getting a bicycle had become the least of his worries. More serious issues loomed ahead on the horizon.

CHAPTER 5

HOW THE OTHER HALF LIVES

Sam had begun having coughing spells intermittently through the night, and Edward could hear his parents' voices in muted conversation after each attack. He couldn't make out what they were saying, but he sensed his father was seriously ill. Each year most people experienced a winter cold and took the usual home remedies to get rid of the annoying symptoms, but Sam's condition had been escalating for years. Several times a week he had to leave the dinner table when he couldn't stem a coughing spell. Retrieving a cotton handkerchief from his pants' pocket to muffle the sound of his suffering, he would go outside or to another room until the spell was over. Edward noted the worried look on his mother's face each time it happened. Something was terribly wrong.

If Edward tried to express his concern to his father, Sam would just pat the observant, young boy's back to reassure him and then simply change the subject. Otherwise, Samuel Edward Randall seemed to be in top shape. His job required heavy physical labor, so he was strong and muscular, and since he never owned a car, he walked every place regardless of the distance. So did the family. They walked to school, church, the local shops and the library. It didn't matter whether or not the sun was shining or it was raining, or snow was piling up on the sidewalk. The Randall family usually walked.

There was one important exception, though, and it offered the entire family a chance to travel anywhere they wanted without paying a dime—railway passes! As an incentive for paying inadequate salaries and providing questionable medical coverage, Norfolk & Western issued railway passes to railroad employees and their families. Supporting a family of five, Sam couldn't afford to buy a car on his salary, but the opportunity for the whole family to be able to travel free to any destination by train was an irresistible incentive.

It gave Sam great pleasure to walk with his family to the nearby train depot down the hill from the Hotel Roanoke. Standing on the platform and awaiting the train, which would whisk them away for a weekend trip to visit relatives, was always entertaining. He loved watching his daughters bursting with excitement and Ora looking beautiful as she proudly carried a picnic basket full of snacks for the trip. Sam would let Edward hold their railway passes for the conductor to punch before herding everyone to their seats and taking his place beside Ora. Seeing his family so happy made all his hard work worth it.

When it came to a vote, the family's favorite trip was a visit with Uncle Henry and Aunt Lily Field. Their farm was about 40 miles northeast of Roanoke, and the train ride up into the lush Shenandoah Valley was breathtaking. Aunt Lily was Sam's sister and she was a great cook, too. She loved children, and she delighted in spoiling her nephew and his sisters. Edward always looked forward to the sumptuous feasts ahead. It didn't have to be a holiday for Aunt Lily to spend most of the day in the kitchen preparing fresh vegetables from the garden and frying one of the chickens retrieved from the hen house or baking a turkey.

By the time she shoved a homemade pie or a chocolate cake into the oven, the enticing aroma of all the food would make waiting unbearable. The children took turns sneaking into the kitchen and begging for just a morsel to stave off starvation, and Aunt Lily usually obliged with a big smile and a sample sliver of juicy turkey from the underside of a golden, butter-basted bird. Sometimes she would hand each of the children a spoon to scrape up the bands of icing that her spatula had missed in the mixing bowl when she frosted a cake.

Aunt Lily's husband Henry Field was always awaiting the Randalls' arrival at the depot in Buena Vista, a bustling village at the junction of the Norfolk & Western Railroads. Uncle Henry worked in a cannery in the small town during the week, and his distinguishing feature was that he often smelled like fish, even after he showered and applied Aqua Velva after shaving. Edward was more than willing to overlook that one drawback, though. Uncle Henry owned a car, and he promised that when Edward was old enough, he'd teach his nephew to drive. That was reason enough for Uncle Henry to be Edward's favorite relative.

The Fields' farm covered 15 acres, and turkeys and chickens roamed free in the front yard while a dairy cow or two munched on the knee-high, tasseled grass beyond the fence in the back. Aunt Lily had surprising skills for a woman. She even butchered hogs, and the garden that she maintained produced enough vegetables to share with friends and family. Ora could count on her generous sister-in-law to fill their picnic basket to the brim with radishes, spring onions, lettuce, and tomatoes at the end of their visit before they left for Roanoke.

Lily and Henry seemed to have dozens of curious neighbors that happened by when the Randalls visited, but they lived at quite a distance. Edward could just barely make out the silhouette of two other farmhouses when he explored the property. If he gazed out of his bedroom window at home, he could count at least a dozen houses in his Gainsboro neighborhood. On the other hand, his uncle's land stretched to the horizon and crops grew to the perimeters. It was like living in a park as far as Edward was concerned. Aunt Lily and Uncle Henry also produced almost all their food, except for staples like flour and sugar. Edward was fascinated by the differences between life on a farm and his life in the outskirts of Roanoke.

As always, the Randalls thoroughly enjoyed their visit, but this time Uncle Henry had a proposition for Edward. After consulting with Sam and Ora, he invited his nephew to spend several weeks on the farm as soon as school was out. Edward could not believe his good fortune. The next two months seemed interminable, but eventually Edward finished sixth grade with flying colors. He packed his rucksack almost to the bursting point as he prepared for an extended visit with the Fields. With his parents' permission, he set out for the train depot by himself. It was his first time to travel solo, and he was proud to have earned his parents' trust. Extending his railway pass for the conductor to punch, he boarded the train.

Settling into his seat, he wondered if the passenger who sat down next to him could tell that it was Edward's very first time to be out on his own. Dressed nattily in a pin-striped suit and sporting a bright red tie, the gentleman removed his black felt hat, placed it in his lap, and leaned back. He closed his eyes and fell fast asleep. Trying to relax and appear travel savvy, Edward mimicked his fellow traveler and soon dozed off himself. It seemed only moments later that the conductor called out "Buena Vista," and as the train approached the depot, Edward peered out the window. There was Uncle Henry in his overalls and thick leather boots. He was waving his favorite weather-beaten hat in welcome.

Aunt Lily and Uncle Henry had planned a working vacation for the youngster because he was approaching his teenage years, and as they had explained to Ora, they could use the help. On the day after his arrival, Edward mirrored everything Uncle Henry did, and the daily chores were completed twice as fast each day. Uncle Henry commended the energetic lad for his all-out effort to accomplish the tasks at hand. He complimented the youth for working as hard as any man, a vote of confidence that made Edward's heart beat faster. Encouraged by his uncle's approval, Edward decided that as soon as he got back home, he would ask his father if he could go to the Norfolk & Western Machine Shop with him. He had noticed his father coughing much more lately, and he was getting thinner, too. Edward knew he had lightened Uncle Henry's load, so maybe he could help his ailing father. He might even be able to get a part-time job and assist with the family finances. Uncle Henry had boosted his self-confidence, and Edward was ready to take on more responsibility.

Meanwhile, to reward their nephew's efforts, the Fields packed up their car to take Edward sightseeing over the weekend in nearby Lexington, the home of the Virginia Military Institute. It was the oldest military academy in America, and President Abraham

Lincoln had once called it the "West Point of the South." Reaching their destination, Edward was impressed by the cadets' deep blue uniforms adorned with gold buttons, and he observed how the erect posture of each young man presented the image of confidence and commitment to country. Edward wondered what you had to do to be accepted at the institution. He wanted to be a pilot, and he knew he needed to have a plan.

Lexington was lush and beautiful to behold. Sheltered by the Allegheny Mountains, on the west and the Blue Ridge Mountains on the east, the area was called the Shenandoah Valley, but Green Valley, its original name, captured it best. It looked like a painting by a famous artist. Edward tried to memorize the magnificent landscape so he could describe it to his parents as soon as he got home.

Every day that Edward spent with Aunt Lily and Uncle Henry was unforgettable, and he realized that was how he wanted to live his life, making every day memorable. Late in the afternoon before Edward was to return to Roanoke, the sky began clouding over and torrents of rain washed away the vivid crimson and gold colors of the sunset. Going to bed early at Aunt Lily's suggestion, Edward closed his eyes and prayed for his father to get well. Raindrops pounded the tin roof of the farmhouse with a hypnotic rhythm, and nature's lullaby soothed the youngster's troubled mind as he fell asleep.

CHAPTER 6

DECISIONS AND CONSEQUENCES

Eager to be home again, Edward opened the front door and placed his rucksack full of dirty clothes on the dusty pine floor of the hallway. Suddenly he overheard his mother. "You are going to leave me here in this house with three children, and you're going to tell me you're going to leave me with a TB patient in the house?" Ora shouted with indignation. Her words and the intensity of her distress startled him. She was such an imposing figure that a mere warning glance usually induced submission. Who was she talking to? Who was she talking about? What was TB?

When Edward entered the room, Ora looked surprised to see her son. She gestured for him to sit down in one of the spindle-back kitchen chairs as she held the phone to her ear and listened. Confused, Edward slumped into his father's chair, propped his elbows on the table, and rested his forehead in the palm of his hands. He waited as Ora turned her back to him and lowered her voice to finish her contentious conversation. She struggled to regain her usual stiff composure as she hung up the phone. Grabbing a small plate of freshly baked sugar cookies and a glass from the cupboard, she opened the ice box, reached for a bottle of milk and walked over to the table. "I wasn't expecting you home so soon," she explained while she filled his glass. "I made cookies," she said and placed the afternoon snack and glass of chilled milk on the table in front of her son. "We missed you. How was your trip?" she asked as she sat down.

Unlike Aunt Lily or Grandma Flood who would give him a bear hug at first sight, Ora was measured in her displays of affection. Edward noticed the nearly dry tears on her cheeks and the open Bible resting on the table, but he said nothing. Instead, he regaled Ora with stories of his adventures on Aunt Lily and Uncle Henry's farm, and he exaggerated just enough to make her laugh at some of his mishaps—a city boy adjusting awkwardly to rural chores. Ora leaned forward and listened more intently as he described the short trip to Lexington and the visit to VMI, the Virginia Military Institute. One way or another, she fully intended to have all three of her children graduate from college, and so she was pleased to see her son take an interest in higher education.

When Edward mentioned that he needed to go to the library to do some research, Ora assumed he wanted to learn more about VMI so she pointed out that there were several hours before his father would be home. He could spend an hour or so at the library before he needed to be back for dinner. Thanking his mother and assuring her he was glad to be home, Edward headed out the front door in search of answers while Ora picked up the family Bible on the kitchen table, went into the bedroom, and closed the door.

Whenever he had a question about a word, Ora would usually say, "Look it up in the dictionary, Edward." Next to the Bible, the dictionary was the most important book in the house, but Edward was older and wiser now and he had learned an even better source of information, the Gainsboro Public Library. Ora had given him a tour and taught him how to use it long ago, and Edward had become such a frequent visitor that the librarian welcomed him by name as soon as he walked through the door. She was a reserved and stately woman who presented the image of authority—hair pulled back tight into a severe knot of a bun and piercing eyes that conveyed her disapproval when visitors' voices broke the silence expected in the library.

After he had asked the librarian for a book about airplanes for nearly the millionth time, the librarian introduced him to the encyclopedia, the most beautiful books he had ever seen. They came as a set that stretched all the way across a high shelf, and the librarian explained to the bright and ever-curious youngster that somewhere in one of those books he could find the answer to every question he had. He knew they were very expensive because the title on each book was written in gold, and every volume had a golden letter of the alphabet on the spine. He felt privileged to be permitted to use one.

The librarian had instructed Edward to ask her whenever he wanted to study about airplanes, and she would retrieve the designated book for him. That's why she was curious that he requested the "T" volume. When he explained he wanted to learn about TB, a worried look crossed her face as she pulled down the appropriate book. She asked him to sit down with her while she flipped through pages almost as thin as onionskin. Then she stopped close to the back of the book and pointed to the word "tuberculosis."

Without speaking a word, the librarian pulled a small notepad and the stub of a pencil from her skirt pocket and handed them to the troubled boy. She watched as Edward picked up the encyclopedia and walked over to one of the library's carrels to begin reading. With each paragraph and accompanying illustration, he grew another year older. He scribbled down words that were new to him and planned to check on what they meant when he returned home. He would have to tiptoe downstairs and sort through the dictionary to do it by flashlight after everyone had gone to bed because he didn't want to arouse suspicion. When he had finally finished the lengthy coverage of the illness, he returned the encyclopedia to the librarian and thanked her before walking out the door. Immersed in emotion, the frightened youngster headed home, leaving his childhood behind in the reference book section of the Gainsboro Library.

Deeply depressed by all he had learned about tuberculosis, Edward faced a dilemma. He was desperate to talk to both of his parents about what he had studied, but he feared it would be unwise to broach the subject with them. His mother frowned on eavesdropping, and since his worries stemmed from the snippet of a private, adult conversation he had overheard, he decided to wait until his parents brought up the subject. Ora was full of adages that succinctly captured concepts, and he pondered one of them, "What you don't know can't hurt you." It no longer applied.

Picking up his pace as he turned the corner and neared the big frame house on Rutledge Avenue, he caught sight of a familiar tall and long-limbed figure. The late afternoon sun reflected off the gentleman's glasses, and his easy gait was unmistakable. Edward couldn't help himself. He raced down the pock-marked sidewalk as fast as he could and embraced his father around the waist the instant he reached him. Surprised but delighted by such a display of pure affection, Sam walked in sync with his son, and Edward didn't let go until they reached their front porch steps.

Suddenly days seemed to evaporate into thin air, and each one was too precious to waste. Two of the new words Edward had learned—contagious and prognosis—were terribly distressing. The only thing he knew to do was be the best son possible and spend every moment he could with his beloved father. Sam was pleased when Edward announced that he wanted to be a champion checker player just like his father. One Saturday morning Sam placed an upended empty crate between two folding chairs and created an outdoor game room in the enclosed section at the end of the front porch. On weekdays when Sam returned home from work, he and Edward often enjoyed a game or two of checkers before dinner. Sam loved watching his son develop strategies in his determination to outsmart his father, but Sam was competitive, too. He never made it easy for the 12-year-old to win. Eventually, Edward emerged victorious more and more frequently, but Sam was still the champion in his son's eyes.

Knowing his father was going to get much sicker, Edward thought checkers would always be something that they could do together. Sam never guessed his son's ulterior motives. Edward wasn't the only one capable of subterfuge, though. Sam bought an erector set to surprise his son at Christmas. He recognized Edward's talent for design and mechanics, and he wanted to encourage the youngster. He also wanted to keep him off that arm-breaking, homemade bicycle Edward had created.

Months passed and Sam's health seemed to be holding so Edward decided his father's frequent trips to the doctor's office must involve some new form of therapy that was working, and he was relieved even though Sam's cough persisted. Edward was on the cusp of becoming a teenager, and the boys his age had begun seriously pressuring each other to take big risks to prove themselves. Whereas he and his close friends had always been well-behaved—never getting into fisticuffs or breaking family rules—he was unprepared to handle the new temptations that surfaced. For a teen whose parents were strapped for money, the opportunity to pick up a dollar or two without much effort was too tempting to pass up.

Sam had taught his son how to play pool at the local YMCA, the only venue for such an activity that was approved by his parents, and that's where Edward met his friends after school on occasion to polish their skills in the sport. Of course, he always informed Ora of his whereabouts before taking off for the "Y," and his mother set the time he was to return home. Edward had reached that point in life where boys are trying to leave childhood behind and establish themselves as young men—an ongoing ritual of measuring themselves in comparison to their peers.

One Friday afternoon when Edward and his buddies were growing bored playing pool at the "Y," an older newcomer to the group announced that he knew a place where you could make big money playing pool if you were good enough, but you had to pay to play. The group decided that Edward was the most skilled player among them so they agreed to support him by chipping in money and betting he would win. "Putting skin in the game," the older boy called it as he persuaded the naïve and impressionable group of youngsters to follow him to one of Gainsboro's pool halls.

Edward won the first game and his adult competitors feigned astonishment as the older boy handed over $52 to Edward. Excitement was at a fever pitch when Edward glanced up at the clock on the wall. Horrified, he explained that he had only five minutes to get home by Ora's deadline. His scruffy male adversaries were none too pleased when their fresh "mark" insisted he absolutely could not play another game. While his three friends testified to the truth of his concerns, Edward divvied up their prize and the youngsters left the pool sharks agape and frustrated that this time they were the ones victimized. Most exasperating of all was that the baby-faced young lads didn't even realize the irony of their victory.

Running all the way home, Edward was breathing hard as he raced up the front steps, banged open the door, and almost careened into his mother. When he proudly handed over his ill-gotten gains to Ora, he expected praise and appreciation. Instead, he received an interrogation. His mother demanded to know where he had gotten $13. That was serious money in 1939. Worst of all was Ora's response to his explanation. She planned to speak to his father when he got home from work.

The wait was interminable. The punishment was worse. Sam sat his son down at the kitchen table, and Edward experienced his first man-to-man encounter—a terse explanation of what had really happened and how Edward had been hooked like a fish, taken in by the pool sharks' scheme. The imagery was embarrassing. Edward was hoping for a spanking. Instead, he was banished to his room without dinner. Trudging upstairs he could hear his younger sisters giggling at his disgrace. The aroma of fried chicken reached his bedroom and that probably meant his mother was serving corn on the cob, dripping with butter, and buttermilk biscuits, too. Leaning on the window sill he watched as night blanketed the neighborhood and lights flipped on in all the houses. The other families were probably gathered around their dinner tables just like his. Hard to believe that his big win resulted in a far bigger loss—his parents' trust. It wouldn't happen again he vowed as he sobbed himself to sleep.

CHAPTER 7

NOTHING BUT THE TRUTH

"I was just out with the boys," Edward responded when Ora demanded to know where he had been. Ora was furious with what she considered his flippant response. Suspicious, she thought she caught a whiff of beer as her son spoke with increasing bravado. She pecked away at him for a more thorough explanation, but Edward knew better than to defend himself. Ora would never understand. Besides, some things are sacred between a boy and his father and not to be divulged to mothers.

Actually, he had been sitting on the curb in front of the YMCA with his friends and bragging about his father while explaining why he would not be going to the pool hall with them again. Although it had been frightening at the time, Edward had quite the story to tell his buddies, and he did so in great detail. He described how his father had marched him to the pool hall, slammed the $13 down on the green felt of the nearest pool table, and announced that his son would not be engaging in any future games. Instead of the expected haggling and possible fisticuffs, a hush fell over the room. Grown men leaned on their cue sticks and stood in awe of Edward's principled and forthright father. Edward knew everyone respected Samuel Edward Randall, but he had never seen his dad in action, a powerful eagle protecting his eaglet.

Edward's friends had hung on his every word, and it was a relief that they would no longer pressure him to join in any further questionable activities. However, he was in hot water at home again and all because he had tried to stand up to his assertive mother.

As soon as Sam arrived from work only minutes later, Ora guided him right back out onto the front porch and closed the door to prying ears. Edward could make out the pitch of his agitated mother's voice growing higher and his father's comforting baritone offsetting it occasionally, but nothing was said when his parents walked back into the house. Throughout dinner Edward squirmed in his chair and awaited his father's verdict. Nothing happened, though he noticed Ora gave him the smallest slice of apple pie.

Hoping for a reprieve, Edward offered to wash the dishes, and his sisters were momentarily delighted until Sam ushered his son by the elbow out to the porch. Expecting the worst, Edward was totally unprepared for what happened next.

Once seated in the windowed nook on the front porch where they had spent so many special moments playing checkers, Sam acknowledged that Edward must be missing the male companionship that he had enjoyed at the Fields' farm. Aunt Lily and Uncle Henry had seven sons and only one daughter, Omega, and Sam knew that his son had instantly become a part of a brotherhood for the first time in his life. Sam shared a few memories of his own boyhood before shifting to the topic he had been avoiding for months.

Edward immediately noted the change of mood as Sam spoke in measured tones about his concerns and plans for the future. At first Edward felt proud to have his father confide in him as a young man instead of treating him as a boy. Then the weight of that responsibility crashed down on him with a relentless power that was suffocating.

Sam stared into his son's eyes as he outlined how the future would probably unfold, and Edward sensed the import of his father's words. At Ora's request, he explained, Norfolk & Western had made an appointment for him with a physician at Burrell Hospital in Gainsboro to determine what was causing his incessant coughing. Tuberculosis was the diagnosis, but Ora questioned its accuracy. She felt the TB diagnosis by a doctor representing the railway company was their effort to avoid compensating Sam and his family for a work-related illness, and so she demanded to see another doctor for a second opinion. She was so persistent that Sam was granted an appointment with a physician at the University of Virginia Hospital in Charlottesville. After performing a far more thorough examination and subjecting Sam to a battery of tests, the university medical staff determined that Sam did not have tuberculosis. Instead, he was in the advanced stage of silicosis.

Edward was momentarily relieved until Sam explained that although there was no cure for silicosis, he would continue taking frequent trips by rail to the university hospital for therapy to alleviate his suffering. Hopefully, he would be able to hold down his job for a few more years. Suddenly, all the puzzle pieces were falling into place. Edward realized that the conversation he had overheard was Ora's fight with the Norfolk & Western Railroad's administration over Sam's initial diagnosis of TB. It was the beginning of her quest to save her husband and her family.

Slumped over and depressed, Edward was stunned by his father's next comments. Sam pointed out that Edward would turn 13 in November, a teenager at last, and that was old enough to hold down a job. Smiling, Sam volunteered to accompany Edward to *The Roanoke Times'* office to apply for a position delivering newspapers to the neighborhood. Of course, that meant Edward would need transportation, and Sam revealed that he had already purchased his son's early birthday present—a bicycle! It was down at Grandma Flood's and Edward could pick it up as soon as they returned from *The Roanoke Times* the following morning. Sam assured his son that he would get the job.

Edward was overwhelmed by his conflicting emotions. His dreams were coming true, but he was losing his father. He thanked Sam profusely and standing up, he leaned over his dad, embraced him, and buried his head in the crook of Sam's neck to hide his tears. Acceptance as a young man had come at a painful price.

Assuming the role of a newsboy was a new experience for Edward. He had to get up by 4:30 a.m. to retrieve his stack of papers from the drugstore, roll them up, and secure them with a wide rubber band before loading them into the huge bag he slung over his shoulder. The best part of the job was pitching them up on the lawns and front porches of his customers before most of the families woke up. Soon he was so proficient that he could return home in time to share breakfast with his dad before the girls woke up.

Edward now followed a specific schedule and maintained a list of his customers with their addresses and phone numbers. The daily paper cost 3 cents, with the Sunday issue a little over twice as much, and on Saturdays Edward was responsible for collecting from his customers. His cut was a penny a paper, which he took out before delivering the money to the newspaper's route manager, an older fellow who took care of any unforeseen problems. Edward's friend, Carroll Swain, was also a newsboy and the morning competition to see who could roll and secure each paper faster made the chore fun. It also honed their skills to the point that it became a race to see who could finish the morning route first. Best of all was an unexpected additional source of income—tips! Edward turned over his salary to Ora in order to help the family, but he kept the tips for himself. *The Roanoke Times* never had such a polite and accommodating newsboy.

Summer was a whirlwind of activity, but as the 1939-1940 school year began, a pall fell over Gainsboro when Germany invaded Poland on September 1st. World War II was escalating. Edward was now reading the newspaper on a regular basis, and his discussions with his father were sobering. His childhood fascination with the countries on the big globe in the Gainsboro Library was replaced with day-to-day updates on what was happening in Europe. Photos of the war effort were featured daily on the front page. The question on everyone's mind was, *Will America enter the war?*

CHAPTER 8

LIVING LIFE TO THE FULLEST

The school year started off well. Edward had become accustomed to his demanding schedule—getting up at 4:30 a.m. to roll and band newspapers with Carroll Swain, distribute them before breakfast with his father, followed by the trek to school. As a result, he was more organized than ever. Edward had learned how to *"fill the unforgiving minute with sixty seconds worth of distance run."* Listening intently in class and taking notes to stay focused, he was excelling in mathematics and auto mechanics, his favorite subjects, and due to Ora's ongoing correction of his grammar, English was a strong suit, too.

By his 13th birthday in November, Edward had already covered an impressive expanse of Gainsboro on his bicycle, and he had picked up a map of Roanoke at the filling station to widen his horizons. In addition to racing off before dawn to deliver newspapers, he had a new destination on Saturdays. It was an area of the Cannady farm north of town. The Cannady family originally leased and eventually sold 136 acres of land to Roanoke city officials who plotted out an airfield. Edward was only old enough to ride a tricycle when the project began taking shape, but in the ensuing 10 years he watched an increasing number of aircraft, launched from the nascent airfield, flying over his house on Rutledge Avenue. Over time the original dirt airfield was transformed into Roanoke Municipal Airport.

When his father was healthier, the two of them hiked over to the airstrip once or twice, but it was quite a distance, which limited the time they could spend at the airfield. Now that he had a bicycle Edward could be there in 10 to 15 minutes and enjoy a lengthy visit before hopping on his bike to return home. Edward believed flight was the future and he intended to be a part of it. He had not given up on his childhood dream of being a pilot.

Across the years Sam had also taken his son to the Norfolk & Western Machine Workshop where he had spent most of his adult life. Entering the machine shop was like stepping into a different world. In the center of the shop was a huge turntable that could accommodate bringing in the mammoth locomotives in need of repair and returning them to the rails when issues were resolved. Even though the facility was open-air, maintenance on the coal-fired locomotives created a dangerous working environment.

The air was filled with pitch-black coal dust and on hot days chemicals released during the cleaning process seemed to remain suspended in air like a lethal dew.

Tragically, silica dust created during the sandblasting procedure settled throughout the shop and in the workers' lungs as well. Everything was filthy, but Edward was mesmerized by the towering size and seeming invincibility of man's magnificent invention. Railroads were uniting the states—transporting both travelers and the products of an emerging industrial power across America.

Even as a young boy Edward was full of questions that revealed his innate talent for mechanics. He was fascinated by the way the workmen broke the locomotives down piece by piece to clean, repair, and reassemble them. It was critical to get the locomotives back on the rails again as soon as possible, and Edward marveled at the way strong men toiled in tandem to get results. In the machine shop, the workers also built dining and sleeping cars designed to attract the upper class as well as those traveling out of necessity. The Norfolk & Western Machine Shop was the most magical place in Gainsboro as far as Edward was concerned.

By the time Sam gave his young son an erector set, Edward already had a working knowledge of mechanics and functional designs. He read and followed complex instructions to assemble intricate metal parts, which he identified by studying the enclosed drawings. In the beginning, he followed the printed and color-coded instructions to produce miniature machines. Soon he drew his own designs and created imaginative vehicles. Edward did not consider his erector set a toy; it was serious business and off limits to his sisters.

Hitting a growth spurt while exercising more than many of his peers, Edward was becoming stronger and more muscular. The transformation in the teenager was remarkable. Everyone noticed—his teachers, friends, the neighbors, his parents, even his sisters. In gym class one afternoon the coach observed Edward's pinpoint accuracy in throwing a football to the intended receiver. Envisioning a potential star quarterback, he suggested Edward tryout for the team. Much to the coach's surprise, Edward politely declined, explaining that he had an important after-school commitment each day so football practice was out of the question. Flabbergasted, the coach wondered what could be more important than football?

Few people were aware that Edward's father was dying, and the youngster was on a mission to spend as much time with his dad as he could. When the last school bell rang each day, Edward was on his way to Norfolk & Western Machine Shop. Jogging down the street with his rucksack full of books and papers on his back, Edward crossed a familiar bridge and hurried down a stairwell to the entrance of the shop. This was his after-school commitment, a daily ritual to brighten his father's day.

Accustomed to seeing him, Sam's fellow railway workers either nodded or managed a quick smile to acknowledge a loyal son before returning to the task at hand. Edward always tried to present his best image to the machine shop workers so his father would be proud of him. Sam was deeply respected by his crew, and they knew the tragedy that awaited the Randall family. Some of them had been in Edward's position when they were boys. They cared.

Edward always tried to arrive in enough time that he could watch the outcome of his father's challenges for the day and discuss it with his dad on the way home. Occasionally, he would hear that all too familiar cough. Sometimes it was one of the other workers, someone else's dear father.

Life came into focus for Edward as he thought back to his brief experience with the pool sharks, cheats dressed in men's clothing. These machine shop workers were real men, sweating and slaving in very dangerous conditions to earn a pittance of a paycheck to support their families and keep America on the move. And in their midst stood Samuel Edward Randall, guiding his crew and giving his all for his family and his country until his last breath.

Closing down for the day and climbing up the stairs to cross the bridge, Edward slowed the pace as he and his father walked home. Sam was struggling to breathe these days, and so Edward would stop frequently to emphasize a point in a story he was telling. It gave Sam a chance to catch his breath and relax for a minute. Even though laughing would often trigger an extended coughing spell, he thoroughly enjoyed listening to his son's daily escapades. They shared a similar sense of humor.

Surprised to hear that Edward had turned down his coach's offer to try out for the football team, Sam held his white cotton handkerchief to his mouth to stifle a cough while Edward embellished his story to the point of absurdity. Soon they were both in hysterics as Edward demonstrated why his extensive experience of throwing newspapers to a designated spot should be patented as a training technique. Jumping in front of his father and walking backwards to finish his story, he proclaimed with a flourish that football programs at major universities would be hiring him to teach football clinics and they'd be rich. Convulsed with laughter, Sam suggested his son's vivid imagination might land him in Hollywood instead.

By the time the two reached home, Sam was in a great mood, which had been Edward's goal all along. Thanksgiving was right around the corner, and Aunt Lily and Uncle Henry would be arriving in a car packed to the brim with kids and delicious food. It was an annual tradition because of the big rivalry on the gridiron between Virginia Polytechnic Institute and Virginia Military Institute. The Randall house would be filled with love and laughter, just what Sam needed. Not all medicine comes in a bottle.

CHAPTER 9

REVERSING ROLES

What a difference a year makes. Through sheer will and determination, Sam had managed to keep his job supervising his crew at Norfolk & Western, but he was losing his strength and his health was failing rapidly. The temperatures in the shop rocked the thermometer in the summer and sapped everyone's energy, but for Sam it was a moment of truth. He was no longer capable of performing his job to the best of his ability. His crew needed an able-bodied man to hold things together. He had no choice but to retire.

The head of personnel had anticipated Sam's decision, but once he made it official the administrator explained that Norfolk & Western would need for him to remain on the job long enough to train his replacement. The abrupt loss of such a knowledgeable and experienced leader would not bode well for a smooth transition. It was an invitation for accidents. Sam was relieved to learn that he would remain fully employed until January 1942 and retained temporarily to retrain his replacement. He was filled with gratitude. At least he could assure his family a joyous Christmas.

Although Ora had successfully stood up to Norfolk & Western Railroad's administration about her husband's health care, she knew Sam would not receive a pension worthy of his dedicated service to the company. Their family of five would struggle to make ends meet. Anticipating a financial crisis looming, she had already secured a position in the library at Lucy Addison High School. Her paycheck wouldn't fully alleviate their situation, but it would help. It would also provide an opportunity to keep track of her children and how they were coping with the impending loss of their father.

When Sam returned home with the news that he would remain on the payroll until after the New Year, Ora was relieved that they had a few more months to prepare for the major changes ahead. She proposed that they have a family discussion with Edward and the girls after dinner. Sam agreed.

Edward and his sisters—Martha and Bernice—were quite surprised to be included in their parents' major decisions. Only Edward was aware of the family's finances. The girls were shocked. The news was unnerving, but each of them offered an opinion when asked. The wheels were in motion. There was no turning back.

Edward realized that the money he earned as a newsboy for *The Roanoke Times* was not substantial enough to make a difference. He would have to seek additional employment. While he and Carroll Swain were sitting on the curb in front of the drugstore rolling and banding newspapers one chilly morning in late November, Edward shared his family's plight with his longtime friend who had a suggestion.

Carroll offered that the Hotel Roanoke sometimes had an opening for a waiter, and his father just happened to know the chef at the prestigious hotel. Perhaps he could be persuaded to put in a good word for Edward. Carroll assured Edward that he had two important qualities that would make him stand out among the many job seekers who usually applied—good manners and correct English.

Heartened by the prospect of being able to earn a steady income, with the additional possibility of receiving generous tips, Edward managed to conceal his inattentiveness behind a pleasant smile throughout his classes all day, and at the sound of the final bell, he rushed home to consult with his father. With Sam's approval, Edward planned to research Hotel Roanoke at the Gainsboro Library before having his father help him set up an interview.

Having gained permission to leave school before lunch, a few days later Edward headed up the hill to the imposing Hotel Roanoke, a Tudor revival style of architecture built in 1882. He had read all about it in the Gainsboro Library, and if he had the chance, he planned to insert a few facts into his interview. Ora had listened to his prepared remarks. but only tapped her fingers rhythmically on the table as he stammered through each revision. "Words matter," his mother finally explained and she offered a few choice ones to polish his presentation. It bothered Edward that his mother was always quick to correct him, but she never seemed to find reason to tell him she loved him. Aunt Lily always hugged her boys, and she had seven of them! Still, he appreciated the interest that Ora took in him when he really needed it.

As he had hoped, the interview went well, and he was hired on the spot with the *caveat* that he was a holiday hire. However, if he proved to be reliable and upheld Hotel Roanoke's lofty standards, he might be considered for the permanent staff after the New Year's Eve gala. Edward made an effort to remain poised, a demeanor his mother had described vividly, but his heart was thumping so hard that he was certain the White man sitting behind the elaborately carved desk in front of him could hear it. Once the gentleman reviewed a series of papers—hotel rules and map as well as the schedule for December—he stood, shook the youngster's hand, and sat down in his padded maroon leather chair.

Without looking up again, he dipped his pen into the crystal inkwell resting on the desk and began writing in broad strokes across a piece of paper. Edward wondered if his new employer was adding *Edward Randall* to the hotel staff roster, but he resisted the urge to ask. Somehow, he managed to contain himself until he walked out the brass-handled front doors, rounded the bend and was absolutely sure that he couldn't be observed by anyone at a hotel window. Then he waved his official papers in the air, whooped with excitement, and ran all the way home to share the good news with his family.

Out of breath and crashing through the front door with the slightly crumpled papers still in his hand, he plopped down in a kitchen chair beside his father. Sam folded the newspaper he had been reading about world news and took off his glasses. Stretching back into his chair and folding his hands, he awaited the outcome of Edward's interview. Clearly, he had gotten the job at Hotel Roanoke, but Sam knew his son wanted to regale him with every little detail. No one in the family had ever been inside the Hotel Roanoke, and Sam was curious as well as proud of his son's accomplishment.

Edward was bursting with enthusiasm and no longer poised, but he gave his father such an animated accounting of his experience that Sam felt as though he had accompanied Edward on the mission. He was an attentive audience, asking questions and complimenting his son for handling the interview with dignity. Receiving praise from his father was gratifying, but Edward still planned to give a repeat performance for Ora and his sisters when they returned home from school.

During his interview Edward had made it clear that he was willing to work every night of the week throughout December, and he was duly scheduled. He found reasons to cover the entire first floor of the massive hotel and familiarize himself with procedures and expectations so he was quite confident as he approached the end of the first week. He was feeling hopeful once again.

On Sunday morning an abiding question was answered and everything changed. The front page of *The Roanoke Times* reduced history to just a few bold words.

Sunday, December 7, 1941.
The Japanese attack Pearl Harbor.
America ensnarled in World War II.

Ora was right. Words matter.

CHAPTER 10

THE SOUND OF SILENCE

Suddenly, life seemed to be moving at warp speed. Edward was struggling to keep up with all his commitments, and so he was relieved to learn that the Hotel Roanoke provided a fresh uniform to wear every evening at work. He certainly didn't have time to prepare two sets of clothing each day. In addition to the convenience of the uniform, Edward was excited about how dapper he looked in the carefully tailored white serge jacket cropped at the waist. The matching white trousers were sharply creased and there were two parallel rows of four decorative brass buttons starting at the waist that traced down the top of the crease. A uniform made a statement, created an identity and commanded respect. He liked the concept.

Throughout the hectic Christmas season, Edward was efficient and unflappable. After just a few days of bussing tables and delivering meals with aplomb, he was promoted to the status of waiter. He was a quick study and with Ora's prompting, he worked out a brief but articulate patter to enhance the dining experience of Hotel Roanoke's guests. He followed the rules but always added a little something extra, much to the diners' pleasure, and he was duly rewarded with a generous tip on most occasions. He continued to study the history of Roanoke and familiarized himself with the major tourist attractions as well as the routes to reach them. If the guests showed an interest, he was fully prepared with answers to their questions.

Equally important was Edward's relationship with the other waiters and the chef. He learned not only the entire menu for the evening but also the origin of a dish, any special ingredients in it, and the appropriate selection of wine to enhance the meal. He was gracious to even the most demanding guests and tried to accommodate every request, regardless of the inconvenience. No matter how tired he was, Edward was the picture of exuberant youth. His manners were impeccable.

Needless to say, Hotel Roanoke felt certain they had landed a long-term employee who

Pictured in a 1941 booklet about the historic Hotel Roanoke, Edward is attired in his waiter's uniform and standing in front of one of the chefs who is giving him directions.
(Photo courtesy of Hotel Roanoke)

would keep customers coming back. He was so cheerful and good-natured, that no one could ever have imagined the deepening sorrow he faced every evening when he reached home late at night. He was missing meals with his family, and he feared every supper might be his father's last. At least he was assuring his dad that he could handle the heavy responsibility of providing for the family.

Usually, Ora and his sisters had gone to bed long before the end of Edward's shift at night, but he knew Sam would be dozing in his favorite upholstered chair and waiting to hear all about his son's day. The bond between father and son grew stronger, making the anticipation of a future without Sam all the more heartbreaking.

Often Sam would reminisce about his life or offer important lessons learned through personal experience. He was trying to squeeze in as much guidance as he could in the waning time he had left. He desperately wanted to prepare his son to face the anticipated challenges of a world at war. He could no longer share adventures with his son—like the day the two took the bus downtown to get a special edition of the December 7th *Roanoke Times*, but he listened faithfully to the radio, and each evening he gave his son an accounting of the escalating hostilities in Europe.

Sam had very much wanted to see his first-born graduate from high school, but now he simply hoped to celebrate Edward's 16th birthday with him. The once sturdy father was making a heroic effort to stay alive, but silicosis is a relentless adversary. By summer Norfolk & Western thanked him for his service in retraining his replacement and permanently retired him. He had reached the point that his coughing shook his entire body, and he often literally gasped for just one more breath. Every movement was laborious. Even neighborhood walks were no longer possible, so he sat in the nook on the front porch and watched the world moving on without him.

Edward wanted to quit school, give his notice at Hotel Roanoke, and stay at home by his father's side, but of course, that was not feasible. Ora counted on him now as she once had relied on Sam. Her only respite was the hours Edward spent with his father when he returned home at night. She tried to get an hour or so of rest while Edward tended to Sam's needs because she was on duty throughout the rest of the night. Sam had become too fragile to travel by rail to the university hospital in Charlottesville for treatment, but it no longer mattered. The attending physician explained there was no more he could do.

Only complete and utter exhaustion permitted Edward to get even snatches of sleep here and there each night. Sam was now sitting upright in his favorite upholstered chair instead of sleeping in the bedroom. It was his effort to give Ora some relief. His long-suffering and all-consuming journey toward death enveloped everyone, including his young daughters—14-year-old Martha and 11-year-old Bernice—who were terrified. Edward had to compartmentalize his emotions in order to function at school and at work.

Without warning on October 15, 1942, the coughing stopped. Samuel Edward Randall was finally at peace. The sound of silence was deafening.

Edward, standing behind Martha and his younger sister Bernice, is well aware of how desperate the family's circumstances are and that he must shoulder as much of the financial load as he can. He no longer is a carefree teenager, but he is willing to take on whatever responsibility is necessary to ease his father's mind and help him live a little longer. Martha and Bernice do their part by continuing to be exemplary students in school, but they are worried about what is going to happen.

Ora immediately shifted into high gear. Although she knew it was futile, she called for an ambulance and all too soon she was planning Sam's Homegoing at St. Paul's Methodist Church. The Fields showed up with their entire brood, and Aunt Lily stayed in the kitchen, helping Ora prepare for all the people who would be dropping by to offer their respects. Grandma Flood came over to join young Omega Field in comforting Martha and Bernice, and Uncle Henry took all his sons and Edward out to the back yard to organize a touch football game. It would have been a glorious occasion if Sam could have been there, but everyone was mostly going through the motions of adjusting to life without the Randalls' beloved patriarch.

By Thanksgiving Ora and her youngsters were numb and lonely, but they turned down invitations to celebrate with other families. Instead, they stayed home to create new traditions and mourn in private.

One month and 16 days after his father's passing, Edward turned 16 years old. Sam had almost made it to his birthday. No gift in the world could assuage a heartbroken son's grief.

Grief-stricken Ora stands beside her younger brother Larry, before they attend her husband Sam's Homegoing.

CHAPTER 11

PICKING UP THE PIECES

Ora had diligently tried to soothe Sam's suffering throughout his illness, but after years of watching silicosis sap her proud and resolute husband of his dignity, his very life, she was exhausted. Only Sam found peace in his passing. As a widow with three children, she could not cave in now. There were expenses, so many expenses, and not enough money to cover all of them. Bereft and losing any façade of being a loving and nurturing mother, Ora tucked away her personal dreams and steeled herself to face the future alone. Instead, she focused with dogged determination on her major goal—the guarantee that her three children would achieve a college degree. At least that would give them a chance in life.

With his father's tragic death, Edward had no expectation of experiencing carefree teenage years like many of his friends at Lucy Addison High. Instead of mooning over the attractive girls in his class who were clearly drawn to his outgoing personality and good looks or pursuing the opportunity that an athletic scholarship might provide, Edward stepped up to the plate. He honored his father by taking on the responsibility of setting a good example for his sisters and being accountable to his mother. The bicycle his father had surprised him with as a youngster now became his means of doing errands and continuing to provide a reliable income as a newspaper boy. Print copy was in greater demand than ever. It was critical for every American family to keep up with news of the war. *The Roanoke Times* served as a barometer for able-bodied men trying to prepare for the great diaspora sweeping up families and their loved ones across America.

During his hours at school, Edward was in survival mode academically. He had little time to fully complete his assignments in his advanced classes at the level of which he was capable because he was clocking extra hours at Hotel Roanoke. He raced straight to the hotel as soon as school was out. Edward had become very popular with the kitchen staff, who knew of his family's struggles, and the chef discreetly wrapped leftovers for the Randall family at the end of the night. Ora disliked taking handouts, but she was grateful.

It helped supplement the meager groceries she could purchase, considering not only the limitations of her budget but also the rationing prompted by the war effort. Plus, she didn't have to worry about Edward's dinner. Hotel Roanoke's leftovers were better than anything she could afford.

The family was gradually making adjustments and falling into new patterns. Martha and Bernice had many empathetic friends and teachers at school and were involved in after-school activities, but Edward was becoming a loner. Ora also worried about her son's declining interest in his academic achievement. Sometimes when she got up early to prepare breakfast, she would find him sound asleep, with his head resting on an open book and an unfinished assignment under his hand. Ora feared that Edward would never reach his potential, that he'd lose sight of his dreams and end up just another tragic statistic.

Ora was working in the Lucy Addison High School library during this challenging period of her life. Instead of being in the classroom where she would have been overwhelmed with grading unending numbers of papers, preparing lectures, responding to parents' expectations, and meeting the standards of the curriculum, she was free to check on Edward during the school day…a fortuitous circumstance as it turned out. One afternoon as she looked out the library window, taking a moment to relax into a daydream, she caught sight of Edward sitting on one of the dozen swings suspended from sturdy metal poles out on the school's playground. Both furious and frightened by the image of yet another Black boy considering dropping out of high school, she raced out of the school doors to confront her son and intimidate him into returning to class.

Descending upon him like a predatory hawk, she admonished him for being a slacker and embarrassing his family with such irresponsible behavior. It was fear for his future that propelled her tirade. She misread the situation, though. In truth, Edward had just been seeking a moment of peace from the relentless cycle that had become his life. Still, the moment was painful for both mother and son. Instead of feeling appreciated, Edward felt denigrated, defeated . . . but only momentarily. Edward was not one to feel sorry for himself.

Embarrassed that one of his classmates might have witnessed the dramatic scene, but also trained to show respect for his mother, he willingly followed Ora back into Lucy Addison High School's empty corridors and headed to the last class of the afternoon. Although Ora never harangued her son about her fears on that day and he didn't harbor resentment toward her, that brief but intense moment remained etched in Edward's memory. It was a turning point . . . time to cut the apron strings.

Ora sensed the change in their relationship and waited for Edward to return home late one weekend evening. She wondered, *How would Sam have handled this situation*? It was clear that Edward needed his father more than ever. She hated to admit it, but she was a poor substitute for her strong and stoic husband. Sam had always seemed to handle crises with a calm but firm hand. The family was at a crossroads, and she needed to help her children make the transition as she tried to pick up the pieces of their life herself.

Edward was surprised to find Ora, dressed in her pink chenille bathrobe and sitting at the kitchen table waiting for him late one Saturday evening after his shift at Hotel Roanoke. Usually, being the focus of his mother's undivided attention was as the result of some serious misjudgment on his part, but Ora insisted that she simply wanted to know about his day. Secretly, she had realized that on Saturdays Edward delivered his newspapers as usual, but disappeared for the rest of the day and did not return until after his shift at the hotel. She was concerned about the company he was keeping in his spare time.

Edward didn't notice the suspicion in her voice, though. At last Ora seemed open and interested in hearing what he had to say. He had big plans for the future, which he had never divulged to anyone but his father. Long suppressed dreams burst out of him like the mesmerizing images of brilliantly colored fireworks exploding in air. He told his mother about the wondrous Saturdays he was now spending at the airstrip adjacent to the Cannady's farm.

Some of the pilots at the airfield had befriended him to the extent that he had a weekly job of hosing down and washing the light aircraft lined up at the far edge of the field. In exchange for his services, a few of the pilots of the privately owned planes provided Edward with the opportunity to go on sightseeing flights over the city of Roanoke with them. Edward was as interested in learning the basics of flight as he was about the intricately interwoven patterns of roads leading to residences, businesses, hospitals, churches, and fire stations arranged like Lilliputian communities hundreds of feet beneath him. Saturdays had become his escape from depression and sorrow.

Rapidly moving his hands with excitement as he shared all he was learning about the principles of flight and the exclusive camaraderie among pilots, Edward explained that flying was his destiny. He informed his mother that he planned to join the newly formed Army Air Force as soon as he graduated from high school. He had already spent time talking to a U.S. Army recruiter after listening to a group of new recruits dressed in their "Pinks and Greens." The young men had recently given a presentation about being in the military to the high school students at Lucy Addison High. Edward was determined to do his part for the war effort by becoming a pilot. He admitted that he had made a personal commitment to the U.S. Army Air Force. Then, he sheepishly revealed he had official papers for her to sign.

Impressed by Edward's resourcefulness and ability to repress significant information,

Ora felt ambivalent. She was worried about her son's obsession with becoming a pilot, but she was also relieved by his candor. He was excited about taking charge of his future, and he was making reasoned decisions, even though he had not consulted her first. Subtlety was not Ora's strong suit, but she recognized that this was an important point in their relationship. They had developed a mother-son dialogue, and she didn't want to risk losing it. Edward was thrilled when Ora reached over, patted him on the shoulder, and smiled as she told her son that she was proud of him. It was a moment to remember. She signed the papers and on 11 March 1944 Edward was officially inducted into the U.S. Army Air Force Reserves.

Edward proudly wears the wings of a prospective air cadet.

By June 1944, the world was shocked by the brazen Allied invasion of Normandy on the shores of France. The historic number of casualties was staggering, especially to a mother whose son was now committed to the military.

Ora silently counted the days as summer faded into September. Edward's senior year was half over. These were his last months at home. Ora was more conflicted over her son's plans than she revealed, but at least he was achieving academically, continuing to hold down two jobs, and adjusting to the loss of his father.

Edward's formal photo as a Class of 1945 graduate of Lucy Addison High School in Roanoke's Gainsboro community.

In August 1945, Edward joins a trainload of soldiers headed to basic training at Keesler Air Base in Biloxi, Mississippi. He is totally focused on one major goal—do whatever is necessary to qualify for the aviation training program at Tuskegee. He intends to succeed.

With his proud mother and sisters in attendance, Edward graduated from Lucy Addison High School in February 1945, and he joined the adult workforce while he awaited the Army Air Force's call to duty. On April 12, 1945, Americans were shaken by President Franklin Delano Roosevelt's untimely death and Vice President Harry Truman's ascension to the presidency. Everyone was on edge worrying about how things were going to unfold until May 8th when the Allied Forces prevailed in Europe!

Americans and all the members of the Allied Forces celebrated Victory in Europe, VE-Day, with grateful jubilation. Meanwhile, the war was still raging in the Far East when the U.S. Army Air Force notified Edward to report to active duty at Keesler Air Base in Biloxi, Mississippi on 13 August 1945.

Then the most shocking news hit the papers on August 6, 1945. The U.S. Army Air Force dropped an atomic bomb on Hiroshima, Japan, and followed up on August 9th with another atomic bomb being dropped on Nagasaki. The world had never witnessed such horror.

A few days later, the Randall clan assembled at the Roanoke Norfolk & Western Depot to see Edward off on his first tour of duty. The mood was somber. Ora was reeling with the thought of losing her first born, but she was also deeply moved that he set up an allotment to be sent to his mother each month. It was automatically taken from his paycheck. The gesture touched her heart, but she withheld her emotions and simply thanked her son. Although only a private, Edward cut a handsome figure as he joined all the other uniformed young men. Waving goodbye to his mother and sisters, Edward looked across the tracks and up the hill to Hotel Roanoke one last time and boarded the train to his future.

CHAPTER 12

STARTING ANEW

Leaving his childhood behind in sleepy Gainsboro, young Private Randall sat midst his peers in the speeding troop train headed southwest of Roanoke. As the powerful locomotive carved its way into the Deep South, he watched out the window of the rail car designated for colored soldiers until it was too dark to see America's vast expanse of pine-forested hills; tended orchards; sweeping fields of waving wheat; and fenced pastures scattered with cattle awaiting a dinner of home-grown silage.

It had been a waiting game for the young recruit. When Edward was inducted into the Army Air Force Reserves in March 1944, he was listed as James E.P. Randall. The U.S. Army dealt with soldiers on a "first name" basis and so Edward was called James or Jim. That was the beginning of many unforeseen changes following his high school graduation in February 1945. In April, President Roosevelt died, and by May, the Allied Forces declared "Victory over Europe." Most shocking of all, though, was President Truman's sanction of nuclear weapons against Japan to force Emperor Hirohito to capitulate. It was mind-boggling, but Jim had finally been called to active duty and he was more than ready as the troop train rolled through unseen vistas shrouded in the secrecy of night.

The following morning, he arrived in Biloxi, Mississippi, disembarked the train, and boarded the waiting buses marked in large block letters with his destination—Keesler AB. Blending into the sea of his khaki-clad compatriots, Jim slung the canvas bag containing all his earthly belongings over his shoulder and reported to the 2143rd Army Air Force (AAF) Squadron A, as Private James Randall, Serial Number 13 181 154.

Groggy from hours on the troop train, Jim almost failed to respond the first few times he was called upon, but he soon adjusted to being summoned by "James" because he needed to distinguish himself from the other recruits. He had to be sharper than his peers in order to achieve his goal of being re-assigned to Tuskegee, Alabama, to earn his pilot's wings. Although listed as a clerk (non-typist) he repeatedly reminded his superiors of his desire to become a pilot. The U.S. War Department had formed the all-Black 99th Pursuit Squadron of the U.S. Army Air Force in January of 1942. The mission was to train young Black pilots using single-engine planes at the segregated Tuskegee Army Air Field—Moton Field—in Tuskegee, Alabama, and Jim was eager to join their numbers.

While most of his contemporaries chose to take a break on weekends, Jim kept his nose to the grindstone. He spent every spare moment studying manuals and preparing to take additional batteries of tests to assure his qualifications for pilot training. In addition to leading an exemplary life as a soldier, he avoided the problems that stalked his peers who made forays into Biloxi, where they were not as readily accepted as their White counterparts. Remaining alone in the barracks over the weekend was also a financial decision since his $50 monthly paycheck was considerably diminished by the allotment the army sent home to his family. By the end of each month, he was counting pennies. His goal had aways been to enter World War II in a cockpit, and though everything was changing, Tuskegee was still the opportunity of a lifetime. Considering that the 1939 census report revealed there were only "125 licensed Negro pilots in the United States" at that time and "none of them were in the U.S. Military," he knew he was lucky.

Jim successfully completed his basic training at Keesler and was transferred to Tuskegee Army Air Field that same year. He was assigned to the Office of the Chief of Safety and once again found himself playing a waiting game. Now it was just a question of when he would be called up for the next pilot training class. Each day Jim watched formations of disciplined young men marching in criss-crossing patterns at Tuskegee, and often he was in the midst of one of the briskly moving units. On other occasions he sat and listened to the increasing chatter among his fellow soldiers about something that both startled and angered him. He had learned how to work within the parameters of segregation in Mississippi at Keesler, but for the first time in his life he was stopped in his tracks by a single word—eugenics. He was shocked by the unscientific assessments of bigots . . . some of them generals!

The scuttlebutt among the soldiers at Tuskegee revolved around the high-ranking White officers who adhered to the idea that the effort to train African American pilots for combat was a futile experiment. Jim learned that as recent as 1925, an Army War College study referred to African Americans as "mentally inferior subspecies of the human race," with "smaller brains that weighed 10 ounces less than whites." General George C. Marshall, the U.S. Army Chief of Staff, expressed his opinion in 1941, when he espoused that "Experiments within the Army in the solution of social problems are fraught with danger to efficiency, discipline, or morale." A year earlier he had also expressed his view that the military was "not the place to change the segregation policies in American society."

Tuskegee was an absurd undertaking to those who opposed what they called the

"Tuskegee Experiment," but for aspiring young pilots like Jim and his contemporaries, it was an incredible opportunity. Jim learned that the Tuskegee Institute was training African American civilian pilots prior to World War II. By 1939, the Civil Aeronautics Administration approved the school as a civilian pilot training facility, so by 1941 when Pearl Harbor catapulted America into the war, things were already in place for President Franklin Delano Roosevelt to sanction the 99th Fighter Squadron as the first African American flying unit to deploy on a combat mission in Spring 1943.

Jim remembered how President Roosevelt's wife Eleanor upstaged him in March of 1941, when she joined Chief Flight instructor, Charles A. ("Chief") Anderson on a flight over rural Alabama. The photo was front page news in *The Roanoke Times*. It stoked Jim's interest in Tuskegee's brief history. At the time, he and his father had even discussed the implication for the future.

However, the latest brouhaha with General Frank O'Driscoll Hunter—a World War I and World War II flying ace who took a stand against colored officers breaking the code and entering a segregated Officers' Club—was unsettling. These intense confrontations could directly affect him and he took note. Growing up in a self-sufficient Black neighborhood had shielded him from much of segregation's cruelty, but Jim was paying attention now. He began researching and reading articles to prepare himself for whatever encounters he might face in his quest to become a pilot because he felt quite sure that airways were not segregated.

In thumbing through military magazines lying around in the barracks, Jim tore out a section of one article which quoted a passage from a 1925 U.S. War Department Study. It read:

In that process of evolution, the American Negro has not progressed as far as the other subspecies of the human family. As a race he has not developed leadership qualities. His mental inferiority and the inherent weakness of his character are factors that must be considered with great care in the preparation of any plans for his employment in war. Even physically the black American is inferior; his normal physical activity is generally small due to his laziness.

Jim carefully folded the clipping, placed it in his black leather wallet, and it remained there for the rest of his life. It was the fuel that fired his unflagging ambition to be the best of the best among the pilots of the fledgling U.S. Army Air Force. Jim was still pondering how to handle controversial situations he might face in the future, when he finally received a call to report to the Personnel Office at 2164 th Headquarters. He couldn't get there fast enough.

This is it, he thought. *At long last I'm going to begin pilot training.* Standing before his commanding officer, he was scarcely able to contain his excitement. A wide grin spread across his face as he snapped to attention and saluted. The ensuing pronouncement about his future was the last thing he expected.

"All training is cancelled," his commander said. "The war in Europe is over and things are winding down."

Noting the look of disillusionment on the young soldier's face, the commander explained that the 2164th AAF Base Unit—the Contract Pilot School which operated the primary flight training school at Tuskegee Institute's Moton Field—was discontinued. The final pilot training class was underway and would graduate on June 30, 1946 but afterwards the Tuskegee Army Air Field was scheduled to be placed on temporary inactive status until further notice…perhaps indefinitely.

Crestfallen, Jim listened to his options. He could remain in the enlisted ranks or enlist in the Reserves, attend college, and become an officer qualified for flight school. What were the odds that the end of war and the beginning of fervently prayed for peace would defer a young man's dreams. On February 23, 1946, Jim received an honorable discharge, and within the week, he boarded a train headed for Roanoke. Exhausted by his unexpected change of fortune, he soon fell asleep thinking about the denigrating article tucked away in his wallet. Jim Randall was more determined than ever to achieve his goals. He had something to prove and nothing was going to stop him.

After completing basic training at Keesler AB, Jim is assigned to Tuskegee Army Air Field, but his career takes an unexpected turn.

CHAPTER 13

WHIRLWIND

It was Jim's first night home and a time to celebrate. The whole Randall family was gathered around the kitchen table once again, and Ora had prepared a celebratory dinner. By the time Ora served Jim's favorite dessert—strawberry rhubarb pie—Martha and Bernice were still chattering away and trying to fill in their big brother on all the things that had happened in his absence. Martha was on the staff of the first yearbook ever published at Lucy Addison High School, and she was very excited about attending Bennett College in the near future while Bernice added that she was the newly elected treasurer of the Math Club. Jim could scarcely believe how grown up they seemed.

Ora pumped her son for all the details of his military experience when she could get a word in edgewise, and Jim obliged by recounting the highlights. Pulling his official discharge papers out of his duffel bag, he placed them on the table and explained what it was like on September 2nd when all the soldiers learned that the Japanese signed a peace treaty and World War II was officially over. There was overwhelming relief and gratitude, but the newsreels showing masses of civilians, even children, caught up in a nuclear blast was horrendous. Everyone agreed that using nuclear weapons to stop the war opened the door to a frightening future.

Exhausted by all the events of the day, Ora and the girls headed to bed after rinsing the dishes and setting them aside for a once over in the morning, but Jim was still unwinding and he remained seated at the kitchen table. He stared at the certificate, which verified that as of 22 February 1946, his new status was veteran. His official Honorable Discharge papers acknowledged that he had received $100 of his $200 Mustering Out pay and $12.50 in travel pay for the journey home. He would also receive the World War II Victory Ribbon. Tracing the embossed U.S. Army of the United States' logo with his finger—a golden eagle bearing both an olive branch and arrows in its talons—Jim wished his father was alive to read the words, "This certificate is awarded as a testimonial of

Honest and Faithful Service to this country." If only his father had lived to see this day . . . After almost seven months of being a world away from Gainsboro, young Jim Randall had developed a broader perspective. He had missed achieving his wings at Tuskegee, but he had been accepted to the program. Although the timing of World War II's conclusion seemed to have devastated a young man's dream, Jim realized the irony of the outcome of the situation. Instead of training with an all-Black unit, he would have the opportunity to enter an integrated pilot training program with White pilots—a privilege guaranteed by President Roosevelt and his successor President Truman. The Tuskegee pilots' outstanding performance in combat situations had bought him a ticket to the new version of the U.S. Army Air Force. He just had to get a few years of college under his belt first.

As a veteran and thanks to the GI Bill, Jim was excited to learn that his college tuition and some of his college expenses would be covered, but he was sorely disappointed that Virginia Military Institute (VMI) would not be an option. As a boy he had not realized that it was segregated. Instead, Jim decided on Hampton Institute, an historic Black college in nearby Hampton, Virginia. Ora intended to make sure that Jim followed through with his decision, and so she fully researched the college and gave it her stamp of approval. As her son adjusted to the civilian world once again, Ora would sit out on the front porch with Jim in the evenings and share all she had learned about Hampton's history.

Hampton Institute was a private research university founded in 1868 by Union Army General Samuel Chapman Armstrong, the son of missionaries. It was established as Hampton Agricultural and Industrial School by both Black and White leaders, primarily representatives of the Congregational and Presbyterian churches, in the American Missionary Association. Their goal was to provide an education to freedmen after the Civil War.

The school was built on the grounds of *Little Scotland*, a former plantation which overlooked Hampton Roads and the Hampton River. In her research Ora learned that the founder, Union Army General Samuel Armstrong, was strongly influenced by his father's method of teaching when he was a missionary to the Polynesians in the Sandwich Islands, which eventually became known as Hawaii. Armstrong used the same approach to develop the curriculum at Hampton—a combination of "cultural uplift with moral and manual training . . . that encompassed the head, the heart, and the hands." In sharing all the history of the school with her son, Ora was heartened by his newly found interest in history.

Noteworthy among donors who endowed Hampton Institute with a substantial amount of money was General William Jackson Palmer, a Union Army cavalry commander from Philadelphia who had been so generous that one of the major buildings on campus was named Palmer Hall in his honor. In spite of his being a Quaker who found violence abhorrent, Palmer felt compelled to serve in the war because of his passion to bring an end to slavery. Awarded the Congressional Medal of Honor for his bravery, Palmer was such an honorable leader that many of his Black soldiers followed him West after the war, and they set down roots in Colorado Springs, the city he founded as he began building the Denver & Rio Grande railroad.

In addition to its intriguing early history, Hampton was about to make history once again. Former Hampton graduate Alonzo Graseano Morón, was to become the first Black acting president of Hampton Institute following his graduation from Harvard Law School.

Jim enrolled at Hampton for the Fall semester in September 1946, and he settled in, along with a few other vets he'd met at registration, to attain the academic credentials that would enhance his chances to be called back into the military for pilot training. Majoring in industrial education, he focused on automotive and diesel engineering. His first year at Hampton delighted Ora and surprised even Jim. He had matured during his stint in

James is very focused on his academic studies throughout his freshman year, although there is one particular girl on campus who has caught his eye. By his sophomore year he makes a point to meet her. Mary Ann Bell of Evanston, Indiana, is studying to become a teacher. James, whose friends at Hampton call him "Jim," is intent upon being accepted as an aviation cadet as soon as he completes two years of college and passes preliminary tests for acceptance into the United States Air Force.

the military, and he had his priorities in order. For the first time, he fully embraced his education and all its nuances.

In autumn of 1947 when he began his sophomore year, he unexpectedly experienced a major distraction. Her name was Mary Ann Bell, and she was from Evansville, Indiana. The female students lived across the campus from where the male dormitory was located, and so Jim didn't see her that often, but that didn't diminish the attraction. Mary Ann was studying to be a teacher and was fascinated that Jim was keenly interested in returning to the military to become a pilot.

Then a letter arrived from the War Department. It was an invitation for Jim to take a physical at Langley AFB, and if he passed, he would be placed in consideration for training in the newly founded United States Air Force. Jim passed the physical as well as a second physical and a battery of tests, including psychological tests administered by a recruiting officer. When Jim continued to excel in every test, the recruiter explained that he felt certain Jim would be called up for pilot training. It was just a matter of time.

By the end of his epic sophomore year, Jim was caught up in a whirlwind of change. He and Mary Ann had developed a serious relationship that worried Ora. She saw the young woman as a diversion that could take precedence over his goals, an impediment to his success, so she was relieved when he left Hampton Institute to await his call to active duty. He was back on track to achieve his dreams. Ora did not realize they now included a certain Mary Ann Bell.

CHAPTER 14

RIDING THE RAILS TO FLIGHT SCHOOL

Returning to Roanoke for an indefinite amount of time as he awaited his pilot training slot, Jim took the opportunity to find temporary employment, something new and challenging. As a World War II vet with two years of college, he had an impressive resume so he applied for the Railway Postal Service. Once again Jim was required to take a battery of tests—a written exam as well as a physical—but he was accustomed to the drill and easily qualified for a position as a mail sorter on the railway route between Roanoke and Bristol, a twin city on the Virginia/Tennessee border.

Although Jim had no intention of remaining in service to the railway system for any length of time, he found the job interesting and he made quite an impression on his superiors. Jim was a team player—focused and resilient; hard-working and consistent—and he immediately adjusted to the demands of the job. He was readily accepted by his older and more experienced counterparts who interacted with precision like the inner workings of a clock. Since as many as 12 postal clerks could be assigned to one railway mail car, the cramped quarters demanded carefully choreographed interactions.

He was familiar with the process of disassembling and repairing engines; building locomotives and railcars; and designing the interior of the various rail cars according to their purpose, but he had never seen a railway mail car designed according to federal specifications. For additional security in the event of an accident, the government had recently decreed that the mail cars were to be made of steel, a safety feature to guarantee the security of the U.S. mail.

The federal government stepped in and organized the use of railway mail cars at the turn of the 20th century to expedite the distribution of mail to an ever-increasing population. Having the U.S. government take responsibility for railway mail cars not only accommodated the demand for faster postal service, but it also generated much needed additional income for Norfolk & Western (to cover the cost of modernizing the railway system).

Norfolk & Western mail cars were positioned at the end of the train, and since the U.S. mail was a federally protected service, the laws regarding the security of the mail were stringent.

First class mail, magazines and newspapers were all sorted, cancelled when necessary, and dispatched to post offices in towns along the route. Registered mail was also handled, and the foreman in charge was required to carry a regulation pistol while on duty to discourage theft of the mail.

An interesting feature of most RPO (Railway Post Office) cars was a hook that could be used to snatch a leather or canvas pouch of outgoing mail hanging on a track-side mail crane at smaller towns where the train did not stop. With the train often operating at 70 mph or more, a postal clerk would have a pouch of mail ready to be dispatched as the train passed the station. In a coordinated movement, the catcher arm was swung out to catch the hanging mail pouch while the clerk stood in the open doorway. The mail pouch had a strap around the middle, and the strap was tightened in preparation for pickup with an approximately equivalent weight of mail in either end of the pouch to prevent the heavier end from pulling the lighter end off the catcher arm. As the inbound pouch slammed into the catcher arm, the clerk kicked the outbound mail pouch out of the car, making certain to kick it far enough that it was not sucked back under the train. Outbound pouches of first class mail were sealed with a locked strap for security. Larger sacks with optional provisions for locking were used for newspapers, magazines, and parcel post. An employee of the local post office would retrieve the pouches and sacks and deliver them to the post office.

Railway mail clerks were subjected to stringent training and ongoing testing of details regarding their handling of the mail. On a given RPO route, each clerk was expected to know not only the post offices and rail junctions along the route, but also specific local delivery details within each of the larger cities served by the route. Periodic testing demanded both accuracy and speed in sorting mail, and a clerk scoring only 96% accuracy would likely receive a warning from the Railway Mail Service division superintendent.

Throughout the holidays, from Thanksgiving through Christmas, Jim was so invaluable to the men on his route that his supervisor suggested he consider becoming a career man. By the New Year there was still no word from the military, and Jim began to wonder if somehow he was going to miss his chance once again. He had almost given up hope when he received a letter with that familiar seal—U.S. War Department. He was directed to report to his recruiting office and to his surprise he was sworn into the newly formed U.S. Air Force with orders to report to Randolph Air Force Base in San Antonio, Texas, by the 25th of March 1949.

After interminable months of waiting, suddenly Jim was frantically racing around and trying to attend to dozens of last-minute details in preparation for the trip west. This was the moment he had been waiting for his whole life. That little boy who gazed out the window of his attic bedroom at airplanes flying overhead to distant vistas . . . who had ridden his red tricycle until the thin rubber tires wore off…who crashed repeatedly on his home-made bicycle that lacked brakes . . . who pedaled his father's gift of a bicycle to the airfield each Saturday to wash private planes in exchange for an airborne moment . . . was headed to flight school as Aviation Cadet James E.P. Randall! A long-deferred dream was coming true!

After a chaotic week of tying up loose ends, jotting a note to Mary Ann about his new address, and sharing one last evening with his family, Jim once again donned his uniform with the newly attached Air Cadet insignia on his shoulders indicating his new status. He picked up his well-worn and heavily packed duffel bag, and after hugging Ora and his sisters goodbye, he hurried to the railway depot down the hill from the Hotel Roanoke. It was a star-studded evening as he boarded the Midnight Special from Roanoke to Cincinnati, Ohio. His plan was to sleep through the rest of the night on the train and arrive in Cincinnati at the break of dawn. It would give him time to check out his orders and re-read the pamphlets about Randolph Air Force Base that the recruiter had given him. He would save the paperback book about San Antonio that Ora had stuck in the top of his duffel bag until later. Straining to remember long ago lectures in his high school history class about San Antonio, he could only recall the war between the United States and Mexico and the battle over the Alamo. Perhaps Ora's book would refresh his memory.

Everything went as planned. Weaving its way northwest to Ohio through the dark of night, the train arrived on schedule in the light of dawn at the big train station in Cincinnati. Jim disembarked and read all the tourist handouts about sights in the city including opera performances at the Cincinnati Zoo. Could that be a misprint? He was especially interested in the predictions about the Cincinnati Reds' upcoming baseball season. Cincinnati sounded like a fascinating place to return to someday. By the time he enjoyed a leisurely breakfast, the loudspeaker announced passengers traveling to San Antonio, Texas, should prepare to board.

Taking a window seat, Jim settled in for the over 1200 miles. It would take several days to reach his destination, but he looked forward to the adventure. He was beginning to feel like a seasoned traveler. It was his first trip to the West, and as he gazed at the changing landscape flying by in flowing watercolor images, he tried to capture what he was seeing in a letter to Mary Ann before he jotted a quick note to Ora.

Finally, reaching his destination days later, Jim stretched to regain his balance after so many hours of sitting. Slinging his heavy duffel bag over his shoulder, he stepped off the train. Searching for some form of conveyance to get to Randolph AFB, he spotted a military transport from Randolph's motor pool idling at the curb and waved his hand to hail the driver. Jim tried to conceal his embarrassment when a young enlisted man stepped out of the vehicle, snapped to attention, and saluted. Jim returned the salute and the soldier opened the back door of the car before stowing Jim's duffel bag in the trunk.

What a difference two years of college and the aviation cadet insignia on your shoulders makes, Jim thought. It was the first time he truly felt he had made it.

The first order of business at Randolph was dormitory room assignments for incoming aviation cadets arriving for basic training. Jim watched the TAC officer assign White cadets two to a room, and as he silently counted the uneven number of men assembled, he figured that he would be the odd man out. Since there were only three Black cadets in the group, he wondered what was going to happen. Braced for discrimination, Jim was pleasantly surprised when Bailey Pendergrass suggested that a double deck bunk and a single bed would resolve the issue, and that's how Bailey Pendergrass and Curtis LaVey ended up as Jim's roommates, an inseparable trio throughout basic training.

Learning to fly the T-6 was an intense experience for Jim. He was a perfectionist and that condescending article about Blacks that he kept in his wallet was a constant source of pressure. He was grateful that Bailey and Curtis were as committed to his success as they were to their own. In the evenings he and his roommates would help one another, going over the training manual and quizzing each other on procedures. It was a time to compare experiences and express concerns—the polar opposite of what he had experienced with many White soldiers at Keesler AB.

Jim excelled in his academic classes. All the years of observing his father working on locomotives in Norfolk & Western's workshop and listening to Sam explain the basic principles of how the huge engines functioned whetted Jim's keen interest in the physics of flight and what made the T-6 such a reliable aircraft. North American had first produced the airplane in 1939, and by World War II, the T-6 was the aerial classroom that most Allied pilots trained in as they transitioned from basic training aircraft to first-line tactical aircraft. "The T-6 trained several hundred thousand pilots in 34 different countries," and North American provided a commonality in training among Allied pilots, which was to their advantage.

Jim appreciated the Pratt & Whitney engine that powered the trainer and the Hamilton Standard propeller that kept it airborne. The aircraft was capable of 205 mph at 5,000 feet, a thrilling experience for an aspiring young man who had only owned pedal-powered bicycles throughout his youth. Even though he had accompanied a few local pilots on quick flights above Roanoke, the power of the T-6 eclipsed the capability of small private planes.

A natural in the academic classroom due to his innate talent for engineering, Jim was frustrated with his progress in flight. San Antonio's oft-erratic spring weather caused quite a few training flights to be cancelled, and Jim was not as confident about his ability in flight as he had expected. After missing several consecutive days of flying, he was relieved when the weather cleared and his flight instructor said, "We'll shoot some landings." Although he felt a bit rusty, Jim managed two good landings and was surprised when his instructor asked him to pull over to a mobile unit in the tasseled grass at the edge of the runway. Climbing out of the aircraft with the engine still "running," the seasoned pilot closed the vents in the back and instructed, "Give me three more touch and go landings."

Filled with both excitement and apprehension, Jim taxied back onto the middle of the runway, revved the engine and took off. Tracking the gears and flaps, Jim made a left hand turn out of traffic. Glancing over at the empty rear cockpit, he began to feel a bit frightened. There was no longer anyone there to help him in the event of an emergency or for just a quick bit of advice. He made his call for his first landing, turned base leg, made the final turn with tail and main gear locked in place, and as he descended and connected with the runway, he hit and bounced. Three times he pulled up, went around, and tried again. Three times he descended with one hand on the gear handle and a death grip on the throttle . . . and he bounced on the landing.

"Turn the throttle loose," the instructor called. "Make a full stop landing, and pick me up!" Unable to admit he had been worried about being by himself, with no one there to help him if something malfunctioned, Jim listened to his instructor's red-faced ranting as he critiqued Jim's landings. Standing with feet wide apart and his hands held tightly behind him, Jim made no effort to defend himself. He was more disappointed in his performance than his instructor was.

Airborne for one more chance at a decent landing, with his instructor once again seated behind him, Jim relaxed as his instructor said, "Settle in," and he glided down to the runway with a much lighter touch. As the two climbed out of the plane, Jim's instructor patted him on the back, congratulated him, and headed to Base Ops without a further word.

That evening Jim was disconsolate when Bailey and Curtis asked about his flight. He went over his experience in great detail, berating himself for such a poor showing. He was both chagrined and surprised by their spontaneous laughter until he listened to their individual experiences at being alone and in control of the T-6 for the first time. Both his roommates had had similar experiences, and their hilarious description of bouncing like a rabbit on their first solo landings had Jim in stitches. He began to see the day through their eyes and appreciate the fact that he had successfully soloed. Perhaps more importantly, he had gained a genuine friendship with his fellow fledgling pilots. So this was what camaraderie among pilots was like. He'd never forget the moment it happened.

The rest of basic training continued without a hiccup. As soon as Jim quit imposing impossible expectations on himself, the more fluid his flight became. His confidence increased with each additional day until he tamed his initial fear of failure, and flying became second nature to him. He no longer questioned himself when he ascended into the heavens alone, and when he reluctantly returned to earth, he occasionally "greased" a landing just like his instructor. He awoke each morning excited about blue skies but prepared for cloudy and overcast ones. Shedding the chrysalis of trepidation and doubt, he emerged one of the best pilots in his class.

Upon completion of this first phase of pilot training and the ensuing graduation ceremony in September 1949, Curtis LaVey was sent to Enid, Oklahoma, to train in the multi-engine B-25. Bailey Pendergrass and Jim ranked high enough in the graduating class to qualify for a single-engine assignment, and they could not conceal their excitement when they learned that they both would be going to Las Vegas Air Force Base in Nevada to begin Advanced Flight Training in the P-51 Mustang with the 3595th Pilot Training Wing. It was a coveted assignment, and they had earned it. Jim felt they had won the trifecta. If they excelled in this next phase of pilot training, they would graduate as fighter pilots, earn their wings, and become 2nd lieutenants in the United States Air Force. Truly, the sky was the limit.

CHAPTER 15

WINGS AND A WEDDING

Ironically, when Bailey and Jim arrived on a Sunday afternoon at Las Vegas Air Force Base, on the outskirts of its namesake city, the officer in charge explained they were shy the necessary number of single rooms in the dormitory for flight students. Clearly, he anticipated a problem since Jim and Bailey were the only Black pilots in the group, but Bailey immediately piped up that he and Jim could share a room in the dormitory. The officer in charge breathed a sigh of relief and briefed the group on the activities for the following day.

Bailey and Jim quickly fell into a rhythm and continued to work in tandem in support of each other. After a busy day on the flight line, they reviewed their performances and compared their experiences. Unlike the quixotic moods of the weather at Randolph AFB in San Antonio, Jim welcomed the desert-like atmosphere in Nevada. Weather was rarely cause for concern, and he quickly adjusted to piloting the P-51.

The competition was keen since the assembled group of young men had graduated at the top of their basic training classes, but Bailey and Jim felt they had the advantage. They studied for tests together and shared insights to help one another overcome challenges and excel. It was a turning point for Jim. He realized that he and Bailey had developed that unspoken bond, which he had watched among the pilots back at the airfield in Roanoke. Bailey and he had forged a life-long friendship that made becoming fighter pilots together an unforgettable experience.

Whereas it had been exciting to master North American's T-6 and graduate high enough in the class to be selected for single-engine aircraft, flying the P-51 Mustang was a pilot's dream. North American's P-51 was originally designed for the British in 1941, but it soon superseded all expectations. Its tried-and-true performance during World War II proved its enormous potential when Allied pilots flying the combat ready P-51 took on Germany's air power, even challenging and conquering the Messerschmitts in fighter sweeps that diminished the readiness of Germany's Luftwaffe.

The tide of the war shifted when P-51s penetrated Germany and peppered the countryside with lethal sorties across the heartland of the enemy. Relentlessly attacking supply trains, depots, and military installations as well as engaging the Luftwaffe in airborne battles, P-51 fighter pilots eventually drained the lifeblood of Germany's airpower and the Allied Forces prevailed. The P-51 Mustang distinguished itself in being the first to reach Berlin and ultimately to join heavy bombers in the devastation of Romania's Ploiesti oil fields. The Axis powers never recovered from the airborne battles and the P-51 Mustang was a major factor in that outcome. By 1944, the Senate War Investigating Committee reported to Vice President Elect Harry S. Truman that the P-51 Mustang was "the most aerodynamically perfect pursuit plane in existence."

Whetted by his passion for the Mustang, Jim had become insatiably interested in military history. Reflecting on his disappointment about World War II ending his dream of achieving his wings at Tuskegee, he was chagrined by his youthful naiveté. As he studied World War II, he was humbled by the exploits of veterans and vowed to honor their sacrifice every time he took flight. He soon developed the habit of hanging around Base Operations (Base Ops) to learn as much as he could about the nerve center of the base. Full of questions but being respectful and unobtrusive, he picked up bits and pieces of conversation that caused him to appreciate all the non-rated people involved in getting pilots airborne each day.

After a while Jim became a fixture at Base Ops, and one afternoon while he lingered on the flight line after his scheduled flight, he was overwhelmed by the ear-splitting roar that rattled windows and almost instantly followed the silent pass of a speeding aircraft. It happened so quickly that he had not locked in on its configuration, but there was no doubt in his mind that it was some type of experimental jet. He couldn't believe what he had just witnessed, but noting the guys at Base Ops looking skyward and laughing in delight, he headed toward them for answers. They surmised that it might have been Chuck Yeager flying the Bell X-1, the first manned aircraft to break the sound barrier. For the first time, Jim envisioned his future in the U.S. Air Force. He knew he wanted to fly "supersonic" one day!

As graduation neared, the tempo increased, and Jim had to set aside time to plan for Mary Ann's arrival. Their long-distance relationship had survived, nurtured only through a robust correspondence. Long distance phone calls were simply too expensive. From the very beginning Jim had established the fact that pilot training would have to take precedence over everything else—even Mary Ann. However, he promised her that once he earned his wings, they could begin planning their future together. Since that moment was soon to become a reality, the young couple faced their first serious problem, conflicting schedules. Jim's graduation from pilot training was in March, and Mary Ann was to graduate from

Hampton with her teaching certificate in June.

He and Bailey had been re-assigned to Brooks AFB on the south side of San Antonio following graduation, so Jim was not going to be able to return to Virginia for Mary Ann's college graduation. It was a conundrum, but he offered her a tempting consolation prize. He planned to cover the cost of Mary Ann's trip to Las Vegas so that she could pin his pilot's wings on his chest. As added incentive, he revealed that he had a big surprise awaiting her when she arrived. How could she resist?

On March 29, 1950, Bailey and Jim graduated from Advanced Flight Training at Las Vegas Air Force Base, and Mary Ann was in attendance! Wearing a bright red silk scarf tucked inside the collar of her dark blue suit and sporting a brand new engagement ring, she looked like a million dollars to Jim. The diamond ring sparkled in the sunshine as the ceremony on the flight line ended, and Jim could not stop grinning as she pinned silver wings on his uniform.

With their pilot wings acknowledged, Jim and Bailey were commissioned together as 2nd Lieutenants in the United States Air Force along with the rest of their classmates. They celebrated by pinning gold bars on each other's shoulders while Mary Ann smiled in anticipation of becoming an officer's wife. Endless partying ensued throughout the night, and all too soon Mary Ann had to return to Virginia. She was torn about leaving but thrilled by the prospect of planning a wedding. Their time together had been far too short, as far as Jim was concerned. He already missed her, but he was impressed by how flexible and supportive she had been. They had compromised and successfully coordinated their schedules—a revealing introduction to military life—and Mary Ann had passed with flying colors.

Jim and Bailey were given an extended leave before they were required to report to P-51 Instructor School at Brooks AFB, and unlike Bailey, Jim headed straight to San Antonio. He intended to avoid the usual frenetic effort to settle into new quarters. He also relished the idea of slowing down, organizing his thoughts and making plans for a future with Mary Ann. How he wished his father could have been at his graduation ceremony in Las Vegas. Sam would have been so proud of him. He would have liked Mary Ann, too. Thinking about how many important father-son talks he had missed, Jim wished he could have just one day to sit on the porch at 126 Rutherford Avenue and seek his father's counsel.

When Bailey showed up in San Antonio after a brief trip home, he tracked down Jim to check out his perspective about Brooks and the Instructor School. He was sure his pal had reconnoitered the entire base, learned about the program, and pestered the guys at Base Ops to let him log a flight or two. Both men were confident about the future when they officially reported to duty on April 30th. Together once again, they expected to graduate at the top of the class! They learned one bit of news, though, that surprised them both. On the very day they attended the indoctrination to Instructor School at Brooks, they were informed that Las Vegas AFB had been renamed. It was now designated as Nellis Air Force Base in honor of 1st Lieutenant William H. Nellis, a P-47 pilot from Las Vegas, who was killed near Bastogne, Belgium during the Battle of the Bulge. It was a reminder of the cost combat can extract.

Once underway, Instructor School proceeded as anticipated. Jim was in his element again as he strapped into the Mustang each day, but the mood quickly changed on June 25th when the North Korean People's Army crossed the 38th Parallel and attacked South Korea without warning. Being a freshly minted fighter pilot took on a whole new meaning for Bailey and Jim. They realized that as instructor pilots they would be responsible for training young men who might be headed for combat missions once they earned their wings. In fact, they might be sent to South Korea themselves. It was a sobering thought.

CHAPTER 16

LOGISTICS

With 2nd Lieutenant bars on his epaulets and wings above his left breast pocket designating that he was now a rated officer, Jim was counting his blessings. He had proven himself and dispelled the denigrating prediction of what some World War II generals believed he could attain. He and Bailey finally had their own dormitory rooms, but their shared sense of humor and relaxed friendship opened the door to a widening circle of confident peers.

Some of the pilots who had graduated with them in Las Vegas were now in Brooks Flight Instructor School, too. They already respected Jim for his prowess in the P-51 Mustang. They had also met his attractive fiancée and delighted in teasing him about his future loss of control as an old married man. Most of them were bachelors and full of bravado.

Being accepted as "one of the guys" was a new and welcome experience for Jim, but he only enjoyed that privileged status on base when wearing his flight suit. On weekends while off the guarded perimeter of Brooks AFB and deep in the heart of Texas everything remained the same in the civilian world, separate and unequal…unless he was in the company of the other pilots. It was a new dance he needed to master before adding Mary Ann to the mix.

He was a tested and true fighter pilot in the air and on military installations, but it was the 1950s, and he was still learning how to navigate the segregated civilian realm. When he went to buy his first car, he decided to drag Bailey along and to wear his uniform, which would verify his socioeconomic status. It worked. Fair or not, he realized he would probably always have to strategize even the most basic of decisions. Fortunately, he loved a challenge. However, it was humbling to realize that he had achieved a lifestyle and source of economic security denied his father. Sam loomed larger than ever as Jim's champion. If only he had lived to be vindicated.

Confident in his skills as a pilot, Jim became intensely interested in the mechanics of flight and every aspect of the engineering that made the P-51 Mustang such a reliable aircraft. In addition to classes on becoming a flight instructor, Jim took a personal interest in talking to flight line mechanics and listening to their experience-based comments about what caused the various problems they had encountered. Their insights supplemented what he was learning in the classroom in a valuable way.

Jim had become accustomed to the process of checking out in two different aircraft and memorizing emergency procedures, but he wanted to be over-prepared when encountering serious problems in flight, especially considering he soon would be responsible for a student pilot's life. He also wanted to be able to fully answer any questions that his future students might ask. That was his initial purpose in becoming acquainted with men who worked on the flight line as well as at Base Ops. Much to his surprise, he ended up the beneficiary of an unexpected bonus. One summer afternoon while lingering at Base Ops after his scheduled flight, he was alerted about a hop to Evansville, Indiana, over the weekend. He jumped at the chance to meet Mary Ann's parents and formally gain their approval. It turned out to be perfect timing.

Jim's visit to see his college sweetheart ended up in a major planning session. It brought the whole Bell family together and laid the groundwork for Jim and Mary Ann's immediate future. Everyone was interested in the complicated logistics involved. Jim and Mary Ann were not just planning a wedding, but they were also dealing with two very different careers.

Women had worked in men's jobs to keep America functioning due to the absence of men serving overseas in World War II, and Mary Ann, like many young women of her age, expected to pursue a career. She had just received the offer of a teaching position in Evansville, but she was reluctant to sign a contract before discussing the matter with Jim. Meanwhile, both Jim and Bailey, prior to completing instructor school at Brooks, had already learned that they were to be re-assigned as flight instructors at Perrin AFB in Texas in September.

There were a lot of factors to consider, but the young couple finally decided on their best option. Mary Ann would accept the teaching position, and Jim could fly up from Perrin in October for their wedding. Mary Ann would complete the first semester of the school year, which she could list on a future resume as job experience, and join Jim at Perrin AFB in January 1951. It all sounded very complicated to Mary Ann's parents, but that's exactly how it happened ... well, almost.

In September Mary Ann adorned her first classroom with brightly colored posters that offered bits of wisdom from sages of the past. Washing the slate blackboard that stretched across the front of the room, she included a few sticks of colored chalk to the traditional white ones in the tray. As an added touch of home, she secured cuttings of plants in small terra cotta pots, which she placed on the counter under the windows that afforded a view of the outdoors. She hummed in happy anticipation of welcoming students to her classroom, unaware of how excited the youngsters were about being assigned to the beautiful new teacher's class. Since Mary Ann knew she would only be there for one semester, she wanted to make it the best learning experience possible for her young charges.

Upon completing Flight Instructor School at Brooks, Jim and Bailey picked up maps at the base service station and plotted their journey to Perrin AFB. It was located about 350 miles northeast of San Antonio on the Texas/Oklahoma border at Denison, Texas, and because each of them would be driving his own car, there was no way to save money other than to drive straight through. They stopped only for snacks when they gassed up at filling stations. Since Jim continued to send an allotment to his mother, money was tight so he appreciated the fact that Mary Ann would have a paycheck, too. Still, he planned to be the main provider. High school math teachers should focus more on budgeting, he decided, as he compared his increasing expenses with the static nature of his monthly income.

Arriving at Perrin AFB in September 1950, Bailey and Jim quickly established themselves as new flight instructors. An avid researcher, Jim had familiarized himself with the history of the base before their arrival. It had been a beehive of activity throughout World War II, graduating 10,000 flight students in support of the war effort, but with the cessation of global hostilities, Perrin was deactivated in the fall of 1946. In September 1947, the Army Air Forces (AAF) were transferred from the Department of the Army to the Department of the Air Force. These big changes were taking place at the same time Jim entered Hampton Institute to gain the credentials necessary to be accepted in the military's new branch.

By April 1948, Perrin was placed on active status once more as the U.S. Air Force continued to develop as a separate military branch. Perrin's mission again became basic single-engine pilot training under USAF's Air Training Command. However, training for additional specialized areas was on the horizon. Now that he had achieved his goal as a rated officer in 1950, Jim tried to stay as informed as possible. He wanted to be on the crest of change.

Planning ahead, Jim managed to snag a weekend hop to Evansville, Indiana, arriving on Friday afternoon, October 20th, in time for the wedding on Saturday. The ceremony was to be held in Mary Ann's home, and the Bell household was a flurry of last-minute wedding preparations. Mary Ann escorted Jim from room to room to meet childhood friends and teaching colleagues as well as excited siblings, but he didn't even try to remember all the names or their relationship to his future wife. He just smiled broadly, shook hands, hugged immediate family, and followed Mary Ann's lead.

Relieved that Jim's arrival was not delayed by weather, everyone was delighted he could join the extended family at dinner prior to the wedding. It was quite a feast. He decided that Mary Ann's mom could rival his Aunt Lily when it came to "putting out a spread." Jim had brought his military hang-up bag with his dress blues to wear for the big occasion, but he couldn't find a spare nook or cranny where he could safely set it aside so he hung it from a door that was ajar upstairs. He was accustomed to his sisters dominating the bathroom as they primped for special occasions, but the Bell house was busier than the flight line at Perrin. A rhythmic hum of animated conversations pervaded every room until late into the evening when Mary Ann's parents reminded houseguests and visitors alike that the bride- and groom-to-be needed to get a few hours of sleep before the main event.

Somehow everything fell into place like scattered puzzle pieces, just as planned. Mary Ann was strikingly elegant in her fashionable bridal attire, and Jim cut a handsome profile in his blue uniform. His silver wings glistened in the candlelight as they exchanged their ceremonial vows in front of the family's minister. The aroma of the sumptuous buffet had filled the room throughout the morning, and the ravenous group of friends and family hurried to the dining room afterward. Each young man loosened the tie under his starched collar, and young women kicked off their heels as they celebrated well into the evening. Jim and Mary Ann had few moments to themselves, but they would have a lifetime together and family mattered. Instead, the young couple savored every moment, knowing that they would enjoy a special honeymoon in the future when they could afford it.

On Sunday morning, Jim returned to Perrin AFB as a married man.

Sitting at the desk in his Bachelors' Officers' Quarters (BOQ) a week or so later, Jim stopped to reflect on all that had happened and to pen a letter to his mother. He had sent Ora and his sisters an invitation to the wedding, but he had not offered to pay for their transportation to Evansville. He simply did not have the funds. He knew they would understand but still be hurt. Instead, he shared photos that Mary Ann sent to him and described his memories of the whirlwind of a wedding.

With the first wave of cold weather and the advent of the holiday season, Jim realized that he really couldn't afford to go anywhere for Christmas since he would be paying for Mary Ann's flight to Perrin when she completed her first semester of teaching in January. It was upsetting that they would miss spending their very first Christmas together, but he had stayed busy spending most of his days interacting with his flight students and much of his nights filling out the required forms assessing their daily progress. Still, most of them would be leaving soon to share the holiday with family, and Perrin would become a ghost town.

By mid-December the holiday exodus was underway, and Jim hung around Base Ops, just to have some company. One afternoon as the sun hung low in the winter sky, Jim was moping around the skeleton crew in Base Ops when his squadron commander Charles DeWitt sauntered in with his hang-up bag slung over his shoulder. Engaging him in friendly conversation, Jim was surprised to learn that DeWitt was leaving on permanent assignment to Craig AFB in Selma, Alabama. Jim admired his commander and instinctively asked how he could be reassigned to Craig, too. Weighing the response, Jim impulsively followed his commander's advice and went straight to personnel to begin all the paperwork for the transfer. Despite his short stint at Perrin, Jim had an enviable record, and his request was approved!

Meanwhile, in Evansville, Indiana, Mary Ann sorted through the day's mail and upon opening the first envelope, she was surprised by Jim's hastily scrawled message on a Christmas card—2nd *Lieutenant and Mrs. James E.P. Randall will be taking a honeymoon trip to Craig AFB in Selma, Alabama.*

CHAPTER 17

INTERNATIONAL STUDENTS IN THE DEEP SOUTH

2nd Lt. James E.P. Randall, son of Mrs. Ora F. Randall, 16 Rutherford Ave, N.W., is married to the former Mary Ann Bell of Evansville, Ind. He has recently arrived at Craig Air Force Base, Ala, where he will be assigned to duty as a flight instructor with the 3615th Pilot Training Wing. He attended Hampton Institute for two years after entering service in August 1945.

Upon arrival in Alabama, Jim opened the mail forwarded to him from Perrin AFB, and read the clipping that his mother sent to him. Ora had never placed a wedding announcement in the Roanoke paper, but on January 18, 1951, she finally acknowledged that Mary Ann was a part of Jim's life. He noticed she still focused primarily on him and his achievements in the article, though. He would have to work on helping Mary Ann to develop a better relationship with his mother who probably was feeling displaced, but there was time to mend fences. Meanwhile, he and Mary Ann were busy setting up their first home, and he was preparing to meet his first flight students at Craig AFB.

The trip from Perrin AFB in Dennison, Texas, across Louisiana and Mississippi to Selma, Alabama, in the heart of the Deep South was the longest period of time that Jim and Mary Ann had ever spent with each other. Mary Ann sat with an unfolded road map in her lap and helped navigate the journey that Jim had plotted out in a wavering red line. The young couple—a teacher and a pilot—were both accustomed to researching for answers, and Mary Ann had checked out historic sights and scenic views they might be able to see as they traveled through the Deep South. Jim, concerned about possible places to stay overnight along the way as well as the area of Alabama where they would be living, took a practical approach. They were off to a good start as they shared their first big adventure together.

By the time the newlyweds reached Selma, Alabama, just west of Montgomery, the state capital in the central part of the state, Mary Ann and Jim had become great traveling companions. Other than Mary Ann's occasional smoking, Jim was excited about their future together. He was reassured that she could readily appreciate and handle the unique circumstances they would probably be facing as a Black couple in Alabama.

He had read that over 83% of Selma's nearly 23,000 residents were Blacks, most of whom could readily trace their family roots in slavery. Although the War Between States long ago ended that form of servitude, segregation still prevailed. The balance of power had not shifted, and minority Whites remained the governing class. Jim and Mary Ann were scheduled to live on base, but Jim knew it was important to understand historic precedents so that he could primarily focus on his position as a military flight instructor rather than engaging in losing battles over civil injustices.

Much like the way Perrin AFB had developed in 1941, during World War II, visionaries in Selma had bought extensive tracts of land—mostly cotton fields and prairie where cattle grazed—to develop an airfield. With the advent of Pearl Harbor, the city fathers agreed to lease Selma's airfield to the U.S. Army as a military advanced flight training base. Jim was interested to learn that Craig AFB, originally Craig Field, was named after 1st Lieutenant Bruce Kilpatrick Craig, a native of Selma who was killed when his British LB-30 Liberator crashed into San Diego Bay while he was on an "acceptance flight" as the flight test engineer. The tradition of honoring departed pilots empowered Jim and gave him a sense of pride for the respect pilots were afforded.

Craig AFB figured prominently in the training of Allied as well as American pilots during World War II. By 1943, Britain's Royal Air Force had 1392 RAF pilots who earned their wings at Craig, and by November 1943, French pilots began arriving at the base in Selma. The Army Air Force (AAF) provided the French three options— advanced single-engine training; P-40 transition training; and pre-flight training. At least 9000 pilots had graduated at the Alabama base by the end of the war, and many of them represented our Allies.

When Jim arrived with Mary Ann in Spring 1951 to join the 3615th Pilot Training Wing as an instructor pilot, he had read about Craig's colorful past and understood why he was assigned only one American and three French flight training students. John A. Inferrera, the sole American, was from Watertown, Massachusetts. The three international student pilots were from different parts of France and had not known each other previously but appreciated being together. English spoken with a Southern drawl was alien to them, and they were grateful Jim spoke in clipped military phrases that were easier to understand. For Jim as well as Mary Ann, the opportunity to learn about France was an unexpected bonus, something they never would have anticipated happening in Alabama.

Michel M. Durand was from Lons-Le-Saunier, the prefecture or capital of the Jura region in eastern France. The city was recognized as being the birthplace of Rouget de

Lisle, the composer of the French national anthem, *La Marseillaise*. It was also the home of Bernard Clavel, an emerging novelist of note. Famous for the thermal, saline waters at the local spa, which had existed since Roman times, the picturesque city was bordered by vineyards. Notable architecture, museums, statues, and fountains attracted both French and international visitors to Durand's hometown.

Claude A. Roumilhac grew up in Bessines-Sur-Gartempe, in the Ilte Vienne region of western France. Bessines was a village bordered by the Gartempe River and surrounded by other villages with medieval architecture.

Claude A. Bonzon hailed from Poissy in the Seine Et Oise region, essentially a suburb of Paris in north-central France. It was a forested area on the banks of the Seine and Oise rivers that claimed historic significance. Louis IX was born there in 1214, and French Catholics met with Huguenots (Protestants) at its former abbey in 1561 to try to reconcile their differences. In more recent times, renowned architect Le Corbusier had completed the Savoye House, a major architectural feat, by 1931.

As members of Class 51-G, Jim's four student pilots quickly bonded and thrived under Jim's patient but demanding guidance. Jim was keenly aware of the possible impediment to safety and success presented by the language barrier for the three French pilots. He could only imagine experiencing advanced flight school in a foreign country while trying to comprehend instructions in a different language. Although he set high standards for all his students, he was sensitive to their unique situation. Late evening conversations with Mary Ann about teaching techniques helped him to develop his own style of instructing and the patience required to ensure his French students' success. They flourished under Jim's meticulous method of teaching. His expertise in the P-51 Mustang soon became clear to them as well as to his instructor colleagues. Jim's international group of students succeeded due to his tutelage and their peer John Infererra's occasional translations of American slang.

Jim also wanted his French students to have a positive experience during their stint in the United States. Considering that Jim and Mary Ann were not readily accepted off-base in Selma, Jim relied on John Infererra, his American student, to introduce the French trio to civilian life in Alabama. Meanwhile, the young couple welcomed the exuberant French men to enjoy American culture by occasionally inviting all four pilots into their home. Mary Ann was familiar with the impeccable reputation of French cuisine, and as a new bride, she was hesitant at first to prepare meals for the novice pilots. She soon realized that the homesick young men were simply happy to be warmly received into the couple's modest quarters on base. It was also a stimulating experience for both Mary and Jim who delighted in learning so much about France, a place they hoped they might visit someday.

Even though there wasn't much of an age difference between the student pilots and their instructor, Jim maintained the appropriate rapport as their leader and by Class 51-G'S graduation on October 27, 1951—the week after Jim and Mary Ann's first anniversary—all of Jim's student pilots proudly received their wings. It was traditional for each class to print a page about their flight training experience in the special publication of *Propwash*, and Jim's students filled their page, "The Sun Spot," with laudatory remarks about Jim. Claude Bonzon wrote, "To my best American friend and my best instructor, too," while Claude Roumilhac penned, "Thank You Sir. Thank you for everything you did for us." Michel Durand added, "*J'espere encore voler dans votre aile et je vous remercier pour tout ce que pour avez fait pour nous.*" (I hope still to fly in your wing, and I thank you for everything you have done for us.)

Inferrera, the American student, scrawled, "To one of the best instructors I know." Jim felt a source of pride in his students and took their remarks to heart. Their assessment of him meant as much as his commanding officer's official write up. He was also deeply touched when Captain Charles W. DeWitt, his fellow instructor to whom the flight students' yearbook was dedicated, wrote, "Lt. Randall, your superior leadership and instruction have made all this possible. Thanks for a very fine job." It was a momentous occasion, reason to celebrate for more reasons than the assembled group knew at the time, and soon Mary Ann would no longer be able to keep it a secret. She was four months pregnant!

By February 1952, while Jim was in the midst of instructing a new class, life shifted dramatically for 1st Lieutenant and Mrs. James E.P. Randall. Jim was assigned to duty as an F-51 fighter pilot with the 12th Fighter Bomber Squadron in the Republic of Korea (ROK). Since Mary Ann was now seven months pregnant, Jim drove her back to Evansville, so that she could be with her family while she awaited the baby's arrival. Trying to fit a lifetime full of conversations into the emotional journey to Indiana, Jim was distraught by the prospect of not being at the delivery of their very first child, one of the most important moments in a couple's marriage. For once in his life, Jim realized that he might never return home again.

Through a tearful parting, Jim tried to burn Mary Ann's expectant image in his brain, like a talisman to protect him. Then he was off to Los Angeles to catch the military transport to South Korea and his destiny.

CHAPTER 18

FROM COMBAT IN KOREA TO DIAPERS IN DOVER

Leaving America behind and flying over 6800 miles into the next day, Jim had time to review his entire life. As a child he had peered out his bedroom window and wondered where the planes flying over the rooftops on Rutherford Avenue were headed when they disappeared into the horizon. Now he was suspended in space over the vast Pacific and headed into a war no one anticipated, certainly not so soon after the conclusion of World War II. After being concerned about his French students dealing with a language barrier at Craig as they learned to pilot the P-51 Mustang, he and his fellow Americans would be strapping into the F-51 Mustang in the Far East and facing not only a language barrier but also an enemy committed to their demise. The irony did not escape him.

Upon arriving in South Korea, Jim and his fellow fighter pilots were shuttled to his new base at Chinhae near Pusan. For expediency, the base was simply referred to as K-10. The bustle and intensity of war-time activity across the country reflected the sense of urgency in everyone. Jim began to realize the importance of quickly familiarizing himself with the configuration of the countryside and being hyper alert at all times. He wished he had access to the librarian back in Gainsboro who always pulled out just the book he needed when he wanted to research a topic. He had been so focused on getting his pregnant wife safely settled with her family in Indiana and preparing for an overseas tour in a war zone that there had been no time to research the history of Korea and what led to the current conflict. He felt unprepared on that account.

Of course, he would be briefed once he was settled on base, but he felt the vulnerability of those who face the danger of being inadequately informed. He was already transitioning into survival mode. As he observed all the Koreans working on the base, a strange thought crossed his mind. He had no way of knowing which of them would be trustworthy and which ones might be deceitful . . . somewhat like the mistrust between races back home. He appreciated how his French students had banded together instinctively and realized that quickly bonding with his American counterparts would be critical. He had already ascertained that he was the only Black fighter pilot in his unit. Never before had interpersonal relationships with his fellow Americans become more important, but he was up for the challenge. So were his colleagues. When it's a matter of life or death, he surmised, common sense trumps learned biases.

Even though Jim's fellow travelers were exhausted from their long journey to the Far East, they were full of adrenalin and eager to orient themselves at the morning briefing the following day. Jim and all the other newly arrived pilots were joining the 12th Fighter Bomber Squadron as part of the 18th Fighter Bomber Wing under 5th Air Force. The wing consisted of 3 squadrons of 30 pilots each. Although billeted at K-10 outside of Pusan, their aircraft were safely housed at K-4, farther southwest on the tip of the Korean peninsula. However, combat missions were launched from K-18, a facility on the eastern coast of South Korea just south of the 38th parallel. Jim was eager to learn more about the missions he would be flying, but he already knew the primary objective—air superiority.

Immersed in the relentless daily schedule of studying maps, listening intently to briefings, and maintaining self-initiated high expectations of himself as a fighter pilot, Jim was taken by surprise when a backlog of letters arrived from home. Of course, Ora had written daily and her younger sister Thelma had penned a letter one afternoon while finishing her work week at the U.S. Mint in Washington D.C. There were even several from his sisters, Martha and Bernice, but it was a bulky one from Indiana that caught his eye, and he ripped it open first. Scanning Mary Ann's letter to learn all the details, he kept glancing back and forth from his wife's handwritten note to the black and white photo she enclosed. Printed neatly on the back, Mary Ann had noted, *Roberta Lynn Randall, born April 19, 1952.* He had been a father for several weeks and had not even known it! Such was life in a war zone.

Letters from home became more treasured than a paycheck, and Jim felt closest to his family when the daily mail call gifted him with a letter from Mary Ann. Just as she made an effort to share the miracle of childbirth with him, Jim tried to capture his life halfway across the world in his letters to her. Surviving life in a combat zone precluded taking photos and buying postcards. Instead, he captured images and emotions in the words he scribbled across sheets of paper…being cautious not to reveal anything that could be significant to the adversary if intercepted.

Jim described Korea as a peninsula that extended like a cupped hand reaching out to the Pacific Ocean. He explained that Pusan was on the southeasterly tip near beaches bathed in the tides of the Sea of Japan. The Yellow Sea licked the shores of Korea's western coast with Seoul, the capital city, located on the coast in the central part of the Korean peninsula, similar to the way Tampa is situated on the west coast of Florida, America's peninsular state.

The expectation was that his tour of duty in Korea would be either one year or the completion of 100 combat missions over North Korea . . . whichever came first. As Mary Ann continued to share photos of Roberta's "firsts" in life, Jim realized all that he was

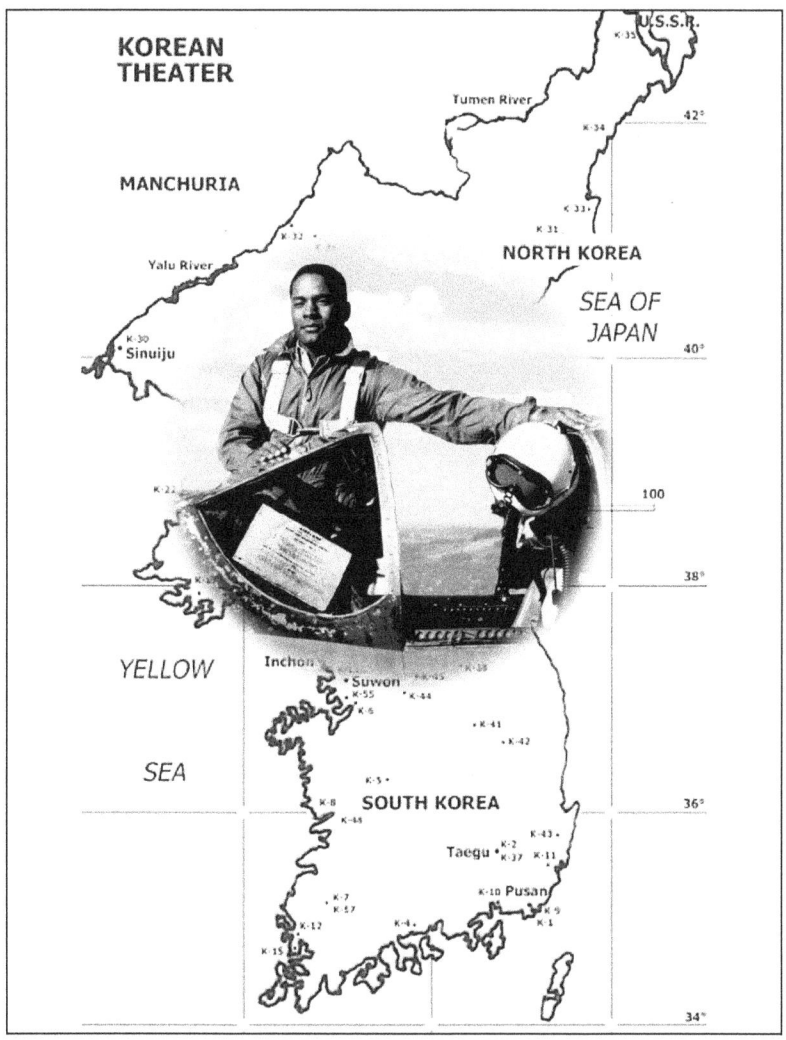

Lt. James Randall stands behind his F-51 after leading a flight of F-51 Mustangs over North Korea to destroy enemy targets. Although Jim completes 75 combat missions and receives citations for his valor, when the F-51 begins to be phased out and replaced by the F-86, Jim is assigned to other duties to meet the requirements of his combat tour—fly 100 missions or serve a full year in Korea. Jim becomes an instructor pilot to Republic of Korea (ROK) pilots until his commander offers him another demanding job, which is a quick ticket home. (Photo courtesy of Regional History & Genealogy, Pikes Peak Library District, Image #412-141)

missing back home. It gave him real incentive to take every available flight north of the 38th parallel.

As much as Jim loved the Mustang, the introduction of Russian MIGs into the mix changed the playing field. Being an experienced pilot and knowing the Mustang inside and out after two years of instructing young pilots, Jim and his counterparts knew how to swoop in swiftly like a hawk, attack a target, and exit at top speed before a MIG had the smaller and older aircraft in its sights. However, the U.S. Air Force was aware that this technique would not work much longer. USAF needed to up the odds in our favor so the F-86 joined the melee. This placed Jim in a quandary. He had completed 75 missions, but 100 missions were required before pilots were eligible for re-assignment.

It was not economical to send Mustang pilots back stateside, train them in the F-86, and return them to Korea to complete the required number of combat missions. As a result, F-51 pilots were assigned other duties. Due to his tenure as a P-51 instructor at Craig AFB with French-speaking students, Jim was initially re-assigned to the 6146th Air Force Advisory Group as a flight instructor for the Republic of Korea (ROK) pilots. Jim was proficient in conveying such complex information and his students were enthusiastic and responsive, but the language barrier created far more challenging circumstances on training missions in a war zone than Jim had ever experienced in instructing his international students in the peaceful skies over Selma, Alabama. Most of the ROK pilots that Jim worked with were very small in stature and sometimes needed 2 pillows to be able to see out of the cockpit. By comparison to the United States Air Force, the ROK's Air Force was a nascent military. It did not have the long history of World War II senior pilots in reserve to train its younger pilots or to create the instinctive level of intense discipline necessary in combat. Still, Jim was very successful in dealing with all the unique aspects of his situation, and it reflected in the numerous citations he received in the process.

Captain [then 1st Lt.] James E.P. Randall, AO-1909934, United States Air Force has distinguished himself by meritorious service in instructing ROKAF pilots as an Advisor to the Republic of Korea Air Force during the period of 1 July 1952 to 20 January 1953. Captain Randall contributed to the Republic of Korea Air Force by instructing forty-one (41) pilots to accomplishment of successful combat missions despite many material shortages as well as language barriers. Through his outstanding performance, Captain Randall actually promoted American-Korean friendship and further proved the effectiveness of a United Nations effort and his example will always be an inspiration to ROKAF officers and men. Captain Randall, by his devotion to duty, brought great credit upon himself, the United States Air Force and the Republic of Korea Air Force.

Although appreciative of the recognition, Jim was anxious to return home and see

Mary Ann and his baby girl. He was reluctant to appear asking for special privileges, but after struggling with the issue for weeks, he finally spoke to his commander about whether or not there was some way he could meet the requirement to return stateside more quickly. He was surprised by the senior officer's solution. If Jim would write up a training syllabus for the ROK, he would not only be permitted reassignment to the 1737th Ferrying Squadron at Dover AFB in Delaware, but he would also return home as a newly minted captain, an early promotion considerably ahead of his peers.

Astonished by such a magnanimous gesture, Jim didn't hesitate to take the offer. "Give me the necessary supplies, data, and a secluded room without anyone calling or bothering me, and I can do that for you, Sir." Jim eagerly reassured his commanding officer that he had picked the right man for the job. Without further adieu, the two struck a deal.

Returning to his home base, Jim went to work immediately. Working from memory, Jim started with Pre-flight and recorded every single aspect of the procedure in great detail. Walking out to the flight line afterward, he actually performed the pre-flight procedure on a F-51 to cross check his actions with what he had written. Once satisfied with the clarity and accuracy of his detailed explanation, he proceeded to document the next step—Pre-start Check on the airplane—starting, taxiing. Jim was a perfectionist. He knew that ROK pilots' lives would depend on an infallible set of instructions so he used a lot of art gum to erase, re-write, amend, re-phrase and produce a precise document. Eventually, Jim was satisfied with his efforts. He submitted a handwritten training manual to the administrative officer, who typed it up and sent it to Headquarters. A month or so later Jim was on his way home to see his baby girl Roberta for the very first time.

In the winter of 1952, Jim Randall, a young lieutenant with an expectant wife, left for Korea as an experienced instructor pilot. In January 1953, less than a year later, he returned to the United States as a new father and a combat-seasoned fighter pilot, a veteran worthy of respect. Unfortunately, his baby girl Roberta Lynn had no idea who he was when he arrived in Evansville, Indiana. Her wide-eyed stare gave Jim fair warning not to make any sudden moves toward her. It was a lesson he quickly learned when he reached out to take his baby girl in his arms for the first time, and she let out an ear-piercing cry. Jim was a brand, new father, who did not speak her language. There would be no sweet-talking this little one into accepting him. Winning over Roberta Lynn Randall would be more of a challenge than those posed by the cultural differences that complicated the training of ROK pilots in Korea.

During his brief visit with the Bell family, Jim felt like a time traveler as he tried to adjust to the pace of family life. He marveled at how Mary Ann seemed to anticipate little

Roberta's every need. She glided from bath time to changing diapers to jostling her little one into a better mood when she whimpered. It seemed second nature to Mary Ann. As Jim prepared their vehicle for the cross-country adventure to his new assignment, Mary Ann neatly organized a myriad of items that were necessary to travel with a baby. Jim watched in awe as Mary Ann deftly packed a diaper bag and placed it strategically in the car so the critical items were within reach. It was as though she had always been a mother. Jim brooded over how to up his game.

Midst tearful goodbyes the trio left for Dover, Delaware, and Jim was relieved when the hum of the car's engine lulled his baby girl to sleep. He hoped that the trip east would be enough time for the three of them to bond as a family. He was accustomed to accomplishing missions at high speeds and with efficiency, and so his introduction to fatherhood after the 6800-mile journey home was a humbling experience. He considered himself reasonable, patient, and focused, but he was an experienced fighter pilot returning from a war zone with finely honed skills that provided little preparation for being a new father. There was an unexpected shift of power in the family, and one adorable little girl was unknowingly in control.

Arriving at Dover AFB, as a new father, a new captain, and a new F-51 squadron commander for the 1737th Ferrying Squadron, Jim was greeted by the three other Black pilots on base—Levi Thornhill, Charles Cooper, and Howard Wilson—who dubbed themselves as the Four Musketeers when Jim joined their ranks. At long last there would be an opportunity for the Randalls to have close friends who perhaps shared similar backgrounds and experiences as young U.S. Air Force couples. Jim had developed his own approach and style to being a confident military member even though he usually was the only Black officer in his unit. On the other hand, when he and Mary Ann married in between assignments, she had no chance to transition to being the only Black officer's wife at Craig AFB in the segregated South. Two years later, a pregnant Mary Ann faced an even greater challenge— giving birth to their first child while worrying about having a husband flying combat in the Far East. At Dover, Mary Ann would finally have the chance to settle in as an Air Force wife and a young mother. At long last it seemed as though their fortunes had changed.

Unlike the civilian world, military rank and responsibility unintentionally grouped military members with their peers. As a result, Air Force families shared a mutual appreciation for one another. Friendships were quick to form, and the Randalls settled into a comfortable routine. Mary Ann enjoyed spontaneous coffee klatches with other young mothers who compared their infants' latest growth benchmarks as well as their favorite recipes.

Meanwhile, Jim thoroughly enjoyed being a family man, especially on weekends, but during the week he intently focused on developing his new command into a cohesive, top-notch unit. Although his colleagues might have been curious—perhaps even jealous—about his early promotion or his experience in Korea, nothing was ever said about his previous tour of duty. Jim didn't recount his exploits with anyone, not even Mary Ann. The transition from war to peace went smoothly until Jim was called into headquarters one morning. Worried about whatever misstep he might have made after such a short time on base, Jim was deeply concerned. Surely there wasn't some mistake in his orders, and as a result, he was returning to the Far East. Instead, Jim's commander explained that he was going to be recognized for his service in Korea. A ceremony was to be held in his honor. His family, friends, and members of his unit were invited to attend. Apparently, the wheels had been set in motion before Jim left Korea, but the paperwork didn't come through until he arrived at his assignment at Dover. He was totally unaware that arrangements had been underway to honor him as soon as he was established in his new leadership role on base.

By direction of the President, Captain JAMES E.P. RANDALL, AO1909934, has been awarded the Distinguished Flying Cross.

CITATION

Captain (then First Lieutenant) JAMES E. P. RANDALL, distinguished himself by meritorious achievement while participating in aerial flight on 29 August 1952. Assigned to the 6146th Air Advisory Group (ROK AF), APO 970, Korea, he was flying combat missions with the 10th Fighter Group, Republic of Korea Air Force as Combat Operations Advisor. Flying number four (4) position in a unit of four (4) F-51 type aircraft, Captain Randall displayed outstanding airmanship and navigational skill when he accompanied his flight through below marginal weather direct to the target area at Pyongyang, Korea. With general purpose bombs and machine guns, Captain Randall attacked factories in that area, pressing successive attacks despite intense heavy automatic and small arms fire. Continuing his attacks until all ammunition had been expended, he personally destroyed two (2) large buildings and damaged an additional one. Having regrouped with the flight, he then proceeded back to his home base. As a result of this highly successful mission, vital enemy equipment and supplies destined to increase the enemy's potential were destroyed. By his high personal courage, skill and devotion to duty, Captain Randall has brought great credit upon himself, his organization and the United States Air Force.

Throughout the reading of the citation, Mary Ann held 10-month-old Roberta tightly as she realized how dangerous her husband's tour in Korea had been, and the hushed members of Jim's unit suddenly had gained a deep respect for their young commander.

If there had been any doubt on Dover AFB about why Jim had received an early promotion to captain, the citation acknowledging his award of the Distinguished Flying Cross dispelled the unasked questions. It encapsulated Jim's courage and prowess as a fighter pilot in the Korean War.

Jim and Mary Ann settled into a comfortable routine, and Roberta Lynn celebrated her first birthday with a party attended by neighbors and their little ones. Unlike flawlessly executed military events, it seemed like organized chaos to Jim. Roberta and her guest toddlers consumed handfuls of cake dripping with icing once the solitary candle was blown out, and little Roberta cooed with delight as she tore through brightly wrapped packages and plopped a big pink bow on her head. She had no idea that Mary Ann was due to deliver her biggest gift in early October. Life was good . . . at least for now.

Jim, in the foreground of a 4-ship flight of F-51s, is leading Republic of Korea (ROK) pilots toward the 38th parallel. The large K on the tail of the F-51 Mustangs designates that the aircraft are Korean, not American. Jim served as an instructor pilot for the ROK Air Force and also produced a handwritten F-51 instructional syllabus for the ROK pilots. (Photo courtesy of Regional History & Genealogy, Pikes Peak Library District, Image #412-142)

CHAPTER 19

ICARUS

In the summer of 1953, the Korean War ended on July 27th. It had already been an historic year for Americans, especially the Randalls. Dwight David Eisenhower had been inaugurated as the 34th President of the United States in January, about the same time that Jim returned home from his combat tour in Korea. Eisenhower, a highly decorated, five-star general during World War II, had served as the sole commander of Supreme Headquarters Allied Expeditionary Forces (SHAEF). In that position he commanded the Allied forces in northwest Europe from late 1943 until the end of the war in Europe, May 8, 1945. During his run for president Eisenhower had made a solemn campaign promise—if elected, he would end the war in Korea. Nearly seven months later Eisenhower fulfilled that promise.

A war-weary public was torn over the outcome in Korea. South Korea had been spared communist domination by its northern counterpart, but the 38th parallel remained the dividing point in the fractured country. Not an inch of ground had changed hands, and yet nearly 40,000 Americans had died for the cause. Jim had his opinions. He was now a seasoned combat veteran and a patriot at heart, but the Randall household was focused on only one thing, Mary Ann's October due date. Would it be a boy or a girl?

The question was answered two months later. After a frantic drive to Bainbridge Naval Hospital in Maryland on a blustery October 1, 1953, Jim and Mary Ann welcomed little Louise Evangeline. Jim was thrilled that this time he would be home for all the baby's "firsts" that he had missed with Roberta. As expected, Thanksgiving and the approaching Christmas holidays accelerated the frenetic pace and level of excitement in every household, but Jim was stunned by the amount of organization having two babies required. Mary Ann seemed to be in perpetual motion during every waking hour, and Jim could understand her mood swings. Having Louise sleep through the night was the only thing the exhausted young couple wanted for Christmas.

By the middle of December, winter had descended upon Dover AFB with a vengeance. When the wind picked up, the damp cold seemed to penetrate a person's very bones and the locals grumbled, but having experienced winter in Korea, Jim far preferred December in Delaware. Mary Ann, on the other hand, worried about avoiding respiratory illnesses and keeping her baby girls healthy. After an epic shopping trip to the Dover Base Exchange, Mary Ann purchased enough baby blankets, winter jackets, flannel pajamas, long-sleeved knit shirts and corduroy jumpers to keep Roberta and newborn Louise bundled for the season.

Although Jim was safely stateside and reunited with his young family, his assignment ferrying aircraft kept him on the move. Temporary duty assignments (TDYs) were the norm. In the beginning he was only required to ferry aircraft stateside, which necessitated his being away from home only a few days. Usually, he came home with gifts or a trinket reminiscent of the area he had just visited, and Roberta soon recognized her father's pattern of early morning departures followed by his returning a few days later laden with gifts for her. She had been afraid of the combat veteran who showed up in her life unannounced, but she had fully adjusted to having an attentive father and greeted his return from each TDY with open arms and a big smile. The Randalls slowly became accustomed to their demanding lifestyle and fell into a fairly predictable routine…at least for a fighter pilot's family. Organization was the key.

Dark winter mornings in coastal Delaware could be bitter, but Jim hardly noticed as he pulled on his olive drab flight suit and hurried to the kitchen. He glanced at the calendar on the wall where Mary Ann tried to keep track of all the events in their busy lives. December 17th was circled, a reminder that he was scheduled to be on the flight line within the hour. Mary Ann had already prepared pancakes, which he found still steaming under a covered plate on the stove. He could hear Roberta's muttered complaints as Mary Ann rustled her awake. Within a few minutes sleepy-eyed Roberta toddled into the kitchen. She was wrapped in her terry cloth bathrobe and followed close behind Mary Ann, who had swaddled 10-week-old Louise in a blue flannel blanket so tightly that only her big brown eyes were visible.

After lifting Roberta up into her high chair, Jim sat down at the breakfast table to enjoy a plate of hot blueberry pancakes dripping with butter. He drizzled maple syrup over the stack while Mary Ann jostled Louise in one arm and served the freshly brewed coffee with her free hand. Jim had a short trip scheduled to ferry an F-51 to Louisville, Kentucky. As usual Jim had his flight plans spread out on the table beside his plate so he could review how changing weather conditions might impact flight patterns. Nothing to worry about, Jim reassured Mary Ann as she finished her coffee and began bundling Roberta in her new snowsuit.

The Randall's small house was situated in a predominately Black section of the neighborhood adjacent to Dover AFB, and many of their neighbors were civil service employees who worked on base. The Black pilots in the 1737th Ferry Squadron who lived close by were Jim's friends, the Musketeers…bachelors Charles Cooper and Levi Thornhill and also Howard Wilson, a family man. Unlike their civilian counterparts who worked daily at jobs with predictable hours that facilitated carpooling, the ferrying pilots dealt with ever-changing schedules and logistics. Consequently, carpooling was not an option for them.

The Randalls, like most of their friends, only had one car so Mary Ann planned to drop Jim off at Base Ops on the flight line and then pick up a few groceries at the commissary before heading home. With Jim gone over the weekend, she also would have the chance to pick up his Christmas present at the Dover Base Exchange and hide it before he returned from his trip. Hustling everyone into the car after breakfast, Mary Ann slid in behind the wheel and headed toward the base. They arrived at the flight line as the sun peeped over the horizon.

Mary Ann turned into the designated parking lot nearest Base Ops and left the motor of their Pontiac running as Jim hugged each of his girls. Waving daddy goodbye and welcoming him home was such a familiar ritual that there were no tears at his departure when he kissed Roberta on the cheek and bent down to smile at Louise one last time. With a quick hug for Mary Ann, Jim jumped out of the car, slung his overnight bag across his shoulder and rushed toward Base Ops. He stopped only once to look back and see the red tail lights of his Pontiac disappear around a corner. With luck, Mary Ann would tuck the children back in bed and have half an hour to herself before the family circus began for the day.

Checking his watch, Jim smiled as he looked down the flight line. He was early, as usual. Punctuality was important to him. He liked to stay ahead of the game. Glancing upward he noted the sky was a beautiful blue, but weather patterns farther south looked like they might present a problem so he scanned the latest weather maps at Base Ops to determine his options in the event he had to take an alternate route.

Striding out onto the runway, Jim searched the line-up of F-51s awaiting the pilots who would ferry them to their final destination. Spotting the one designated for him, Jim stopped momentarily to chat with a crew chief and then headed to his aircraft. He was looking forward to this trip. It was highly unlikely, since these missions were usually such a quick turn-around, but perhaps he could surprise Mary Ann and get a little Christmas shopping done before returning home.

Jim wanted to get something extra special for Mary Ann for Christmas. She had sacrificed her teaching career to become a young mother of two as well as an Air Force wife, and it was a full-time job. In the first three years of their marriage, she had spent a year in the South when Jim was an instructor pilot at Craig AFB, followed by a year at home with her parents and her new baby in Evansville, Indiana, while Jim was on combat duty in Korea. The assignment to Dover AFB in Delaware had been a welcome change. Three moves and a war in the first three years of their marriage had been challenging for a young couple in their twenties; Dover was the first place that seemed like home. Eventually, flights to ferry F-51s included destinations in Europe, but at this point, Jim was often able to return home by late evening. It was the closest thing to a normal life the Randalls had known.

After finishing his pre-flight, Jim climbed into the cockpit of the F-51 he was scheduled to deliver to Standiford Field in Louisville, Kentucky. If all went well, he would arrive in time for lunch and hopefully enjoy some good old Southern cooking like his mother Ora always had waiting for him when he headed back to Roanoke for the holidays during his college years at Hampton Institute.

Flying at an altitude of about 5000 feet, the young captain checked his instruments frequently as he headed south. He had determined that the most direct route was Dover to Washington D.C. to Charlotte, North Carolina. Then he would swing over to Knoxville, Tennessee, en route to Kentucky. Instead, as he neared Charlotte, North Carolina, the weather along the route he had planned to fly was breaking up. Cloud formations were roiling and ominously dark. The dramatic sight before him suggested a change of plans was in order. A big storm was surging right through his flight path.

Initially, Jim was not concerned. He knew the country like the back of his hand. Compared to situations he experienced during his year of flying combat missions in Korea, this was a minor blip in his plans. At least the skies over the Carolinas were free of flak, and the people on the ground were *friendlies*…well, for the most part. Still, it was better to err on the side of caution

Looking over the map strapped to his knee, he made several calculations, but as he decided the best course of action and changed his coordinates, the engine suddenly began running rough. The 145 high octane gas that fueled the F-51 was heavily leaded and sometimes coated the spark plugs to the extent that a pilot had to run the engine at full power for one minute to de-lead them. Jim performed the maneuver but to no avail. He became alarmed as he realized the temperature of the engine was elevated and climbing rapidly.

Then it happened.

Steam and smoke began pouring out of the left side of the aircraft, and Jim's visibility was obscured by the smoke billowing out of the right side of the plane, too. He briefly considered bailing out, but after quickly assessing the circumstances, he realized he was going to have to bring the Mustang down. Hopefully, he could belly in without incident.

As he scrutinized the landscape below in search of a suitable site to make an emergency landing, he hoped to find the answer to his dilemma. Like all the southern states, North Carolina was polka-dotted with centuries-old oak trees. There were few areas long and open enough to land his F-51. Checking his altimeter as he descended dangerously low, Jim suddenly spotted a beautiful sight.

It was a flowing expanse of grass extending far enough that it would accommodate an emergency landing. Of course, it would be rough because the ordinary ground would not support the weight of his plane like the airstrip at Dover, and even though he was an experienced combat pilot who had trained for situations like this, Jim looked up and his worst fears were realized. What had appeared to be a wide area of solid ground when he was at 4,500 feet was actually a field of winter wheat. It was gracefully flowing in the wind, and since the soil had been tilled for the crop, the ground was not going to be the compact surface he was expecting.

He did not have enough altitude to climb skyward and search for a more suitable area to land, and he was far too low to bail out. With no alternatives, Jim mentally prepared himself for what he realized would be an unpleasant outcome . . . landing right in the middle of some farmer's cash crop.

Without time to do anything more than stabilize the feisty F-51 Mustang before the aircraft touched the ground, Jim braced himself for the unexpected. In spite of the temptation, he remembered the axiom: Do not put the gear down in an emergency like this. Once the wheels hit the ground they will dig in, causing the plane to pitch forward and roll—an invitation to "meet your Maker." There was no time to consider the irony of his predicament. After a year of flying combat in Southeast Asia, Captain James Randall of Roanoke, Virginia, was about to crash in a wheat field in the boonies of North Carolina.

When the belly of the plane hit the ground with a thud, the unbalanced aircraft traveling at 100 miles per hour bounced high into the air like a basketball. Airborne momentarily, Jim had only nanoseconds to decide his course of action, and he had no good options. He realized that the wheat field was terraced and that eliminated the possibility of achieving any degree of stability upon landing.

Clenching the stick with the intention of maintaining an upright position when the plane touched down again, he managed to keep the aircraft from pitching forward and toppling over, but he soon bounced high into the air again. His once sleek and powerful F-51 was out-of-control and the next few seconds would determine the outcome for both the aircraft and the young father trying to manage some semblance of control over the plane as well as himself.

When the careening Mustang reached the ground for a third time, it proved an old adage to be true. *The third time's the charm.* The once powerful aircraft had lost its *ballon*, and powerless, it came to rest in the midst of crumpled, ankle-high winter wheat. A battered trail through the once willowy stalks marked the path of the Mustang's erratic emergency landing.

Scared as hell, a rattled Jim sat stunned for a moment, realizing he had survived. Then he scrambled out of the cockpit to reach a safe distance from his seriously damaged aircraft. It had the potential of exploding into flames at any minute. In the distance, Jim heard shouting, and he spun around to see a group of people racing toward him. He assumed he was about to meet the owner of his temporary landing strip, and he was certain his unanticipated arrival would not receive a gracious Southern welcome.

Dusting himself off, Jim stretched up to his full height of 5'8" and prepared himself for a dressing down. Dealing with a bunch of irate farmers would probably be a rehearsal for the looming audience he would soon be having with his squadron commander when he returned to Dover and had to explain why he had just lost a $52,000 aircraft. It would be a matter of pure economics. The cost of losing an F-51 would be the first consideration, never mind that Jim was priceless to his wife and two innocent little girls back in Delaware. Surviving the dangerous landing was one thing. Beating the military's first instinct to lean toward "pilot error" as an explanation for the loss of the aircraft would be the next hurdle.

Farmers, their neighbors, and curious youngsters—most all of them Black—had watched the F-51s dramatic descent from the heavens, and within minutes they rushed toward the landing site where the plane had bellied in. Suddenly, everybody stopped dead in their tracks, and a hush fell over the motley crowd as they stared at the sight of the pilot who had fallen from the sky. He was Black! Instead of the anticipated barrage of anger Jim anticipated, he received what amounted to a hero's welcome. It was an historic moment for the farming community that stretched between Shelby and Kings Mountain, North Carolina.

The huge plumes of smoke that filled the air had alerted members of the local sheriff's department, and they arrived on the scene, too. Watching as the uniformed sheriff and his deputies hurried toward him, Jim began to experience twinges of pain. He realized that he had sustained a neck injury during the violent landing, but at this point he was more concerned about contacting his commander at Dover than seeking medical attention. In the ensuing conversation with the sheriff, he was relieved to learn that the police had notified officials at a nearby base. Officials at Dover would know what had happened by now.

Soon the military legal team showed up and began asking Jim questions. Unnoticed by the excited crowd, an overalls clad farmer wearing a long, heavy overcoat weeded his way through the fringes of the assembled group. It was his crop that had been partially destroyed, and he was as interested as the assortment of curiosity seekers to see the plane that was permanently grounded in the heart of his wheat field.

Realizing that Mr. Oates had arrived, the crowd parted a pathway for their widely respected senior member of the farming community, and they waited for his reaction. Mr. Oates was clearly surprised to see that the young pilot in the midst of the investigative team of officials was not what he had expected. Jim was standing in the sun, but with only a windbreaker added to his flight suit, he was shivering both from December's chill as well as shock. When Jim introduced himself as the culprit in the incident, he apologized profusely as the farmer studied the young Black pilot with a look of amazement on his weathered face. He shook Jim's outstretched hand and quietly introduced himself.

The older man cocked his head and listened carefully as the sheriff advised Mr. Oates that he could be reimbursed for his losses by the government, but when he was asked what he wanted to do, Mr. Oates did not respond immediately. Instead, he slowly took off his heavy overcoat and draped it around Jim's shoulders before quietly responding that he did not choose to file a claim against the government for damages. Surprised by this outcome, the puzzled investigative team looked askance at one another as the stooped and aging farmer slowly turned and walked away.

Intent on absorbing every minute of the dramatic event, the crowd remained until Jim was taken to the military facility in Charlotte where he made a personal call to Dover before checking into the Visiting Officers' Quarters (VOQ) for the night. Using the voucher provided for his flight out of Kentucky, he made arrangements to fly home to Dover late the next afternoon via a commercial flight out of Charlotte, North Carolina, instead of Louisville, Kentucky. It had been a sobering experience and he was thankful to have lived through it…a Christmas miracle he would never forget.

CHAPTER 20

THE PULL OF GRAVITY

Deep in thought, Jim climbed aboard the flight to Delaware. Was it really only December 18th? His mind was crowded with images of all that had happened in the span of a mere 24 hours. In contrast to the other travelers, who chattered with anticipation about the Christmas holidays, Jim silently stowed his overnight bag, adjusted his uniform, and stretched out in the comfortable, upholstered seat of the commercial airliner. Facing away from his buoyant fellow passenger, the young captain slipped into a reverie of reflections. His close call with death demanded his undivided attention to consider his priorities, his perspective on what was important in life. Jim was long overdue for this personal assessment.

The familiar sound of the aircraft engine's high-pitched roar muffled the conversations of the holiday crowd as the DC-3 hurtled down the runway like a pole-vaulter seeking a higher leap into space. Airborne once more, Jim drifted into a collage of worrisome memories. The only voice he recognized was of his mother Ora, who seemed to reside in his subconscious and surface in his thoughts during stressful times. More his teacher than a nurturing mother, Ora had constantly critiqued his actions and measured his efforts throughout his youth. She guided him intellectually and morally, and she set the parameters for her expectations of him. She had done her best to dissuade her son from becoming a pilot, but her efforts were futile. Flying was his passion. Still, she continued to worry about his safety. Jim knew she would be distraught to learn about his accident.

His father Sam was his heart, his role model of a man who dearly loved his family. Sam was stoic but he had literally willed himself to remain alive as long as he could in order to protect his children. It was a testament to the depth of his love. In spite of unimaginable suffering, Sam had managed to create a bond with his son that reached beyond death.

For the first time Jim began to think as a parent rather than as a pilot. What if he had not survived crash landing his Mustang in Mr. Oates' wheat field? Little Roberta would have suffered the biting loneliness of his loss for the rest of her life. He knew how that felt.

He had never gotten over his father's death. Louise was so young that she would not have experienced the protective imprint of his love, a reality Jim could not bear. How could he have been so blind? He had jumped right back into life when he returned home from Korea. He never considered slowing down and fully enriching the moments he spent during his waking hours with his family. He needed to become a more involved father.

By the time his flight touched down in Delaware and a military transport shuttled him to Dover AFB, Jim had experienced an epiphany that led him to organize his thoughts and shift his priorities. Mary Ann, Roberta, and baby Louise would be his sole focus throughout the Christmas holidays, he decided. He was grateful for second chances.

There were the brief pre-emptory interviews about the accident upon his return, and Jim obliged with a detailed description of the entire sequence of events. His demeanor was deceptively calm, considering all that he had experienced, but no one questioning him could have imagined the complexity of his thoughts. He had envisioned his entire lifetime on the trip home, and the young pilot had matured years beyond his age. He had survived crash landing his Mustang in a southern wheat field and avoided causing any casualties in the small rural community where he landed. Perhaps more importantly, Jim had embraced fatherhood. As a result, Christmas 1953 was an especially joyous occasion in the Randall household, a turning point.

By January 1954, Jim was immersed in the official investigation of his accident. He had always spent as much time as possible at Base Ops and on the flight line with the crew chiefs discussing mechanical problems, safety issues, and emergency procedures, not only regarding the F-51, but also all the other aircraft in the inventory. Whenever he saw the opportunity, he even requested the chance to check out in other aircraft. He was insatiably curious and incredibly interested in every aspect of flight. No one doubted his dedication or professionalism.

Eventually, Jim had a chance to read the accident report about his ferrying flight on December 17th. It revealed that he blew a head gasket at full power. What continued to gnaw away at him, though, was the elderly Black farmer who turned down the monetary compensation for the losses Jim had caused. He never forgot the look on Mr. Oates' face as he searched the young Black pilot's countenance to assess his character. Jim always felt in his heart that the farmer's decision was one of grace. He didn't want to pursue legal action that might jeopardize the young Black pilot's chances at a better life. It was a defining moment for both men.

Jim had escaped death and kept his career intact in spite of losing his aircraft, but that was not the end of the story…not by a long shot. Eventually, the large skeletal fragments of Jim's Mustang were cleared from Mr. Oates' wheat field, but the detritus embedded in the ground remained a fascination to the curious young boys who frequently adventured through the field to find treasured pieces to keep as souvenirs.

Meanwhile, the military investigation of the crash ended with Jim's exoneration, and he was selected to attend Air Force All Weather Training at Tyndall AFB on the gulf coast of Florida. He was relieved that his career was back on course, but there was a catch. The course was only six weeks long so it was considered a temporary duty assignment. It was not practical to move the family to Florida since he would be returning to duty at Dover. Consequently, Jim reported to the 3626th Flying Training Group at Tyndall sans Mary Ann and his little girls.

The trade-off was that, based on his performance in All Weather Training, Jim would qualify for ferrying flights to destinations across the Atlantic Ocean. Excelling in the course would also certify his increasing proficiency as a pilot. The only way Jim could justify leaving his family for an extended TDY after being home for only a year after a combat tour would be to graduate at the top of his class and that became his goal.

Tyndall AFB was about 12 miles from Panama City, Florida, so the other pilots studied during the week but hit the road to party in town during the weekend. Jim had already experienced this scenario when he was at Perrin AFB in Texas and again at Craig AFB in Alabama. As a young Black man, Jim reasoned that he was probably safer flying combat missions than partying on weekends in Panama City, Florida, in 1954. Instead, he disciplined himself to study each day after class during the week and also throughout the day on weekends, but during lonely weekend evenings when the base was like a ghost town, he treated himself to long-distance calls to Dover.

Mary Ann kept her promise to snap photographs for him, but like 2-dimensional paintings of landscapes that fail to capture the sound of the wind or the warmth of the sun, his wife's photographs never quite conveyed the bustle of family life like those phone calls. It meant a lot to hear Mary Ann's recounting of the week's events. Even though she was clearly overwhelmed with all the responsibility, she always described Roberta's antics with humor and captured how rapidly Louise was growing. The most special moments, though, were when Roberta tried to carry on a conversation while Louise whimpered for attention in the background.

By April 9th, Jim read Captain John Ottenstein's assessment of his performance during the All Weather Training Course. Jim had logged 26 hours 40 minutes in the T-33 and 12 hours in the synthetic trainer that simulated different challenges in flight often due to weather. Captain Ottenstein noted, "Capt. Randall entered this course with an instrument flying proficiency well above average. He maintained this proficiency throughout the entire course in both his basic instrument flying and also his radio work."

These comments, listed as a "Word Picture of Students' Progress," were laudatory and very rewarding to Jim. However, it was the handwritten comments at the bottom of the page by the commanding officer that filled Jim with pride as he read—

This is the highest grade given since (the) course started at Tyndall in July 1953.

Jim's flying training grade listed him as #1 in the class.

Upon his return to Dover the following week, Jim embraced Mary Ann and the girls in happy reunion. He relished every moment of being back home again and playing with his daughters. He created an epic mess in the kitchen dyeing Easter eggs with Roberta and jostled Louise in his arms when she was cranky. On Easter Sunday he proudly escorted his family into the base chapel for the service, which was followed by an Easter egg hunt for all the children in the congregation. Grateful to experience Easter through his children's eyes, Jim smiled when Roberta squealed in delight as she discovered a brightly colored egg nestled in the branches of a bush and little Louise tugged at her first frilly Easter bonnet.

Jim continued to ferry aircraft to bases across the United States, but he had also begun to ferry planes across the Atlantic Ocean on a regular basis. For the international flights, he was transported by military aircraft or commercial flight to either Warner Robins AFB in Georgia or Brookley AFB in Mobile, Alabama—the point of origin where he picked up the aircraft he was to ferry abroad. Since he took every opportunity to check out in as many different types of airplanes as possible, he became increasingly skilled in various aircraft, which made him exceptionally valuable as a ferrying pilot.

Proficient in piloting the T-33, F-84G, F-84F, and RF-84F, Jim personally delivered a variety of aircraft to Goosebay, Labrador; Bluie West 1, Greenland; Keflavik-Reykjavik, Iceland; and Prestwick, Scotland. The flights to Prestwick, Scotland, were primarily a stopping off point prior to continuing to destinations in Stravanger, Norway; Furstenfeldbruch, Germany; Yugoslavia; Turkey; and the Netherlands.

Covering such a large cross section of the globe, Jim encountered unending climatic challenges, but he dealt confidently with the sometimes-radical shifts in the weather. He was unflappable . . . until August 13, 1955.

Hurricanes Connie and Diane were both heading toward Delaware, but Jim had a ferrying trip that could not be cancelled, not even by the military. Mary Ann was in labor with their 3rd child, and Jim was on a mission to get her safely to the base hospital at Dover for the delivery. As often happens when major storms affect the barometer, pregnant women are equally affected and sometimes deliver ahead of schedule. Stressed when William Edward Randall arrived in the midst of competing tropical storms, Jim was excited to have a boy, at last. As he stood gazing at his newborn son for the first time, he was simply thankful that the baby was healthy "with ten fingers and ten toes."

Jim continued to have a sporadic schedule, punctuated with ferrying flights across America, interspersed with international flights to intriguing places. By December 5th he was surprised to receive a letter of achievement from Brigadier General B.E. Allen, the 1708th Ferrying Wing Commander at Kelly AFB, Texas. General Allen congratulated him for "successful completion of six (6) jet trans-ocean crossings as a pilot during the period March 1953 to 24 October 1955." In recognition of the accomplishment, Jim was awarded the Military Air Transport Service Award for Safety in Military Aviation. The commander also noted that he was attaching a copy of his letter to Jim's official military records. Needless to say, Jim was very happy that the award would supersede any mention of the ill-fated F-51 that never made it past Mr. Oates' winter wheat field in North Carolina.

By the beginning of November 1955, it was undeniable. We were at war in Vietnam. Jim had been keeping track of our involvement in Southeast Asia and knew he might be flying combat missions again. He planned to continue preparing for any eventuality.

Meanwhile, Mary Ann had her hands full taking care of three children who were 3 years old or younger. The logistics of running the Randall household became as complex as the mission of the crew chiefs on the flight line, but Mary Ann managed somehow, though she was smoking heavily now. She had picked up the habit in college and had vacillated between giving it up when she was pregnant but drifting back to smoking as the children became toddlers. Whereas smoking relaxed Mary Ann, it stressed Jim. It had become a divisive issue between them.

By mid-December, Mary Ann was looking forward to having Jim home for the Christmas holidays. He was so good with the children, and it was such a relief when he was around to help, but her expectations were soon diminished by what was actually good news. Jim was notified that he had been selected for Squadron Officer School, an acknowledgement of his stellar performance as a young officer. It was a TDY assignment to the Air University at Maxwell AFB in Montgomery, Alabama, and he was to report to Maxwell prior to the beginning of classes on 6 January 1956. Being selected for the three-month course assured that his next assignment would continue to advance his career, and since it appeared that the ferrying squadron at Dover was eventually going to be phased out, graduating with distinction from Squadron Officer School was an important step toward his next goal—making major. It also put him in the mix for a plum assignment in the near future.

With another separation from the family looming in January, Jim and Mary Ann made sure Christmas 1955 at the Randalls was a grand production. Roberta was constantly underfoot in the kitchen as soon as Mary Ann began baking holiday treats. At three, Roberta was familiar with family rituals, and she eagerly awaited the chance to decorate holiday cookies and lick the colorful icing left over in the mixing bowl. Jim was in his element as he adorned the Christmas tree with twinkling lights and then helped 2-year-old Louise hang ornaments on the aromatic branches. With Christmas carols on the radio adding background music, Jim lifted Roberta so that she could add the finishing touch to the project, a shiny star for the top of the tree. Too young to be trusted with breakable decorations, a wide-eyed Billy could only squeal in delight over all the commotion. With Jim's mother Ora arriving to meet her new grandson and Jim's colleagues, the Musketeers, dropping by for a visit, the Randall household overflowed with holiday merriment.

All too soon the joyous celebration of Christmas was over and the New Year was lying in wait. Mary Ann braced herself for yet another lengthy separation as she piled three sleepy little ones into the car to take Jim to the flight line. Jim had planned ahead and was lucky to catch a hop to Alabama. Once again, the family would remain behind in Dover while Jim settled into the Bachelors' Officers' Quarters on Maxwell AFB for the duration of Squadron Officer School.

Mary Ann vicariously experienced her husband's days through his letters about the rigorous but interesting classes he was taking. He explained everything in considerable detail, adding anecdotes to amuse her, but it wasn't the same as being there. She realized the gravity of his coursework, though. The content of the courses was both critical and expansive to prepare field grade officers, those ranking as major and above, for future commands. Jim sent her a copy of the military's synopsis of each course:

"WORLD AFFAIRS the political, ideological, economic, and military factors which impact the current international relations with other countries

AIR POWER the nature and characteristics of air power as well as the development and employment of air units.

COMMANDER AND STAFF ethics and the responsibilities of leadership and command in addition to community and information services and the organization and functions of command and staff elements.

COMMUNICATION SKILLS counseling and conference techniques; written and oral communication; logical thinking; problem solving; and professional reading.

FIELD LEADERSHIP field problems, athletics, ceremonies, etc.

RELATED ACTIVITIES a potpourri of proficiency flying, processing, examinations, and independent study and research."

After a documented 616 hours of attendance and continuous interaction with his fellow participants at USAF's Squadron Officer School, Jim attained a new level of confidence in himself as he read his final Training Report. He was described as a "friendly, sincere, and effective officer [who] maintained a positive approach to increasing his capabilities and exhibited a high level of interest and enthusiasm toward all phases of the curriculum."

This opening observation was positive, but as Jim continued to read his evaluation, he noted how the key words and phrases singled out those officers who exhibited the ability to achieve excellence as commanders as well as superiority in the cockpit. The remainder of his evaluation made it clear that Jim had the qualities the military was searching for—

A very effective team worker, he showed a superior ability to work in harmony for and with others. He readily accepted additional responsibility and produced above average results. A consistently good leader, with an excellent ability to grasp a situation and develop correct and logical conclusions, he was aggressive when the situation required and developed above average cooperation and teamwork. He was an active and willing participant in conferences, staff work, and problem solving activities and his contributions to the group effort reflected a slightly above average degree of constructive originality and resourcefulness.

There had been an asterisk on the list when Jim was promoted to captain. It noted that Jim was "Negro." On Section Leader W.J. Baugh's assessment of Jim's performance at Squadron Officer School, Jim was acknowledged for being exceptional among his peers based solely on his performance without denoting his race. For over a decade he had kept the folded article in his wallet that claimed Negroes were not capable of measuring up to Whites. On 16 April 1956, Jim had written proof of the absurdity of that generalization…a silent but very satisfying victory.

One year later when Roberta was old enough to attend kindergarten, Jim was reassigned to Nellis AFB. Jim was only 31 years old, but he had completed 75 combat sorties in Korea, flown across the Atlantic 8 times, travelled the world and logged more hours in the cockpit than most of his contemporaries. At 29, Mary Ann had spent most of her waking hours at home tending to the children and waiting for her husband to return home from his latest TDY…disparate lives heading in different directions. Even radar could not predict whether they could weather the storm as the Randalls headed west to Jim's new assignment, Nellis Air Force Base in Las Vegas, Nevada.

Baby William sits in his infant seat entertaining his big sisters, Louise on the left and Roberta on the right. The girls are dressed up and waiting to hear their parents' plan for the day.

CHAPTER 21

A NEW START IN THE WEST

Traveling almost 2500 miles from Dover, Delaware, to Las Vegas, Nevada, with three very young children required as much organization and far more critical supplies than preparing for a trans-ocean ferrying flight, but it was a rare opportunity to experience the majesty of America. Jim knew the children were too young to remember all that they had seen, but he had fought for his country, and he wanted to take Mary Ann and his children on this journey with him. Too often he'd had to leave them behind.

Mary Ann was as excited as Jim when they finally arrived at Nellis AFB. She had fond memories of being in attendance when Jim received his wings there in March 1950.

It had been called Las Vegas AFB at the time, but a lot had changed over the span of 7 years. One of the most exciting developments was that the 3600th Air Demonstration Team had transitioned to flying F-100 Super Sabres and had recently been re-assigned from Luke AFB in Arizona to Nellis; as the Thunderbirds, they did brief shows for base personnel each time they returned from performing in both the United States and abroad.

Mary Ann was relieved that Jim was eligible for base housing, and since their moving van arrived on base ahead of the family, the Randalls could move into their quarters once the van was unloaded. Jim officially checked into base headquarters and arranged for the family's brief stay in the Visiting Officers' Quarters (VOQ). It was cramped for a family of five, but having ready access to their base quarters, as they moved in, outweighed the inconvenience. Once the movers transferred all the Randalls' possessions into their new home, they assisted Jim in assembling the essentials—cribs and assorted items of furniture. One of the perks of living on base was that the units were equipped with major appliances for the kitchen and laundry, and additional furniture was available to supplement what the family had previously acquired to furnish their off-base rental at Dover.

After an endless morning of shifting furniture around according to Mary Ann's directions and helping her set up the bedrooms so that the family could leave the VOQ and begin settling the children into their new home, Jim shifted his priorities. Leaving Mary Ann to unpack the boxes marked "kitchen," Jim located his lawnmower and headed to the base filling station with an empty 5-gallon gas can. The temperature in Las Vegas would have set records in Delaware this time of year, and the grass in front of their new quarters clearly had not been mown in quite a while. He planned to spruce up the front yard in an effort to show that his family would be good neighbors.

Once he returned home and had the mower up and running, Jim made overlapping but parallel passes to tame the unruly grass. He was sweating profusely but making progress when a tall, good-looking White guy in Bermuda shorts sauntered out of the quarters across the street, slipped on the pair of flip flops on his front steps, and ambled over to welcome Jim to the neighborhood. Jim turned off his lawnmower as the guy extended his hand and introduced himself as Dean Pogreba. Jim, in fun, dubbed him Pogie for short.

 A few brief comments between the two turned into an animated conversation destined to last for hours…two fighter pilots exchanging stories. Pogreba had the last laugh when he topped Jim's story about falling in love with speed and flight as he pedaled his tricycle almost fast enough to become airborne. Pogreba countered with his oft told story about how his brothers helped him affix wings to his tricycle so that he could appear in his hometown's parade honoring veterans. He couldn't resist adding that it was also the year he met his future wife, Maxine. "She was six years old at the time," he added, to win the point. Soon the two fighter pilots "raced back and forth across the street like kids," according to Maxine's version of the budding friendship. Though both had a serious side, they shared a sense of humor that peppered most of their conversations with gales of laughter.

Pogreba was four years older than Jim so he had earned his wings at Nellis in 1944 and married Maxine, his childhood sweetheart, immediately afterwards. Though he had been bent on being a fighter pilot, he logged his 100 combat flights in the C-46 in the China-Burma-India theater shuttling supplies to the British 14th Army. As Jim shared his experience in World War II, the two men found it interesting that they had both left the military after the world-wide conflict. Jim had taken off for college, but Pogreba, being older, returned to his home state of Montana where he helped establish Montana's National Guard with P-51 Mustangs. When the United States became embroiled in the Korean War, Pogreba was soon back on active duty as a combat pilot flying the F-86. Although their lives did not intersect in Korea, both Jim and Pogreba became fast friends at Nellis AFB from the moment they met as across-the-street neighbors in 1957.

Pogreba and his wife Maxine had children about the same age as the Randalls, so a friendship was forged that would last for a lifetime. Due largely to the GI Bill following World War II, it was possible for most Americans to become homeowners and remain rooted. On the other hand, the U.S. Air Force continued to expand, so military families were more mobile than their civilian counterparts. Making friends quickly at each new assignment made it easier to leave old friends behind. Children as well as their parents had to be resilient. Jim counted himself lucky the day Pogreba and his family welcomed the Randalls into their life.

Jim was put in charge of Base Operations at Nellis, a demanding job. It entailed making certain that the flight lines were well maintained and that taxiways were checked regularly to make sure there was no debris that could be sucked up into an aircraft's engine. He made himself available 24/7 to ground crews so that schedules were always met in spite of unexpected incidents that necessitated being flexible. Jim ran a tight ship, keeping everything in sync. Since the one thing he could not control was the weather, he had contingency plans for every eventuality. Keeping the flight line functioning like a finely honed machine was gratifying, but Jim was a fighter pilot at heart, so each time he had the chance, he checked out in every available aircraft to increase his knowledge and rating as a pilot. Within the first year of his tour at Nellis, he qualified in the T-33, B-25, L-20, C-45, C-47, and T-39. He even received tutelage from Jacob "Shorty" Manch, who was an instructor pilot at Nellis at that time. Nicknamed "Shorty" to facetiously acknowledge his 6'7" frame, Manch had managed to earn his wings despite military regulations, and he became one of the heroes of World War II as a Doolittle Raider.

Getting to know the older pilots who had served so honorably was truly rewarding to Jim, but he was chafing at the bit to be accepted into the Fighter Weapon School to become an F-100 pilot. He felt it was his destiny. Even so, he remained dedicated to every aspect of his designated mission. Jim was also very skilled at dealing with the puzzles that the aircraft maintenance crews faced. Although his fellow pilots had often worked on their jalopies as teenagers and were mechanically inclined, Jim never had access to a car when he was young. His family couldn't afford one. Instead, he had spent his after-school hours in the midst of the huge engines that his father built, repaired, and maintained for the Norfork & Western railway system in Roanoke. He was a natural at dealing with both the maintenance and malfunctions of huge machines. His commander soon learned to trust Jim's judgment in discerning the root of mishaps and often called on him to assess a situation.

Jim was amenable to doing his time on the ground and keeping everything functioning at the highest level, but he never stopped planning ahead for his own career. Getting back into the cockpit full time was always his goal. He had established a good relationship with his commander as well as his team on the flight line, but he was hesitant to discuss his desire to be airborne once again. He felt he had to earn that privilege. Patiently, he waited for the propitious moment to ask about upgrading to the powerful jet aircraft that were now making loud and impressive appearances on the Nellis flight line. After almost two years of focusing intensely on the job at hand while dreaming of the future, Jim sensed the time was right.

With trepidation, he approached his commanding officer with a request to attend the 8th Fighter Weapons School at Nellis. When his commander began explaining why he could not afford to lose Jim at Base Ops during a lengthy stint at the prestigious school, Jim prepared for rejection. Instead, the senior officer offered an alternative. He made arrangements for his loyal Ops Officer to be accepted into an abbreviated version of the course and to receive personal training from one of the school's instructor pilots. Jim worked overtime at Base Ops while training in the F-100, but he was on Cloud Nine.

As his commander had expected, Jim sailed through training in the F-100. The only thing he needed to do to be fully qualified in the F-100 was night training, and he would have to go TDY in order to accomplish that requirement. Again, his commanding officer made accommodations and granted Jim temporary leave to train elsewhere, knowing full well he had just guaranteed that he was about to lose the best Base Operations officer he would ever have. He was right. Not long after Jim returned fully qualified as an F-100 pilot, he was ordered TDY to the Survival School at Reno, Nevada, as preparation for his assignment to Etain, France.

Since it was not logistically possible for his family to accompany him when he was to depart for Europe in February 1959, Jim drove Mary Ann and the children to Evansville, Indiana, to stay with Mary Ann's parents until his family was cleared to join him. Roberta had finished kindergarten and was in first grade at the base elementary school on Nellis, while Louise was in the midst of kindergarten. Jim realized that his children's education would continue to be an important consideration each time he was reassigned, and this was the first major test of their resilience. The family had really enjoyed living in Las Vegas, especially Mary Ann, but the adventure of living in Europe appealed to her. The children were too young to understand why they were being uprooted, though.

A few days later, Jim stepped aboard his flight to France with mixed emotions. Picturing the sorrowful scene in Indiana at his departure—three sobbing children begging him not to go— Jim pondered how his career would impact the arc of their lives. He was being promoted ahead of his peers, recognized for his proficiency serving in a command position, and respected for his prowess as a pilot. He was on track career-wise, but he had to consider how well he was doing in the most important job in life, being a father. He reflected critically on his success in that role until the familiar drone of flight lulled him to sleep.

CHAPTER 22

LIFE IN POST-WORLD WAR II EUROPE

Jim was jet-lagged from his military transport flight across the Atlantic when he landed in France in April 1959, but that was only the first leg of his journey. He had to travel by rail to reach his final destination at Etain Air Base where he had been reassigned to the 49th TAC Fighter Wing as a member of the 8th Fighter Squadron USAFE (United States Air Force Europe). Just as he had anticipated, there was a chill in the air and the wind was picking up as he boarded the train. Spoiled by the moderate temperatures and endless days of sunshine in Las Vegas, he braced himself for the year ahead. He had read that the highest winter temperatures in France were about the same as the desert's coldest nights at Nellis.

Ever the researcher, Jim had also discovered that Etain Air Base and Nellis AFB had one unenviable thing in common. Few people were aware that both installations were adjacent to huge swaths of land, which were deemed toxic and uninhabitable after World War II. About 75 miles distance from Nellis was the Nevada Test Site. Beginning in 1951, while he was flying combat missions in Korea, that high security area of Nevada was used to test nuclear weapons and nuclear bombs, a practice that lasted until 1992, and forever changed the environment.

Etain, on the other hand, was near a 460 square mile area deemed by the French government as *Zone Rouge*, the Red Zone. From February 21st to December 18th, 1916, the area was a World War I battleground between the French and their German invaders. There were 400,000 French casualties and 350,000 German casualties near Verdun, only 12 miles from Etain. Somme, France, where casualties in World War I numbered over one million, was over 200 miles away.

Restoration of the war-ravaged areas of Verdun and Somme would have been astronomical for a country trying to recover economically as well as emotionally from the ravages of war, and so the French Ministry for Liberated Territories deemed the entire area as Code Red—"unfit for human habitation or commitment." Over time nature reclaimed the land, its horrors concealed by an overgrowth of spindly trees, displaced boulders, and dense vegetation. Undetonated bombs and ordnance pitted the topography, creating unnatural hills and dangerous depths. Bodies of combatants, indistinguishable between French patriots and their German adversaries, became one with the earth in an expansive, unplanned cemetery created by Mother Nature.

Still deep in thought about how winning as well as losing in war extracts unbearable losses, Jim was jolted awake when the train slowed to a screeching stop and the conductor announced their arrival in Etain. The chill of an April shower captured Jim's breath in filmy wisps as he stepped down off the train, but he could see a young man in uniform frantically waving his hand and rushing toward him.

Red-faced and apologetic for running late, Jim's host saluted and introduced himself before driving Jim over to the trailers where unaccompanied officers at Etain Air Base resided. As he helped Jim unload his gear, he handed him several flyers about the local area and a detailed map of the major facilities on base before wishing him well and heading off to his duty station. Compared to Bachelor Officers' Quarters stateside, the trailers were hardly commodious, but this was to be a brief though important tour of duty focused on ferrying aircraft to other Allied locations and closing down American control of the base at Etain. Jim was more than qualified to handle his role in the transition.

Everything seemed stabilized and falling into place like clockwork on base, but American pilots at Etain remained combat ready. Franco-American relations had continued to deteriorate ever since former General Charles de Gaulle's election as president in December 1958. De Gaulle decried what he considered "British ambiguity" and "American isolationism." He pulled France's military out of NATO, recognized China, and was demanding French control over American forces, weaponry and military inventory that were based in France. President Dwight David Eisenhower—the former Supreme Commander of Allied Expeditionary Forces in Europe during World War II—and his Cabinet were never going to let that happen, and gradually the U.S. bases in Germany expanded with a *largesse* of American military equipment and military forces, which were being shuttled out of de Gaulle's France to a receptive Germany.

By June 1959, Jim's family was scheduled to join him for his remaining three months at Etain, and he was faced with a dilemma. His modest trailer was pathetically inadequate and would be cramped for a family of five so he added house hunting to his busy schedule. He found the answer to his quest in Virton, Belgium, where a local family was willing to rent the upper floor of their home to Jim's family for the duration of his time at Etain Air Base. When Mary Ann arrived a day or so early with Roberta, Louise and Billy in tow, their temporary home in Belgium was not yet available, so the family endured living like sardines in a tin can until a day or so later.

Jim and Mary Ann were able to re-establish their household in Belgium fairly easily, and they marveled at how quickly their children adjusted. They would gather with the Belgian family's children out in front of the house and play with one another until the sun set. It was a glorious summer, and the sounds of Belgique (a Belgian form of French) and English blended together like magic as the youngsters communicated through pantomime and gestured directions followed by raucous laughter. Despite not being able to speak the same language, they understood each other perfectly. One evening as Jim and Mary Ann stood on the deck overlooking the front yard and watched all the children thoroughly immersed in entertaining one another, Jim realized that his children instinctively understood the path to world peace. They were living it. It touched his heart.

Although Jim always refrained from being involved in politics, he was a voracious reader, and it was becoming increasingly clear that diplomatic efforts to deal with de Gaulle had failed. U.S. personnel as well as airplanes and military equipment were being strategically re-positioned at bases in England, in addition to Germany, at an accelerated clip. Soon only Jim and his shrinking unit remained as part of the skeletal crew maintaining security at Etain Air Base until its final days. By August 1959, the last vestiges of American military might had left Etain. De Gaulle had finally bullied his way into getting control of U.S. military installations in the country, sans America's highly trained military personnel and the enviable inventory of U.S. advanced aircraft and military equipment he coveted. Pride can excise a heavy price.

As he anticipated, Jim received official orders to Germany, and so he decided to leave his family comfortably settled in Belgium while he reported to duty at Spangdahlem and arranged for family housing on the base. On a bright August morning Mary Ann and his children stood on the platform at the train station and waved good-bye as he boarded the train to his new assignment—Spangdahlem Air Base in southwestern Germany across the border from Belgium.

Less than two hours later, after a few stops along the way, Jim arrived at his destination in Germany. Within minutes he was met at the station by his sponsor, an enthusiastic young officer intent on giving him a tour of the area. Jim explained that he had left his wife and three children behind in Belgium and was eager to arrange for family housing on base as quickly as possible. Aware that Jim was anxious to settle in as well as learn what was expected of him, his younger host was quick to assure Jim that he was going to love the officer he would be working for—the Chief of Safety.

Instead of responding with further conversation, Jim fell silent at the dread of being placed in a paper-pushing job. He spent the waning moments of the drive to Spangdahlem

Air Base plotting how he was going to gain control of his destiny by petitioning his new commander for a position in a unit where the focus was flying. He didn't know the Wing Commander, but as soon as he had the chance, he intended to meet him and pursue a change of assignment.

Reaching the Visiting Officers' Quarters, the young officer was still chatting away and offering to be of service, but Jim politely declined, grabbed his gear, and rushed into the VOQ. Once in his room, he showered quickly, changed into a fresh uniform and headed over to the Officers' Club for dinner. Reaching the facility, he was surprised when the door opened from the other side and the colonel who was coming out shouted, "JIM! What the hell are you doing here?" It was one of his former commanders when he was assigned to Dover AFB…an unbelievable stroke of luck.

As the two reminisced, Jim explained that he had just arrived and learned that he was to be Vice Chief of Safety, an assignment that he felt was not the best use of his flying ability or work ethic. As diplomatically as possible, he expressed his desire to be the Operations Officer of one of the squadrons at Spangdahlem. The senior officer nodded as he listened to Jim's concerns, and he arranged to meet with him the following day to discuss an idea of how to come to a suitable compromise.

Based on his extensive experience and unflagging dedication to the mission at hand, Jim commanded a level of respect among his commanders as well as his colleagues, and so he was confident when he sat down in the colonel's office the next morning. He was both honest and direct when he expressed his desire for a job that provided him with more responsibility as well as promotion potential. The colonel was sympathetic but explained that his Chief of Safety was in the hospital in Wiesbaden, Germany, so he needed Jim to fulfill the position in Safety Ops temporarily. He quickly added that upon the Chief of Safety's return, he planned to assign Jim to operate the Alert Facility. Jim suppressed his instinct to shout with excitement and gave a sharp salute before departing to be the best Safety Officer on record…temporarily.

Having been given a few days to retrieve his family in Belgium and bring the Randall clan back to Spangdahlem to move into the large brick buildings set aside for accompanied officers, Jim returned to Virton, Belgium. After consolidating their belongings into trunks and thanking their Belgian landlords for their kind hospitality, Jim and Mary Ann boarded their three excited children onto the train headed toward new adventures in Germany.

Mary Ann was relieved when she walked into their fully furnished quarters, "stairwell, apartment-like units" with the refrigerator stocked with groceries thanks to Jim's quick thinking and his hasty shopping trip to the commissary before traveling to Virton. She immediately began sorting through the trunks and putting all the children's clothing away first. School would be starting soon and she wanted everything organized in advance. It was important that Roberta and Louise felt comfortable in their new surroundings before stepping into a classroom as the "new kids."

Meanwhile, Jim headed to the flight line. He was doing double duty as the acting Safety Officer and preparing for the role of Alert Facility Commander. In his absence, the Randall household was caught up in a whirlwind of activity as a steady stream of USAF moms from neighboring apartments dropped by with kids in hand to welcome the Randalls with freshly baked casseroles and desserts sure to please the children. The relaxed moments in pastoral Virton, Belgium, already seemed like a distant memory.

Every Alert Facility had extremely important equipment assigned to it, and when Jim took command of the one at Spangdahlem, he set about making changes in the organization that facilitated its becoming a highly efficient and cohesive unit. Eight F-100s were assigned to the unit and the pilots were scheduled so that there was always a group on alert for specific intervals. Consequently, even the dining facility staff maintained a schedule to accommodate the 24-hour daily period of alert.

The grounds around the Alert Facility were fenced and there was a guard at the entry, but for added security Jim stipulated that no civilian vehicles were permitted inside the fence. He also had everyone assigned to the Alert Facility, including the dining facility staff, participate in a refresher course on gun safety. Safety was of the utmost importance, and Jim was intent that everyone went about their duties with that in mind. Soon the unit operated like a well-oiled machine. Morale was at an all-time high.

The Wing Commander was especially proud of how Jim had taken charge and how his men continued to respond with positive attitudes and pride. *Esprit de corps* was on full display. Each time high-ranking officers or dignitaries came to visit Spandahlem, the Wing Commander would take them to the Alert Facility for lunch with Jim and his crew. He was proud to show off the Alert Facility for its exemplary performance, which also reflected well on him.

As an F-100 pilot, Jim was assigned to 8th Squadron, and he took part in the unit's bombing flights over a range at Wheelus Air Base in North Africa in order to qualify and remain proficient in bombing and gunnery capability. One morning when Jim was strapped into the cockpit and rolling down the taxiway to join the squadron, he had to pull over to one side as a stream of traffic came racing toward him—an ambulance, fire truck, military police, the Wing Commander, and the DO (Duty Officer). Every vehicle in line was heading straight as an arrow in the direction of Jim's Alert Facility! His thoughts raced to all that had taken place earlier that morning. There had been no incidents when munitions had been attached to aircraft. Everything had taken place in accordance with procedure…just like every other day. Still, there was an alarming number of emergency vehicles and high-ranking officers rushing to Jim's Alert Facility as he was headed with his squadron to North Africa. He was desperate to know what in heaven's name was going on, but there was no turning back.

It took determination to remain focused on the mission at hand, but Jim knew the danger of distraction and was relieved when his flight of F-100s was finally headed home to Germany. As soon he was back on the ground, he parked his airplane, jumped in his car and raced to the gate of the Alert Facility. Leaning out the window, he yelled to the guard and demanded, "What in the hell is going on?" The guard quickly explained that the NCO in charge of maintenance in the dining facility had shot himself. Horrified, Jim drove into the fenced area, jumped out of his car and breathlessly ran into the Alert Facility. How could he have missed the signs of despondence that led his trusted sergeant to such an act? What had happened? Had he survived? Was anyone else hurt? Jim was full of questions as he faced his crew expecting the worst. He was caught totally off guard by their answer.

Apparently, Jim's trustworthy sergeant had accidentally shot himself with his .45 pistol and though injured, he was going to be fine…except for the repercussions that follow such an incident. Jim experienced a deluge of conflicting emotions, but he controlled himself until he was safely in his office behind a closed door. Sitting at his desk he took deep breaths to calm down, and then he mentally reviewed everything he had told the instructors who led the gun safety course. He had explained exactly what he expected them to cover and emphasized that only one gun was to be loaded and unloaded at a time. Then he pulled out a yellow legal pad and began writing notes for the inquiry that was probably already underway.

Fortunately, Jim's commander knew him well and was aware that accidents still happen in spite of extensive preparation. However, the incident also reflected upon him, so Jim listened respectfully as his commander spoke in minced words to convey his level of dissatisfaction, which was about a 10 on the Richter Scale, Jim guessed. A review of the gun safety course for the entire unit was in order as soon as the chagrined sergeant returned to work. That was expected, but also, in the future Jim would have a chase plane following him each time he was flying. Fortunately, there were no further incidents. One was more than enough to emphasize the importance of safety.

On occasion the Squadron Commander would ask Jim to take the DO (Duty Officer) with him to qualify on bombing runs and see the latest procedures being adopted. The flight to Wheelus Air Base was only about 1½ hours from Spangdahlem, and the Mediterranean sparkled as they approached Libya's coast. Wheelus had an interesting history. The Italian Air Force had originally constructed an airfield there in 1923 only to have the British

Eighth Army capture it two decades later in January 1943 during World War II. Ironically, the 376th Bombardment Group of the U.S. 12th Air Force launched B-24 Liberators from the same area to bomb Italy, which had joined the Axis powers—Germany and Japan—in World War II.

After World War II numerous agreements were signed between Libya and the United States across the years, welcoming the U.S. to operate Wheelus Air Base and permitting U.S. Air Forces in Europe (USAFE) fighter-bomber units to continue using the gunnery range at Wheelus for training. Since Libya was a poor country, these agreements were to Libya's benefit economically. However, it was 1959 and significant sources of oil had been discovered. Flights from Spangdahlem to Wheelus were still occurring, but the balance of power would ultimately be shifting yet again.

Once over the gunnery range, Jim's expertise as an instructor in the F-100 back at Nellis kicked in, and he enjoyed alternately letting the DO practice weapons delivery and then taking control again for the next run. He was always at the top of his game, but the DO probably thought Jim was just having a good day. Few of his colleagues knew that when he attended Fighter Weapons School at Nellis, he could outshoot everyone in the squadron. Jim's accuracy was legendary, but he never flaunted his talent. Like a coach, he had the heart of an instructor and genuinely enjoyed seeing his students and his military colleagues shine.

By Christmas Roberta and Louise had learned a lot about Germany and its holiday traditions, and they brought home crafts that they had made at school to celebrate. Mary Ann enjoyed taking the girls and Billy to all the little shops in nearby Spang and Dahlem, separate villages whose combined names became the designation for Spangdahlem, the air base. Germans were noted for their finely handcrafted wooden toys—wooden work benches with wooden tools; play kitchens with wooden sinks, stoves, and refrigerators full of brightly painted wooden vegetables; puzzles made of wood—all of them treasures that would last long enough to become heirlooms in the family. At Christmas time the shops also featured wooden carousels that would turn when all the candles on the base were lit.

The Randall children had loved seeing all the fluorescent neon lights on the imaginative signs in Las Vegas when Jim was stationed at Nellis, but Christmas in Germany was a magical experience, like being in a fairytale. At night they could look out the window of their 4th story apartment and even see the lights of Trier, a town almost 20 miles away. When it snowed, everything seemed to glisten with the beauty of the season's message. Jim had never seen Mary Ann quite so happy or engaging so often with other military wives, but the proximity of apartment dwellers made interaction frequent and natural.

As the New Year rolled around, the 1960s began with a furor. John F. Kennedy was running for the presidency, a young World War II hero ready to step into the White House with big ideas. Meanwhile, Fidel Castro won his revolution against Cuba's entrenched political system, but immediately afterwards, he shocked the public by embracing communism instead of democracy. The decade started off with America facing a communist country—supported by the USSR's leader, Nikita Khrushchev—right off the southern shores of Florida.

Jim, along with his Alert Unit, felt increasingly pressured as the balance of world power following World War II seemed to be shifting in a dangerous direction. However, he had always left his military responsibilities behind him when he walked in the door to be with his family. Instead of discussing his concerns with Mary Ann, he scheduled short trips so that the children could learn about the German culture as well as visit important sights in neighboring countries. He wanted Roberta, Louise, and Billy to experience what Europe had to offer and fall in love with learning as he had as a boy. When they took a jaunt down to Pisa, Italy, he showed Billy how to pose with the Leaning Tower of Pisa in the background so that it seemed as though the child kept it from falling down. The Italians probably were sick and tired of the daily photo ritual among tourists, but they loved children and indulged them in the joke.

On another occasion the family returned to Virton and stayed briefly with their Belgian friends. Then they ventured through the French countryside, stopping frequently to visit small villages and enjoy French cuisine. As spring turned into summer, Jim scheduled trips across Germany to see all the beautiful gardens and enjoy picnics along the way. The Randalls had developed a lifestyle that brought them together in a manner that had never seemed possible in the States. European countries were smaller in comparison to many of the states in America, and so it was easier to travel from country to country in Europe. There were also extensive rail systems that saved parents from driving distances. They could sit with their children and watch all the scenery passing by like vibrantly painted landscapes in the Louvre.

At the end of the summer of 1960, Roberta and Louise had become experienced travelers with photos and trinkets from various countries that they looked forward to sharing with classmates once the fall semester of school started. Jim was thrilled to see how they were thriving in the DOD (Department of Defense) school they attended, and he promised a very disappointed little Billy that it wouldn't be long before he could join his sisters and register for his first year of school. Though he could appreciate Billy's loneliness, he was pleased that his son was so determined to go to school. Perhaps he would become the scholar in the family.

By November the whole world was abuzz about the election of John F. Kennedy as the

United States President—a young World War II hero replacing a revered 5-star general who had served both his country and the world as the Supreme Allied Commander during World War II and then had gone back home to serve as President of the United States. The news was full of stories about the Kennedy clan and for young couples like the Randalls, it was easy to identify with JFK, as he was being called, and his beautiful and fashionable wife Jackie. They had a lovely little girl named Caroline and when her precious baby brother, John F. Kennedy, Jr., arrived on November 25, 1960, soon after his father's election, even Roberta and Louise were excited to talk about it at school.

At Christmas, the Randalls combined their own holiday traditions with the German rituals they had learned. It was a glorious time for the whole family. That's why when they once again welcomed in another year on a snowy New Year's Eve, they could not begin to imagine what lay ahead. John F. Kennedy was inaugurated on January 20,1961, the official designation for the elaborate occasion, and his beautiful young family was on full display. People were beginning to refer to Kennedy's presidency as Camelot, but trouble was brewing and by April, the political fault lines between America and Cuba cracked wide open with the Bay of Pigs debacle, a desperate effort conceived by Cuban refugees to save their homeland from communism. President Kennedy had supported the plan but things did not go well, and Khrushchev boldly inserted himself into the equation in support of Cuba's communist government. The Cold War was heating up and for the first time since World War II, world peace as well as America's security was in question.

Things were tightening up all across the world, especially at the Spangdahlem Alert Facility, but Jim tried to keep family life as normal as possible. He still planned occasional outings with the family, but sightseeing was mainly accomplished by driving across the German countryside on one-day jaunts. That became increasingly important since Mary Ann was now pregnant with their fourth child and was tiring more easily. Still, the family enjoyed short visits to nearby villages and picnics on the plush green lawns in the local parks. The Randalls loved Germany. The countryside was absolutely beautiful. Even the cemeteries that dotted hillsides flourished with flowers and foliage like well-tended gardens.

Summer faded into autumn and with the advent of another school year, Roberta and Louise were eager to get back to class and all their friends. Billy fretted about going to kindergarten. There was so much going on that he felt lost in the shuffle, but Mary Ann reassured him everything would be fine. Meanwhile she quietly gave thanks that she was in her last months of pregnancy. Then on August 13, 1961, the unthinkable happened. When everyone across Germany woke up that morning, there was an impenetrable wall encircling the nation's capital Berlin like a boa constrictor. It physically separated West Germany from East Germany, which had been under Russian control since the end of World War II.

As Commander of the Alert Facility at Spangdahlem, Germany, Jim experienced historic moments of sword-rattling between Superpowers. He was responsible for maintaining flights on high alert for 24 hours a day, 7 days a week. In the photo Jim is standing at the left, camera in hand, with an entourage of military officers viewing the gate between the Western and Eastern sectors of Berlin, Germany. The Berlin Wall was erected on 13 August 1961 and remained for 28 years, from 1961 to 1989, but democracy ultimately prevailed. (Photo courtesy of Regional History & Genealogy, Pikes Peak Library District, Image #412-113)

Jim immediately rushed to the Alert Facility along with everybody else reporting to duty stations across the base. The threat was immediate. Bombing and gunnery runs over Germany became daily and now included napalm, a highly volatile mixture of gasoline and kerosene that has devastating results. If the situation escalated, the goal was to seal off all routes into East Germany to protect West Germany. Prepared to drop ordnance if ordered to do so, Jim and his crew prayed it would never come to that point, but Jim feared war was imminent.

Jim and his fellow fighter pilots at the Alert Facility continued making daily flights over Germany, and they were ready to drop ordnance if the standoff with Khrushchev escalated. The purpose of their mission was no longer theoretical, and it was stressful since their own families could become enmeshed in the dangerous situation. After the Berlin Wall sprang up overnight like a poisonous mushroom, each time Jim returned home from the Alert Facility, he made a conscious effort to conceal his personal depth of concern. Roberta and Louise were too young to understand the dangerous implications of its existence, but all their elementary school friends now knew far more about international relations than most stateside youngsters in the primary grades. It was becoming harder to protect their innocence. As the months passed, tensions eased somewhat. Still, Khrushchev gave no indication that he was willing to remove the Berlin Wall. Life in Germany had changed overnight.

In the meantime, Jim was on alert for a very different reason. On October 4th, 1961, after calling a neighbor to stay with Roberta, Louise, and Billy, an anxious Jim helped Mary Ann into their car for a hasty 6-mile drive to the hospital on Bitburg Air Base, where little Patricia Elaine arrived to complete the Randall family. Jim was overjoyed as he returned to their apartment to tell his children the big news. Accustomed to planning major events, Jim organized the family into a team. He was well-prepared to fix meals, and get the children off to school each morning, but he enlisted the aid of a neighbor to provide a safe haven at the end of the school day. Roberta and Louise were responsible for picking up Billy after school and the three of them were to go straight to the neighbor's apartment and do their homework until Jim returned from the Alert Facility to pick them up. Jim was confident he had everything under control until he realized he had no idea how to fix the girls' hair—a major deficit in his planning.

Fortunately, a wife on another floor was known as an expert in braiding, and his temporary babysitter connected Jim with her. Each day before breakfast, Jim marched the girls upstairs for their early appointment to have their hair braided before school while Jim enlisted Billy to help with setting the table and assisting his dad with preparing breakfast. With Billy and the girls off to school, Jim headed to work.

At the end of his work day, Jim raced over to the hospital for a quick visit with Mary Ann and his bouncing baby daughter before retrieving all three children from the neighbor and begin preparing dinner with the help of Roberta and Louise. The children thought it was great fun, but Jim had developed a new perspective about motherhood and was glad when Mary Ann returned home with darling, little Patricia. He had not realized all the logistics involved in being a mom. The Christmas holidays were more exciting than ever with a bright-eyed baby girl in the house, and the Randalls celebrated the message of Christmas with a new understanding.

Life became increasingly complicated with the advent of the New Year. Although Jim received a "recommendation for promotion ahead of his contemporaries" by the Deputy Commander of Operations, 49th Tactical Fighter Wing, USAFE (United States Air Force Europe), he was already brooding about what his next assignment might be since 1962 was to be the final year of his tour in Germany. As it turned out there was far more than that to worry about in the future.

Mary Ann was more cautious about taking Patricia on long trips and exposing her to crowds so the family remained closer to home during the winter months. By late spring the weather warmed up enough for the Randalls to pursue short adventures again, which was particularly fun because little Patricia was delighted by everything. It was all new to her and her reactions were quite entertaining. The way she expressed herself with the limited vocabulary of a baby sometimes sounded like a foreign language. It seemed as though she was trying to speak German instead of English.

By summer Billy was ecstatic that he finally would be in first grade. He was no longer the baby of the family. There was the usual hubbub of shopping for school clothes and supplies. The girls had outgrown nearly everything, and now Billy was included in all the excitement of dressing room fittings and shopping bags full of purchases. Jim was a bystander in the phenomena, but he frequently asked Billy about the latest shopping trips with all the girls, baby Patricia included. He was surprised but delighted when Billy explained that he wanted to talk about first grade instead of shopping. Then he proudly announced that he planned to walk to school all by himself on the first day of classes.

At last the long-awaited day finally arrived, and Mary Ann prepared a special breakfast to celebrate the important occasion before sending the children off to school in a good mood. Roberta and Louise left early to meet with their friends, but Billy was still insisting that he wanted to walk to school by himself, though he didn't seem quite as confident as he had been. Jim had made arrangements to go to work later than usual, in case Billy changed his mind, and so he was still sitting at the kitchen table enjoying a second cup of coffee as Mary Ann ushered Billy to the door. Jim offered once more to walk with him or at least accompany him down to the first floor of the building, but Billy adjusted his backpack and answered with a shaky, "No."

Mary Ann shook her head with a "What do you think we should do?" expression on her face as Jim walked to the window and looked out to see Billy slowly stumbling through the grassy field outside the apartment building. He was still heading toward school, but his hesitant pace finally slowed to a stop. He dropped to his knees, placed his tiny hands over his eyes, and Jim could see his little body heave in defeat.

Sensing Billy's desperation, Jim raced out of the apartment building to help his son, and as soon as he reached him, he hugged the shaking child and commended him for a valiant effort. Then he helped him to his feet, took him by the hand, and walked the rest of the distance to school with him. The teacher seemed a bit surprised to see the teary-eyed little boy escorted by a young captain in uniform and a tardy arrival at that, but Jim didn't need to explain. Department of Defense (DOD) teachers were well-versed in the challenges of living abroad, and she welcomed Billy as though it were the best day of his life. Jim mouthed, "Thank you," before slipping away to go to the Alert Facility. He would never forget the moment when Billy first struggled to have courage. He was proud of his son.

With the three older children busy with school activities, Mary Ann and Jim kept track of all the weekly events on the kitchen calendar and so when Mary Ann flipped it to the month of October, Thursday the 4th was circled in red. Everyone in the family knew what that meant except Patricia who was toddling around the apartment and pestering Mary Ann for attention. The kitchen was filled with the wonderful aroma of a cake baking in the oven, and Patricia was hungry. She had no idea what a birthday party was or that Mary Ann was baking a cake in honor of her busy little daughter's very first birthday. When Roberta, Louise, and Billy raced through the door after an eventful day at school, they kept their baby sister entertained so Mary Ann could finish all the preparations before Jim returned home from the Alert Facility.

Once the entire family was gathered around the table, they enjoyed having dinner together until Mary Ann disappeared into the kitchen. Squirming in her high chair and trying to see why her mother had disappeared, Patricia squealed with delight when Mary Ann re-entered the room holding a small but beautifully iced birthday cake with one flickering candle placed in the center. After Mary Ann cut the cake and put a slice on each of the dessert plates assembled on the tablecloth near her, the girls served everyone seated at the table. The whole family joined in at slightly different pitches to sing "Happy Birthday" to the youngest member in the room as Mary Ann placed a slice of cake on Patricia's highchair tray. Patricia was not entirely sure what the whole ritual was about, but she understood that she was the center of attention and she was free to eat her cake with her hands instead of with that thing called a fork. Jim saved a mental image of the joyous moment in the photo album that he kept in his thoughts. It was a Norman Rockwell moment.

Twelve days later, on October 16, 1962, the headlines screamed that a Cuban Missile Crisis was underway. One *New York Times* headline spelled out the danger in bold print, **U.S. Imposes Arms Blockade on Cuba on Finding Offensive-Missile Sites. Kennedy Ready for Soviet Showdown.** Articles printed in all the languages spoken world-wide reported that Russian leader Nikita Khrushchev had ordered the strategic placement of Soviet missile installations in Cuba that were capable of launching nuclear warheads toward the U.S. in retaliation for the Bay of Pigs. Since Cuba was only about 90 miles from the southernmost point in Florida, Jim thought of all the military at Tyndall AFB, and how incredibly vulnerable they were, but in truth the entire Southeast was a target.

Every alert facility across the planet was on edge as negotiations between President Kennedy and Khrushchev intensified. In Germany the formidable Wall, which was virtually assembled overnight in mid-August, was proof of Khrushchev's determination to stand democratic countries down. Optimism waned as negotiations dragged on, but after 12 unendingly long days of nail-biting tension, Khrushchev announced that the missiles would be removed from Cuba, a huge relief to America's young president who had survived his first international showdown.

Jim's tour in Germany as the Commander of Spangdahlem's Alert Facility was during one of the most volatile periods during the Cold War. Jim was promoted to major at the end of the tour.

CHAPTER 23

SHOWDOWN IN SOUTH CAROLINA

Jim's suspicions had finally been confirmed. He was being reassigned to Shaw AFB, 13 miles distance from Sumter, South Carolina. He was already working toward a change of assignment, but he was going to have to report to duty in January 1963, regardless. Mary Ann had been explicit that she never wanted to return to the Deep South. He dreaded sharing the news with her, but there was a major move ahead and they needed to begin getting organized.

As he feared, Mary Ann was stressed beyond words and had begun smoking more frequently once again. Roberta, an enthusiastic fifth grader, found Mary Ann in tears one afternoon after she returned home from school, and though her distraught mother didn't go into detail, it was clear to the youngster that she dreaded going to South Carolina. It was troubling, frightening.

After years of thriving in Germany, Jim watched with a heavy heart as family life began fragmenting. At the Alert Facility he still performed at the top of his game. He remained on high alert and logged almost daily hours in the F-100, but the atmosphere at home was deteriorating. Hoping for a miracle, Jim researched significant sites in Germany and neighboring countries that the family could visit before his tour was over. Planning those trips together as well as including his wife and the children in his research ameliorated the situation somewhat.

By December and the advent of the Christmas holidays, there were mixed feelings in the Randall household since Jim's tour in Germany was coming to an end. The children had developed special friendships, and they were melancholy about leaving Germany at Christmas. They found solace in knowing their family would be spending the holiday back in the United States splitting their time between grandparents, Jim's mother Ora in the East and Mary Ann's parents in Evansville, Indiana. It would be the older generation's first chance to see their youngest grandchild, Patricia. For Jim, Mary Ann and the children the anticipation of being back home with family members that they had not seen in several years lightened everyone's spirits.

Midst myriads of Christmas lights shimmering across snowy expanses of Germany's countryside and sentimental parties honoring Jim and his family upon their departure, the Randalls left the country that the children had considered home for 3½ action-packed years and returned to the welcoming arms of excited grandparents.

Christmas 1962 was a pleasantly distracting bustle of shopping in elaborately decorated department stores, having joyful reunions with relatives, enjoying sumptuous feasts, and the exchanging of beautifully wrapped gifts. The Randall children were caught up in the exhilaration of being the center of attention. Saying goodbye to loved ones and moving in January 1963 to South Carolina was the depressing antithesis.

There were issues from the moment Jim arrived at Shaw AFB. Although he was a newly promoted major, base housing slots were issued according to DOR (date of rank) and there was another major ahead of him, so the Randalls were temporarily accommodated in Guest Housing on Shaw. After 3½ years in the excellent Department of Defense (DOD) school at Spangdahlem, Roberta had completed the first semester of 5th grade and Louise, the first semester of 4th grade. Billy was looking forward to completing 2nd grade.

For military families, registering and settling their children back into school following a change of assignment is of foremost importance, but the Randalls were still awaiting housing, an equally critical issue. It looked as though the family was going to miss important deadlines, but at the last minute a unit at 313 Maple Drive became available and the Randalls were caught up in the tumult of moving vans, stacks of boxes to unpack, furniture to arrange—the whole process of settling into their new home on base.

When the first day of school arrived and the second semester in Sumter schools was ready to begin, Mary Ann made sure the children were dressed warmly enough and that their backpacks were loaded with all the supplies that they were instructed to take to school. Jim was on the phone at home arranging an appointment to meet with his new commander at Shaw AFB Headquarters, where he was assigned to a non-flying position. He was eager to state his case for a change of station and start the ball rolling for reassignment, but he reached out for a hug from each of his children, commented on how great they looked in their Christmas-gift clothing, and wished them well. Meanwhile Mary Ann, with a warmly bundled Patricia in her arms, opened the door for Roberta, Louise, and Billy and walked them to an area near base housing where an idling bus was waiting to transport eager young students to school.

The White male driver ushered a flock of anxious military youngsters onto his bus, noting a few by name and offering encouragement and good luck, but as Roberta and

Louise stepped forward, he quickly closed the door to the vehicle and stepped on the accelerator. Mary Ann tightened her grip on Billy's hand so he wouldn't run toward the bus, and she told the girls to wait with her. She explained that they would be boarding another vehicle. Confused, the girls stood quietly as the blinking tail lights of the yellow bus disappeared into the wintry early morning of January 1963 and headed toward Shaw Heights School in Sumter.

A few minutes later a second bus appeared and the Black woman driver pulled it forward along the curb. The Randall children boarded with the remainder of those left behind and once everyone was seated, the driver turned in the direction of Ebenezer School in Dalzell, a town nine or so miles northwest of Sumter. It was the Randall children's first experience of being singled out and excluded because of race, a puzzling situation for them since they had no idea what school segregation was. They had always attended schools with Whites in both Spangdahlem, Germany, and at Nellis AFB in Nevada. The three youngsters were nervous and didn't know what to expect so they sat huddled together trying to summon the courage to face whatever lay ahead for them.

Usually, when children return from the first day of class, most parents ask the traditional question, "What happened at school today?" With military families who have just experienced yet another move, it is a barometer to determine how well children are adjusting to new and perhaps challenging circumstances. Needless to say, Roberta, Louise, and Billy could not stop talking about the unexpected situations they had faced. They were accustomed to the disciplined environment, advanced academics, and high expectations of the DOD school in Germany and at Nellis AFB, too, and so they were shocked by their first, endless day in a segregated South Carolina school.

Their distress was evident as they described poorly equipped classrooms filled with a student-teacher ratio that would confound even a master educator. Louise and Roberta were very articulate in expressing how far behind their classes at Ebenezer School seemed to be in comparison to their school at Spangdahlem. Horrified and afraid that they would lose ground academically, they begged to be sent to a different school. Billy was only a second grader, but his observations were the most worrisome. He revealed that the instructor didn't get to teach very much because she had to spend most of the day trying to keep her class under control.

Mary Ann was distraught, but Jim was livid. He had attended all-Black schools in Gainsboro, but the scenario that his son described would never have happened during Jim's school days. Parents like Ora demanded high standards of their children as well as the teachers. Many Gainsboro students went on to attend college and became successful adults. In fact, Jim had been strongly influenced as a teenager when two former Lucy Addison

High School graduates spoke to the high school students at their alma mater. Dressed in military uniforms as freshly minted Tuskegee Airmen, they personified Jim's dream and gave him hope.

During World War II, Jim was sent to Tuskegee after he completed basic training and qualified for pilot training, but with the end of the war and his dream deferred, he pursued a college degree at Hampton Institute. After two years of studying industrial education and engineering, he qualified a second time for pilot training. Achieving his wings in a newly integrated U.S. Air Force, Jim had flown 75 combat missions over North Korea at the behest of his country. He had ferried an impressive inventory of F-51s across the Atlantic to support America's European Allies in maintaining world peace. He had been entrusted to train French pilots in the Deep South and had checked out in every type of aircraft available to him at his various assignments.

Proficient as an F-100 pilot, Jim had flown planes out of France to Germany during America's international standoff with de Gaulle. He had commanded Spangdahlem's Alert Facility during the tense times of the Bay of Pigs and ensuing Cuban Missile Crisis back home, as well as remaining on alert to defend West Germany during the dawn of the Berlin Wall. Advancing in rank faster than the majority of his peers, Jim had managed to circumvent racial issues by mastering his talents and serving his country with a patriotic heart. He was an American fighter pilot, tested and true, but he was about to take on the fight of a lifetime—racial injustice in South Carolina.

Faced with the possibility of censure or worse, Jim was determined to champion his children and the youngsters of other Black military fathers on Shaw AFB who were struggling with the same situation. It was outrageous. Seething internally but calm and razor-focused in appearance, he set about righting an egregious wrong, something that not even Thurgood Marshall's success with Brown v. Board of Education had accomplished as far as South Carolina was concerned. Shockingly, "South Carolina was the last state in the South with no desegregated public schools below college level," thanks to stolid leaders determined to maintain the status quo.

Jim was a combat-ready Senior Pilot plunged into a paper-pushing desk job in Shaw's Headquarters, but he was ready for a fight. He was not facing aerial combat as a member of the U.S. Air Force. Instead, he was taking a stand against formidable opponents—political figures who denied his children the right to attend school with their peers in an educational setting appropriate to their capabilities. The Germans had a word for such mistreatment—*schadenfreude!* Jim intended to win the battle for justice.

Jim immediately contacted the Judge Advocate General (JAG) on base to outline the abysmal circumstances of his children's situation. He planned to re-locate his family in

Indiana near their maternal grandparents in Evansville, so that they could attend superior schools, which were integrated. Then he intended to return to Shaw to complete his assignment there. However, to do so he needed a military leave of absence. Instead, the JAG offered an alternative and Jim agreed.

Through deft machinations with Sumter School District 2, which was responsible for the public education of Shaw AFB students, the JAG persuaded the school district officials to make an exception to their formalized agreement with Shaw and permit the Randall children to transfer to Liberty Street School, an all-Black facility in downtown Sumter. It took until February, but finally the Randall children were permitted to board a bus transporting students to all-White St. Anne Catholic School, also in downtown Sumter. The bus made a second stop at Liberty Street for the Randall children.

Segregation was a state of "1000 cuts," brief incidents that excised long-lasting suffering as they piled up, especially in a child's psyche. One sweltering hot day toward the end of the school year, the bus driver stopped to permit students to get a drink at a public facility. Roberta was seated with Louise and Billy at the rear of the bus, but she got up and followed the White students ahead of her. She was thirsty. A nun with the White students stopped her without explanation…a moment when Roberta realized the price of being Black in South Carolina in 1963. Looking out the bus window as she returned to her seat, Roberta caught a glimpse of the sign by the water fountain that made everything clear—Whites Only.

Although their circumstances improved somewhat, the Randall children struggled to adjust to an environment that cast them as pariahs. After being accepted as equals throughout their whole life and attending school with confidence, they had become fearful and uncertain. By June, the school year was over, but their education about the struggles ahead had just begun. The Randall children should have felt free to run through sprinklers and set up lemonade stands or sit against the huge trunk of a sheltering live oak to read a colorfully illustrated book of fairy tales or laugh at cartoons in the heat of the day. Instead, images of snarling police dogs and police using fire hoses to control civil rights protestors dominated the newspapers, magazines, and television channels. Newscasts on the family's television set became vivid conveyors of history-in-the-making.

On June 11, 1963, pompous Governor George Wallace of Alabama stretched his 5'7" frame to look imposing and stood staunchly in front of the University of Alabama's Foster Auditorium to deny African American students' admission. In response to Wallace's hateful, outward display of disrespect for the U.S. Constitution and the justice system, President John F. Kennedy addressed the nation that evening. The Randalls watched solemnly as Kennedy emphasized that he found racial discrimination in public schools abhorrent. He challenged the American public to consider whether or not they would accept being judged solely by the color of their skin or tolerate the sluggish effort to create a more equitable culture if they were the ones being targeted.

Kennedy was a World War II hero, who privately struggled with injuries he endured in August 1943 while saving his PT-109 crew after the boat was rammed by a Japanese destroyer. He challenged Americans to be introspective and have the courage to change. Jim was inspired by Kennedy's speech and decided to take more deliberate action to effect change in the Sumter school system on behalf of his children. On June 12th, the night after Governor Wallace's incendiary action, the Randalls turned on the television, and breaking news again shocked the nation. Medgar Evers was assassinated in front of his home in Jackson, Mississippi. He had recently been honored to speak to the first Black cadets accepted at the Air Force Academy, and now he was gone. Vanquished! Horrified, Jim plotted the course of his actions, and he did not deviate. His target was injustice.

By September as a new school year was about to begin, the Randalls initiated a federal civil suit on behalf of their three children—Roberta Lynn, Louise Evangeline, and William Edward. In the complaint they filed with the U.S. District Court in Columbia, South Carolina's capital, they named Sumter School District 2 as the defendant and demanded that the district cease the practice of school segregation.

Thirteen other Black military families joined the Randalls and signed the complaint, and the group became known as the Shaw Fourteen. Attorneys from the NAACP, who had been involved in numerous other civil rights cases, came forward to represent the group, and for the first time they were optimistic. The case would involve more than the oft political and legal maneuvering of adversaries. This time plaintiffs were more than names on documents. The case clearly captured the essence of those being denied rights guaranteed in the U.S. Constitution— military men who were serving their country with honor and their young children who faced the transient life of a military family while constantly adjusting to new schools. The legal system, the press, and the public would have to face the reality of segregation. Black military members who risked their lives to protect the rights of their fellow Americans were being denied the same rights for their own children. Finally, the focus was on the truth.

The team of NAACP attorneys for the plaintiffs were Ernest A. Finney, Jr., Jack Greenberg, Ira Kaye, and Matthew Perry. Ernest Finney and Matthew Perry were Black attorneys who were graduates of South Carolina State College Law School, an all-Black school about an hour's drive southwest of Sumter in Orangeburg. Ironically, South Carolina State College Law School was opened in 1946 after a Black World War II veteran sued when he was not permitted to register at all-White University of South Carolina

School of Law. The judge in the case ruled in favor of the plaintiff, and he offered the state government three possible solutions to resolving the crisis: 1. Permit the plaintiff to enter the University of South Carolina School of Law; or 2. Open a law school for Blacks; or 3. Close the South Carolina School of Law. The South Carolina state government chose to open the South Carolina State College Law School. As graduates, Finney and Perry were experienced in civil rights issues and eager to take on the Randall case.

Ira Kaye and Jack Greenburg were White attorneys. Kaye, a respected Sumter resident, was active in the Jewish community. Jack Greenberg lived in New York City where he led the Legal Defense Fund for the NAACP so he consulted by phone. He had served with Thurgood Marshall in the Brown V. Board of Education case. It was a well-prepared and determined group of attorneys, which was fortunate because the defense attorneys were relentless with their arguments, the most offensive being that "desegregation would upset the cultural, ethnic, and social harmony of Sumter's schools."

Particularly insulting was the defense attorneys support of the argument when Judge Robert W. Hemphill reviewed the case. The district claimed that school desegregation would cause "undue duress in Sumter County's schools because of irreconcilable differences between African American and White students." The defense attorneys became even more vitriolic by adding, "There are certain ethnic, cultural, racial, intellectual, anthropological and physical differences between Negroes and Whites…that form a sufficient rational basis to allow segregation in the public schools of Sumter County."

Jim left the Shaw Fourteen's case in the capable hands of the NAACP team of attorneys because he had serious military responsibilities to fulfill, but in reading some of the defense attorney's arguments, he immediately thought of the frayed article he had folded and angrily put in his wallet when he was an aspiring young Black airman, hoping for a slot at Tuskegee. He pulled it out and read it again.

In that process of evolution the American Negro has not progressed as far as the other subspecies of the human family. As a race he has not developed leadership qualities. His mental inferiority and the inherent weakness of his character are factors that must be considered with great care in the preparation of any plans for his employment in War. Even physically the black American is inferior; his normal physical activity is generally small due to his laziness."

The tired tropes of nearly 20 years were still being used to demean and define members of the Black race. Jim had more than proved them wrong, but he was incensed that such hateful accusations were now being used against his children. He folded the article along its deep creases and returned it to his wallet.

Summer was coming to a close and the school year was about to begin again. The children knew what to expect so they were not enthusiastic about returning. Mary Ann was disconsolate and chain smoking, and Jim was diligently fulfilling his duties at Shaw Headquarters while assiduously pursuing an early change of assignment. The expectation was that he would complete a minimum of three years at Shaw, but he remained in constant contact with his commander about the outcome of the many queries he sent to possible sources of assistance to resolve his dilemma.

By September 1963, General Lawrence Tanberg arrived at Shaw as the new Deputy for Operations of Ninth Air Force. Jim, as the Communications Officer in the Command Post, was overqualified for the position, but he was very effective in sorting through the myriad of issues that arose with mixed race crews due to the stranglehold of segregation in every aspect of life for the military at Shaw. General Tanberg realized Jim's talents and appreciated the young major's determination to resolve issues amicably. Jim continued to point out that the U.S. Air Force was not utilizing his talents as a pilot, however. He never mentioned how his own family continually dealt with the suppression of segregation, and Tanberg grew to appreciate his diplomacy. Just as Jim felt as though he was beginning to get a handle on the challenges he and his family faced, the unthinkable happened.

President John F. Kennedy was assassinated on November 22, 1963, in Dallas, Texas.

President Kennedy and his lovely wife Jackie were riding in an open-top 1961 Lincoln Continental convertible with Governor John Connally and his wife Nellie while Lee Harvey Oswald lay in wait on an upper floor of the Texas School Book Depository until the motorcade was in full view. Waving to the massive crowds attending the parade in his honor, Kennedy had just responded to Nellie Connally's comment, "Mr. President, they can't make you believe now that there are not some in Dallas who love and appreciate you, can they?" Kennedy replied, "No, they sure can't—" Seconds later he was mortally wounded by the assassin's bullet.

The Randall family sat weeping in front of their television set and watched the news coverage of the American tragedy. They had been looking forward to celebrating Thanksgiving on Thursday, but they were so shocked and broken-hearted that grief overwhelmed them. It was inconceivable that the president they admired so much was gone.

By Christmas, the beautiful memories of the Randall family happily celebrating with Germans and Americans alike stood out in vivid contrast to the situation in South Carolina where Jim and his family were not accepted by many of their fellow Americans. It was ludicrous, but it was reality. Like most bases at Christmas time, many non-essential organizations were operating with a smaller crew, and so Jim decided to retrieve the manual at Headquarters regarding the regulations concerning reassignment of senior officers.

Jim was wearing the gold leaves of a major now so the young clerk was concerned about being subordinate, but he stood his ground and said the manual could not be removed from the office. He had no answer, though, when Jim asked exactly how many times had anyone requested to see the manual. Unable to come up with a good argument, the young airman reluctantly handed it over, and Jim promised to return it first thing Monday morning. Over the weekend while Mary Ann and the children put up Christmas decorations, Jim sat tucked away in the bedroom reading every word of the manual and was able to glean the information he needed.

Drafting a masterfully worded letter to the Inspector General, which he planned to submit through his commander according to procedure, Jim outlined all the reasons that he should be reassigned to another base. His primary argument centered around his credentials and how his talents were being under-utilized in his current position. He made no mention of segregation practices that undermined the quality of life for Black pilots at Shaw. He left that issue to the JAG and the NAACP lawyers working on the case waged by the Shaw Fourteen.

Jim submitted his carefully crafted letter to his commander and prayed he would get results.

Much to his amazement he received a telegram 2 days before Christmas. It informed Jim that he was one of 5 officers to be reassigned; he was given several options. Jim chose to be reassigned to McConnell AFB in Wichita, Kansas. He would be joining the 562nd TAC Fighter Squadron as the Ops Officer. It was the best Christmas present ever. He and the family had to endure 6 more months at Shaw, but at least they could see the light at the end of the tunnel.

By June 1964, Jim had made arrangements to take Mary Ann and the children to Evansville, Indiana, for the summer so that they could enjoy being with family while he traveled to Wichita, Kansas, to ensure that the Randalls would have suitable housing as soon as they arrived. It had been a grueling 18 months in South Carolina, and he didn't want his family to ever endure such a situation again.

General Tanberg called Jim into his office before he left the gates of Shaw for the last time, and he thanked him for facilitating easy relationships within mixed race crews. He also expressed his appreciation for Jim's handling of the situation with segregated schools. Tanberg expressed his admiration about how Jim had managed to keep those major issues separate from his military mission. All the hoopla over South Carolina's recalcitrance to desegregate public schools remained within the justice system, and Jim had continued to fulfill his military duties without creating a distraction.

It was a rare and personal moment shared between a young Black major and a White two-star general that was the ultimate vindication. General Tanberg saw Jim as the man he was striving to be.

CHAPTER 24

ON A WING AND A PRAYER

"Hey! Pogreba! POGIE! What are you doing here?" Jim yelled across the street to a tall uniformed officer who was walking toward the McConnell Base Exchange.

The fellow spun around, pulled down his dark aviator sunglasses with a look of surprise and yelled, "I'm stationed here! What in heaven's name are you doing here, Randall?" Excited to see a familiar face, Jim raced across the busy road and the former neighbors from Nellis slapped each other on the back and hugged in genuine surprise at being reunited once again. At least six years had passed, intense and action-packed years for both of them.

Shoppers both entering and exiting the Base Exchange smiled at the reunion of friends and walked around the two while the men chatted away in the middle of the sidewalk. Jim explained that he had just been reassigned to McConnell from Shaw AFB in South Carolina and that he was trying to set up base housing for his family before he retrieved Mary Ann and the four children from her folks' house in Evansville, Indiana. Pogreba noted that the Randalls had added a family member since their kids played together on base in Las Vegas, and Jim proudly described his latest addition, little Patricia.

It was June and there was usually a big turnover of personnel on military bases in the summer months. Military members with families tried to schedule their moves to coincide with school schedules to minimize the struggle for their children who constantly faced adjusting to yet another school. Being able to start at the beginning of the school year with everyone else made the transition a bit easier, and considering all the trauma Roberta, Louise, and Billy had been through, it was especially important that they have a positive experience. At least they would be attending integrated schools. Consequently, Jim had checked in at the VOQ and immediately followed through with all the necessary procedures to secure base housing. As a major he was assured that a unit would become available. It was just a question of time. Meanwhile, he planned to stay at the VOQ. He had already reported for duty.

Pogreba described where he was living—a house with a finished basement. He offered Jim a bedroom and bath downstairs in his home until base housing became available. That way, he explained, they could "finish their conversation." Jim laughed and agreed it was going to be a long one. They had a lot of catching up to do, so he gladly accepted Pogreba's generous offer.

Trailing behind Pogreba as he picked up essential items on his wife Maxine's list, Jim assisted his fellow fighter pilot in the mission, and then the two headed to the VOQ where Pogreba made a call to Maxine to let her know they would be having a guest for dinner that night, a house guest who would be staying for a while. With arrangements underway to pick up Jim at the end of the day, Pogreba raced back to work. Until the chance meeting with Jim, he had only planned to run a few errands at noon so he was about to be late for a briefing.

Meanwhile, Jim organized and repacked his gear. Then he wrapped the small gift he had purchased at the Base Exchange (BX) while helping Pogreba with his shopping list. Jim planned to give it to Maxine as a token of his appreciation. He didn't want to arrive empty handed. By the time Pogreba dropped by the VOQ after work, Jim was out front of the building and sitting on his luggage in the late afternoon sun.

Pogreba had kept the identity of their houseguest a secret because he enjoyed surprising Maxine and the children, and so the minute he pulled in the driveway, the whole family poured out of the house in excitement. Maxine gave Jim a big hug as the kids asked dozens of questions about Roberta, Louise, and Billy. They wanted to hear all about the Randall kids and see their photos. To be welcomed back into the Pogreba family with such affection meant the world to Jim. His family's personal experience with segregation in South Carolina had been very hurtful, but being accepted as a beloved friend by the Pogrebas restored Jim's faith in his fellow man. He tried to express the depth of his gratitude, but Pogreba just smiled and said, "You would have done the same for me." Of course, he was right.

Jim's time with the Pogrebas was an unexpected gift. Like fitting a missing piece into a puzzle, the family graciously made him feel at home. It gave him a chance to catch his breath before the flurry of getting his family moved from Indiana to McConnell in Kansas. Once they arrived, there would be a lot of work to do—moving into new quarters at 2427 N. Chatauqua; shopping for school clothes; and preparing three children for school. The family's needs competed for attention with his new job as Ops Officer for the 562nd Tactical Fighter Squadron, but that was life in the military.

Somehow military families managed it all. Once the dust settled, Jim's focus was to put aside the trials and tribulations that segregation in South Carolina had presented for his children. He was determined to help the family start anew in Kansas, while giving his best effort to his job on the flight line. He had promised not to seek another assignment within a designated time frame, and he intended to be worthy of the consideration he had been given by being permitted to leave Shaw early. He needed to get checked out in the F-105 at least sometime in the fall, but that would have to wait. The F-105 was a very complicated airplane with complex systems and capabilities. It was his understanding that he would probably have to go to Nellis for the training. Jim was anxious to be fully prepared, but he would just have to be patient. Life seemed to be falling into place once again when early one morning the new Wing Commander walked into Base Ops and asked for Jim. When Jim identified himself, his commander explained that he would like to see him in his office. Jim's heart sank. Had something already gone wrong? He hurried to complete the task at hand and rushed across the street for the impromptu meeting. His new boss was still in a briefing, but he excused himself to talk to Jim. This must be serious, Jim felt. He followed his commander into his office and awaited the verdict.

Much to Jim's relief, the Wing Commander was also focused on quickly getting settled into his new command. He wanted to know the "health of the wing" so he asked Jim to create a butcher paper briefing for him, an overview of the entire wing. To accomplish the task Jim would have to study the Manning Document, a voluminous amount of information, but he agreed to get started right away. Shaking hands with his commander, he saluted and returned to his job at Base Ops while planning how to complete the heady task. However, he had an advantage. He had undertaken a major project like this once before in Korea when he was far younger and much less experienced. He set to work immediately.

It took almost one month to study the Manning Document in its entirety and create a succinct briefing, but once Jim felt fully prepared, he contacted his commander and presented the detailed information. The older officer listened intently and asked an occasional question but was generally positive when Jim concluded. "As far as manning in your Wing, you are very healthy. As far as experience in the Wing, you are lacking in some areas." The commander had another meeting scheduled, but seemed pleased. He thanked Jim and hurried off to meet with a group assembled in the boardroom.

A week or so later, Jim was working at his desk at Base Ops when he received a call from the Wing Commander's secretary explaining that the Wing Commander needed to see him right away. Headquarters was right across the street from Base Ops so Jim rushed over, worrying about the urgency in the secretary's voice. He figured he had either done a poor job with his briefing or the corollary was true—he had done a good job and he was going to end up a project officer for months until he was finally sent to Nellis for F-105 training. Neither situation was appealing so he took a bold step and once he was in the Wing Commander's office, he explained that he wanted to focus on flight and the F-105, not paper work.

He was not expecting his commander's reaction.

"How 'd you like to work for a captain?"

"Sir, I'm a—" Jim was about to mention that he was a major, but his commander anticipated his reaction and laughed as he explained that he did not want to lose precious time with Jim's leaving for Nellis so he had arranged for him to be trained in the F-105 right at McConnell. He had talked to personnel at Air Force Headquarters, others at Dover AFB and Tyndall AFB, and also consulted with the U.S. senator from the area. Before requesting permission for Jim to be checked out locally, he had confirmed Jim's outstanding flight record and after considerable effort, he had received the necessary authorization. No one had ever been checked out in the F-105 without going through the school at Nellis, he explained, but he had gotten permission for that to happen. He smiled proudly as he added, "Now do you understand why you'll be working for a captain, Major Randall?"

"Yes, sir!" Jim saluted. "When do I begin?"

Jim's instructor was Captain Russ Schoonover.

The two got started with the unique training situation right away and on the very day Jim was originally set to leave for training at Nellis AFB, he soloed in the F-105 at McConnell. He had learned all the systems in the airplane and proven his proficiency in utilizing them, including firing missiles. The only phase he hadn't had the opportunity to train in was refueling at night. Base Ops was not able to coordinate with a tanker outfit to accomplish the task until several weeks later. By then, Jim was flying the F-105 every day and racking up hours of experience.

One morning the squadron commander walked into Base Ops and announced, "We are going to Hawaii for a month to fly close air support training for the 25th U.S. Army Infantry Division. You will be working with forward air controllers and dropping live ordnance." He reminded Jim that probably the only pilots in the squadron who had experience in dropping live ordnance were Jim, his Assistant Ops Officer, and the squadron commander himself. However, when he took off for Hawaii with a 6-ship flight of F-105s for the mission, Jim would be the only one with previous experience in dropping live ordnance on a target. His combat tour flying bombing missions over North Korea would be extremely important in thoroughly briefing and de-briefing his crew each day.

With only a few days to prepare for the mission, Jim led the flight of F-105s across the Pacific to Oahu, where the 25th U.S. Army Infantry Division was in training. The flight to Hawaii was exhilarating. Jim had flown 8 missions over the Atlantic while ferrying planes from Dover AFB in Delaware to U.S. Allies in Europe, but he had to wear exposure suits while flying at those northern latitudes. In the event of an emergency, ejection over the north Atlantic meant dealing with deathly cold oceanic temperatures, which was less of an issue with the vast expanse of the Pacific.

Connecting with tankers and re-fueling at Santa Barbara, California, went like clockwork and once the flight landed in Oahu, Jim linked up with the army commander to set maneuvers in motion for the month of March 1965.

Captain Russ Schoonover congratulates his student, Major James E.P. Randall for successfully checking out in the F-105 and completing his first solo flight.

Jim proudly exits his F-105 after soloing. (Photo courtesy of Regional History & Genealogy, Pikes Peak Library District, Image # 412-120)

A Crew Chief holds Jim's flight records as Jim signs off his solo flight

The new Wing Commander at McConnell AFB congratulates Major James Randall, Ops Officer for the 562nd TAC Fighter Squadron, after his successful solo check-out flight in the F-105. Jim earned the opportunity by fulfilling the Wing Commander's request: Prepare a "butcher paper" briefing about all the members of his squadron, a manning document. This entailed identifying every military person in every slot in the unit-- pilots, weapons officers, maintenance, etc. The project included as many as 500 people, and Jim listed each individual according to rank, AFSC, pay grade, and related data...beginning with the Wing Commander. It was a voluminous amount of work to undertake in addition to Jim's maintaining standards of excellence in his position on the flight line as Ops Officer. However, it was a win-win situation for both men. Jim was able to check out in the F-105 and later in the F-111 as well. (Photo courtesy of Regional History & Genealogy, Pikes Peak Library District, Image #412-115)

Coordination between the Army's 25th Infantry Division and the flight of F-105s from McConnell, assisted by A1-E Skyraiders calling targets, went flawlessly throughout the month and by the first of April, Jim received orders from their squadron commander to bring the crew back home.

The weather was nearly perfect on the return flight, but Jim noted that they were 15 minutes behind schedule when they reached Santa Barbara. Jim was meticulous about every aspect of a mission, and he was a stickler for details, especially being punctual. He quickly calculated the time for the remainder of the trip to McConnell and decided that if they continued on the route he had planned—Santa Barbara to Albuquerque to Amarillo to Wichita—they would be 15 minutes late when they reached Wichita. He didn't want to leave everyone standing out on the ramp awaiting their delayed 5 o'clock arrival.

Checking with the other pilots, he asked, "How are your birds running?"

"Purring like a kitten," was the general response.

Confident in his decision, Jim directed them, "Push 'em up!" and the 6-flight gained time between Albuquerque and Amarillo. He had to fudge a little bit when he called Denver Center, but he explained that he had 5 airplanes with him and they had encountered cumulus clouds ahead. As a result, he wanted to circumvent the weather. He received permission and the slight deviation in course achieved his goal.

The flight of F-105s touched down exactly at 5 o'clock to a cheering group on the ground. Not only had they arrived on time, but the general who commanded the 25th Infantry Division had sent a letter of commendation to Jim's squadron commander. The army general congratulated Jim and his pilots and thanked their commander for sending a "highly proficient bunch of guys" to do the job for him.

For Jim it was a moment enshrined in memory—friendships forged in the unflagging trust that your colleagues will give their all to support the mission.

Leading flights across the Pacific became more and more frequent for Jim due to the military's growing concern about the F-105s attrition rate as the engagement over North Vietnam increased. Every factor was taken into consideration, down to the smallest detail. At one point even the camouflage paint job was questioned, and so Jim was tasked to pick up a freshly painted F-105 and lead a 4-ship across the Pacific to judge how the aircraft might be impacted in comparison to the other three unpainted planes. Jim recorded copious notes throughout the long flight, and the conclusion was that the camouflage paint had virtually no effect on the F-105's performance. Although it might have seemed a foregone conclusion, when an American pilot's life is concerned, there can be no cutting corners.

Not only was Jim depended upon for leading flights over to Thailand to replace 105s that were lost in combat, but he also was extremely perceptive in analyzing whether or not an accident was the result of malfunctioning aircraft systems. His commander valued Jim's assessments and relied heavily on him.

Jim was in the thick of things and well aware of the rotation of crews leaving McConnell to fly combat missions out of Thailand to North Vietnam. Eventually, his number was called. As far as his family was concerned, Jim was being sent on another TDY, but Jim knew he would be flying combat missions. It was August 1965, and Operation Rolling Thunder was underway. The Department of Defense's intention was to stun the enemy by relentless bombing attacks with the objective of destroying bridges and main thoroughfares, which were transporting weaponry; disrupting anti-aircraft missile sites; and blowing up munitions plants.

Jim, seated in the camouflaged F-105 on the left, prepares to lead a 4-ship flight to Southeast Asia to assess how the paint might affect flight, especially in combat.

The U.S. government was not openly acknowledging that such flights were taking place, but Jim knew that the war in Southeast Asia was escalating as he arrived by military transport with the 562nd TAC Fighter Squadron members to settle in at Takhli AB in Thailand. Jim hoped to return home some time in December.

Although Takhli was a Royal Thai Air Base, the government of Thailand had originally made a gentleman's agreement to accept the U.S. Air Force as tenants back in the 1950s when the Dalai Lama's government was under siege by China. The agreement continued to be honored as first one crisis after another plagued Southeast Asia. Takhli AB was situated northwest of Bangkok, and Thai military forces maintained the base and provided security, but U.S. presence was the main source of security for that area of Southeast Asia. By 1965 things had really heated up and in some places, it was boiling over.

Once on the ground, Jim wanted to get settled quickly. He reported to duty, listened to an orientation briefing, and headed out to familiarize himself with the base. Locating the area of metal tent-like structures where many of the pilots bunked, he set up his meager possessions in one of the units and took off for the Officers' Mess. The dining hall was buzzing with conversations between the pilots who were coming to the end of their rotation and the ones just entering the combat arena. The exchanges were not war stories. Instead, they shared insights gained through experience that could prove valuable for incoming combat pilots. Everyone was on the same team. Unity mattered.

The following morning Jim was excited to get down to the flight line and attend the briefing about the day's target. It had been 13 years since he flew combat missions in the F-51 over North Korea. Like a champion athlete getting ready to compete again at the beginning of a new season, he was eager to get in the cockpit of the F-105 and master the mission. Once he was airborne again, he felt in control and ready to push the limits to get the job done. Still, he was mindful of his responsibility to all the members of the flight that he led, and he lived up to expectations.

With his combat experience in Korea kicking in, Jim confidently led a successful mission and the de-briefing re-established his leadership among his colleagues. The group strolled over to have dinner together at the mess hall and share their personal observations about their first encounter with ground fire over the outskirts of Hanoi. It was a productive conversation, and so Jim made a practice of listening to the scuttlebutt among the pilots at dinner each night. He soon fell into rhythm with the routine at Takhli. Consequently, when he heard a squadron was rotating in from Yokota, Japan, he decided to amble over to the flight line and welcome them. Considering the circumstances, camaraderie was a saving grace.

As the first pilot disembarked from the plane, Jim's mouth dropped open in awe and he called out "Pogreba?" A big smile spread across Dean Pogreba's face as he sauntered over to Jim and put his arm around his shoulder. Since they were in different units at McConnell, Jim didn't realize that Pogreba had been shipped to Yokota and was part of the group of rotating replacements.

"I can't believe this. I just cannot believe this! Are you going to be here with the squadron as long as they're deployed?" Jim asked. Pogreba explained that he was the Ops Officer and would remain with the unit. He was planning to see if he could get a room in the BOQ. All Jim had was a very small room with a hang up locker, a foot locker, and a bunk, but he knew he could scrounge up another bunk so he invited Pogreba to stay with him in the cramped metal tent. Agreeing with a nod and a smile, Pogreba picked up his gear and followed Jim to his humble abode. Nothing is quite as special as being with a friend when facing stressful circumstances, and few things are as stressful as war.

Each night the two men would lie in their cots and share all they had experienced together, from Nellis to Germany to McConnell and finally Thailand. What were the chances that their lives would cross paths four times as they almost circumnavigated the globe. They laughed over their children's antics and remembered many of the wild things that they had done as children themselves. Like two brothers recounting the highlights of their lives with one another, Jim and Pogreba truly became family. The evening conversations before they fell asleep softened the harsh reality of each day.

Humor also has a special role in war, and Jim quite unintentionally provided it a few weeks later. He had noticed that one of his flight members always had a plug of tobacco tucked in his cheek, especially when they took off on a mission. He apparently also loved Cokes because he always had a bottle handy. He was a cool character, and so Jim, being curious about the appeal of chewing tobacco, decided to give it a try. He purchased a pouch at the BX and one afternoon, he went back to his tent, cut off a plug, put it in his mouth and began chewing. He thought to himself, *Now I'm one of the boys.* As the sweetened wad of tobacco began dissolving into a pithy liquid, he swallowed and almost choked as the toxic liquid seared his throat.

Feeling dizzy and beginning to vomit, Jim was too embarrassed to seek help so he decided to try a drink of water, which only exacerbated the situation. With his stomach cramping and no relief in sight, he realized he was in serious trouble. Fortunately, Pogreba didn't see him at dinner and was worried so he finally decided to check their tent. He burst into laughter listening to Jim's account of what he had done, but tobacco poisoning is serious so he dragged his friend to the flight surgeon, who admonished Jim roundly. Activated charcoal worked like an antidote, binding with the toxic nicotine in his stomach so it could be eliminated from his body.

It took a few days before he was well enough to fly again. Since he didn't die, Jim became fair game for all the jokes about the hot fighter pilot who survived anti-missile attacks over Hanoi but almost met his Maker when he naively swallowed chewing tobacco. Jim was a good sport about the whole thing and laughed each time his colleagues teased him, but he was more curious than ever about why the fighter pilot he was trying to emulate never got sick. He finally got up the nerve to ask him. He was surprised to learn that the fellow actually was spitting out tobacco juice into the Coke bottle he always stuck in the pocket on the side of his flight suit. Though the bottle looked as though it was Coca Cola, it was actually tobacco juice spit.

Days in Thailand could be sweltering, but nights were hardly comfortable, even though the structure Pogie and Jim stayed in had a sluggish air conditioner. One night the power went out, and with no air conditioning whatsoever, it was as hot as Hades. The humidity was so thick that you could cut it, but it had begun to rain outside, a pretty good shower, and so Jim impulsively stripped his pajamas off, picked up one of the metal chairs in the room and yelled, "Come on, Pogie. Get your pajamas off!" He walked out into the rain, grounded his chair in the grass, and slumped down in the seat. A few seconds later Pogreba joined him and the two sat buck-naked in the rain to continue their conversation. Sopping wet but cooler, they finally went back inside, toweled off, and slept until dawn. They laughed about it the following morning and imagined they would still be telling the story when they were old men.

Several weeks later, Pogreba was shot down on one of his missions but he was rescued immediately and sustained no serious injuries, so he and Jim had a somber conversation that night. It was very disturbing to Jim, but Pogreba was such a gifted aviator and so experienced as a combat pilot that he tried to think of the whole episode as an isolated incident. Meanwhile, Pogreba continued to be unflappable, invincible…until October 5th. When Jim returned from his flight over North Vietnam that day, his heart sank when he heard the news. Pogreba still had not returned from his mission.

Jim sat slumped and dejected as he stared at his dinner that night. He could hardly eat. The other pilots respected his grief and left him to his thoughts. Returning to his quarters in the row of metal tents, he crawled onto his bunk and looked over to the empty one. He was shrouded in the silence of Pogreba's absence. He had never felt so alone. He tossed and turned throughout the muggy night fighting off unfinished nightmares.

Sitting and listening intently to the briefing for his mission the next morning, Jim felt better when he crawled into the cockpit of his F-105. He was responsible for the safety of the other members of the flight, and he did not let his mind drift from that duty. Although eventful and checkered with intense moments, the mission went as planned, and upon his return to Takhli Jim immediately checked on Pogreba's status. There was still no word of his whereabouts, but pilots who had been part of his flight speculated that he had somehow flown off course. He had called in that his navigation system was malfunctioning.

For the next 7 days Jim fell into a vicious loop—breakfast, briefing on the mission, reaching the designated target and accomplishing the mission, de-briefing, checking on

Pogreba. Every day it was the same answer—still no word.

The weather on October 13, 1965, was stellar. Anyone would have appreciated being in an airplane flying around in the bright ultramarine blue skies and enjoying the lush emerald foliage of the jungle below, but Jim and his flight of F-105s were on a mission. As they left Takhli and dropped off the re-fueling tanker at Ubon, northern Thailand, they crossed the Mekong River and Jim led his flight north to their assigned target— a railroad bridge across the Black River northwest of Hanoi. The ride up to the target area was peaceful, though— not a cloud in the sky and the winds were calm, so Jim just cruised along and enjoyed the beauty of the earth. There had been nothing out of the ordinary or foreboding to cause the flight of fighter pilots to be wary at that point in time, a rare moment to relish.

Jim had experienced few other missions that started off with climatic conditions as peaceful as this particular day was. In fact, he had sometimes flown in weather so horrible, especially during the monsoon season, that keeping track of his exact location in airspace when he flew from Thailand to the target area in North Vietnam, was the biggest challenge of the mission. The weather could sometimes seem more of a threat than the armed adversaries on the ground below.

On this particular day, though, it was just a pleasure to be airborne and cruising along at 8 miles a minute. The cloudless, bright blue sky made visual references easily recognizable, and Jim had no reason to be concerned about reaching their destination within the designated time frame. He had marked checkpoints on the map strapped to his knee that were 8 miles a minute apart, and so all he had to do was keep track of the time between checkpoints. If he was getting ahead of schedule, he simply pulled the power back a little and slowed down to keep on schedule over the ground; 8 miles a minute was the key. The flight of F-105s had a smooth run north, but as soon as Jim sighted the target—while still moving at 15 to 25 miles south of the river and the designated bridge—he radioed the other fighter pilots on the mission and alerted them to be ready. "Arm up. Target in sight. Time to go to work."

With Jim in the lead, each pilot swooped down like a predatory bird and dropped ordnance on the bridge before pulling up for another run at the target. Synchronized like an organized swarm of mosquitoes, the F-105s attacked the target relentlessly. The plan was to re-join afterwards at the rendezvous point that Jim had selected in advance and then head home.

The bombing run went as planned, but the final time Jim pulled off the target, he heard an explosion in the aft section of his airplane. He immediately checked his instrument panel and the controls in the airplane indicated he was rapidly losing hydraulic power. That could only mean one thing. He was about to lose control of the airplane.

Sure enough, Jim pulled up and that was the last time he was able to move the controls and re-position the airplane to start climbing toward a mountain a bit off in the distance. When the hydraulics completely failed, the F-105 began a very slow roll to his left. Rapidly recounting the emergency procedure, he reached down and made sure all his equipment was secure—his helmet was on tight, his visor was down, and his belts were all secured.

Reaching down and feeling for the ejection handles on the side of his seat, he fired one ejection that separated the canopy from the airplane. He tried once again to right the F-105 but it was continuing the slow roll to his left and he muttered to himself, *I'm going to have to get out of here before I'm in a compromised attitude.* If he were to be seated in other than the upright position, there was danger of injury when he ejected from the airplane.

With each millisecond mattering, he squeezed the trigger beside the seat and everything went dark as he was thrust into space from his F-105, which was hurtling through the sky at over 575 miles per hour.

The power and pressure of the ejection was violent and overpowered lucid thought, erasing all memory of exactly what happened, but like coming out of a nightmare, he found himself drifting through the sky in a dreamlike state of suspension with a sunlit halo of parachute silk blossoming overhead. Suddenly, loud blasts of ordnance jolted him back to reality as he realized the enemy was waiting for him below.

Jim looked up at his parachute to be sure that no panels had ripped due to the speed of ejection and once reassured that everything was intact, he searched the ground to locate where his airplane had crashed. Twisting to follow the mushrooming cloud of dust in the distance, he spotted the bridge his flight of F-105s had bombed. He rotated his chute to have a panoramic view of the whole area, and he could see for miles. All at once it became so quiet and peaceful that he relaxed, almost hypnotized by the experience until he looked down and realized he was directly above a village.

He thought to himself, *James, you are not going home tonight.*

When he looked around again, the village had disappeared. Was he hallucinating? It didn't take him but a second to remember that in the pre-flight briefing for the mission, he was told that the winds were forecast to be from the northeast at 13 knots, and that gave him an idea of why the village had disappeared. He was drifting across the ground at 13 knots. Trying to find a grain of hope in his observations, he continued to talk himself through the perilous situation. "Now if I can just stay up here long enough and drift across this valley, I will be able to reach the edge of the jungle by the time I touch ground."

Sure enough, by maneuvering the silken parachute overhead, Jim made it all the way across the valley, and when he landed, he rolled the chute into a tight knot and got rid of it. He had a large but heavy survival kit, so he ditched it, too, and ran as fast as he could into the edge of the jungle. The first thing that he saw was a cave and he darted toward it for cover, but then he thought, *No, no, no. You don't want to go in that cave. That's the first place they'll look.* All the survival training he had received was beginning to kick in.

Deciding it was safer to keep moving, he climbed up through the brush on the side of the hill, grabbing for exposed roots and branches to keep from falling. Progress was painfully slow, and every twig that broke under his footsteps sounded like a firecracker identifying the escape route he was taking. As he climbed higher and higher he could hear the excited voices of the villagers looking for him. Were they getting close? Had they spotted him yet?

He began to worry about how much noise he was making as he thrashed through the thick underbrush, so he stopped running and instead, he crawled up along a rock ledge. Pressing his body as tightly against the ledge as possible, he slowly turned his head to look back towards where he had shed his parachute, and there they were! Men were crowding together and picking up his equipment that he had left behind. Had they noticed him clinging to life in the distance?

He breathed a sigh of relief when they turned away and headed in the direction of where his airplane had crashed, and when he felt they were out of hearing distance, he pulled out one of his two radios and reached the channel that connected him with his flight. He assured them that he was safe for the moment, but he cautioned them not to fly over his position. There were local villagers hunting him down and they all had long barrel guns.

Once he had alerted his flight crew, he scampered further up the hill. Slithering through high grass and breathing heavily from the climb, he finally reached a clearing. He didn't want to expose his position to his enemies, so he remained in the patch of undergrowth at the edge of the field. If a rescue helicopter was searching for him and managed to locate him, he was going to have to be in a relatively clear area so that the rotors wouldn't become entangled in all of the underbrush. For a moment he had hope that he might escape capture as he lay on the ground gasping for breath. Then he looked back down the steep hill and panicked.

He had made his way through tall grass to reach the clearing, and from his vantage point above his frantic scramble toward the crest of the hill, he could clearly discern the path he had taken. The grass was tamped down and his route stuck out like a road map leading directly toward his hiding place. Crawling in erratic patterns back down through the grass, he made an effort to stand it back up to its natural state. His heart was pounding when he finally finished the task and zigzagged back to a different area at the edge of the clearing. Had he been seen? Did the enemy have binoculars? Had they detected unusual patterns of movement in the grass? He didn't hear anything, but maybe they were quietly crawling on their bellies through the grass just as he had.

Trying to determine what else he could get rid of in case he needed to move quickly to another area, he decided to ditch his anti-gravity suit. He lay quietly on the ground and began to unzip the tight-fitting flight suit, but when he got to the left leg, he was startled to find it was moist and oozing. Sitting up he was surprised that the leg of his flight suit had a hole in it. Concerned, he wiggled his toes in his boots and was distressed to learn that the boot was sopping with blood.

He thought to himself, *I got out of the airplane safely. I made it safely to the ground. Thus far I've avoided the enemy, but now I'm going to lie up here and bleed to death.*

Feeling woozy but knowing that he had to keep assessing his situation, Jim struggled to remain prone as he removed the antigravity suit. When he sat up to examine his leg, his worst suspicions were confirmed. There was a hole inside the calf of his left leg and it was pulsing with blood. What now?

He had left his big survival kit behind so that limited his options, but as he sat staring at his wound, he realized that the blood in some areas around the perimeter were coagulating. That meant that the wound would eventually stop bleeding. Remaining still and calm and conserving his energy was the best choice. He would just lie there and wait for his rescuers to come.

He no longer had any sense of time, but at the faint sound of a helicopter in the distance he popped up as the whirlybird went right by him. Jim had a Mae West and as he struggled to stand up, he waved it frantically, but the helicopter kept going. Grabbing his radio, Jim called for help and an A1-E Skyraider flying somewhere in the area responded. At last! They were looking for him and now his rescuers had his location.

Apparently, the helicopter was directed to turn back around, because the copter pilot and his crew finally sighted Jim and hovered over him like a mother eagle. A copter crew member reached down and Jim managed to make a wristlock with him.

Looking upward Jim summoned all his strength, but he was sweating profusely so that when his rescuer slowly lifted him up to the edge of the helicopter, the wristlock slipped and Jim fell back to the ground. He was on the edge of losing consciousness now and his leg was dripping blood.

The helicopter pilot deftly repositioned his craft so that two crew members were able to reach down and make a wristlock once again. Cautiously, they pulled Jim upward and into the helicopter. As soon as the pilot received a thumbs up to indicate Jim was safely secured aboard, he quickly lifted up into the sky and flew to safer air space.

Jim had remained able to think logically and be decisive throughout the whole ordeal but once aboard the helicopter he shivered and began shaking violently as he suddenly felt cold and faint. He was desperately thirsty and cried out for water. He'd had nothing to drink since he left Thailand, and he was dehydrated. There was no water aboard the helicopter, but one resourceful crew member reached for his lunchbox and pulled out an orange. Slowly peeling it, he gave Jim a section at a time so that he could slowly suck the juice. It was an unforgettable act of mercy.

Jim was still shivering so another crew member pulled out an old, greasy piece of heavy tarp lying at the back of the copter and he covered Jim with it. Jim seemed to be doing better, but suddenly he burst into tears so the crew member sitting beside him, put his arms around Jim to calm their wounded patient. Jim had been so rational up until this point that he couldn't understand why he was suddenly so overwhelmed with emotion, but the helicopter crewmembers were experienced and recognized all the signs of severe shock. They knew exactly what to do.

Stabilized and tucked safely in the midst of the attentive helicopter crew, Jim had no defining frame of reference to determine the sequence of events unfolding…no segues linking him to reality. He had always been a fighter pilot capable of pinpoint accuracy in timing—traveling 8 miles to the minute to reach his target in North Vietnam on the morning of October 13th—but now he was emotionally drifting in and out of a drama.

Without memory of landing on the ground or even thanking the guardian angels who had rescued him, Jim found himself in a medical facility with a team of medics pulling off his dirt-caked boots and helping him out of his dirty, bloodstained flight suit. He welcomed the comfort of safety…the warm spray of a shower as it cleaned his wounded leg… blood pooling in the water at his feet and draining away the fear…being helped like a child into roomy, soft clothes…returning to the human race…falling asleep in the arms of security.

A bright light flicked on. Where was he? Was someone speaking French? Startled, Jim suddenly realized there were several men standing at the foot of his bed…civilians…asking questions.

"Did you have a weapon?"

"An 8-round, snub nose .38," Jim replied.

Struggling to focus his mind as well as his eyes, Jim tried to remember answers until the youngest and shortest member of the interrogators asked such an absurd question that he snapped back with an acerbic retort. Was this a dream? Surely these were not military men.

"Did you have to use it?" the young fellow asked.

"What a ridiculous question. Using a .38 against dozens of villagers hunting me down with long guns?" he answered with a frown. Safety, not confrontation, was the obvious choice. He was through with the group, whoever they were. He lay back down and turned his head aside to end the questioning as the men muttered to each other and flicked off the light as they left.

When he woke up again, medics were helping him out of bed. His legs had stiffened to the point that he couldn't walk. He still didn't know exactly where he was or how long he had been there, but his medical attendants were Caucasians, not Vietnamese. Thank god! He had survived capture.

Jim was shot down on a Thursday, but by Sunday doctors decided he was well enough to be transported back to Takhli and familiar faces. Eager to check on whether Pogreba had been found, he was crestfallen to learn that there was still no word. With each passing day, hope of finding Pogie alive was fading. Then on the 22nd of October, war extracted its price once again. Fred Cherry, another Black pilot and a Virginian like Jim, was shot down. Only the Randall children would be welcoming their father home.

4-Star Air Force Chief of Staff John Paul McConnell visits Major James Randall at Takhli AB in Thailand after his shoot down over North Vietnam.
(Photo courtesy of Regional History & Genealogy, Pikes Peak Library District, Image #412-146)

Air Force Chief of Staff General John Paul McConnell and PACAF Commander Lt. General Joseph D. Moore listen intently as Jim gives a detailed account of his experience being shot down over North Vietnam on October 13, 1965. Jim is able to provide valuable insights in the lengthy informational interviews.

CHAPTER 25

ENCORE AT NELLIS

Military transports aren't built for comfort or equipped with luxurious accommodations, but Jim was simply grateful for the "ride." Heading out on the flight line he was suddenly overcome with emotion as a corpsman assisted him aboard the aircraft. At last, he was going home! Leaving Thailand's throbbing heat behind, he knew how lucky he was. As tears welled up in his eyes, he rubbed the sleeve of his uniform across his face and settled into a seat near the front of the aircraft. He couldn't stop thinking of Pogreba and Fred Cherry when the airplane roared up into the sky. His friends should have been sitting there beside him, sharing his good fortune. He'd often heard that tragedy descends upon us in threes. Why was he the one spared? Survivor's guilt crept through his thoughts and tamped down his joy.

Jim had been on a temporary duty assignment (TDY) from McConnell AFB to fly combat missions over North Vietnam out of Takhli, Thailand. Now that he was deemed healthy enough to make the long journey back to Kansas, he was airborne for the first time since his dramatic rescue over North Vietnam and the eventual flight back to Takhli in Thailand. As he closed his eyes, vivid images flashed across his mind and captured October's drama. He could still see Fred Cherry smile and wave to him from the cockpit as he taxied the length of the runway to head north toward Hanoi. It had been a challenge to amble down to Takhli's flight line to see Cherry off. Jim was struggling to walk again after his fateful flight 9 days ago, but somehow, he felt compelled to make the effort. He wondered what prompted him to do that? Neither fighter pilot could have known that Cherry was headed toward an interminable 7-year stint in a prison camp.

And Pogreba? Oh, Pogreba! By some quirk of Tactical Air Command scheduling he and Pogreba had been assigned to the same base four different times. Their friendship meant the world to Jim, but he never actually expressed it in words. He always thought he would see Pogreba again. The finality of it all was more excruciating than Jim's physical injuries. It seemed as though he re-lived his entire life on that flight back to McConnell AFB. The fighter pilot who had left for Thailand was not returning to Kansas as the same man. All the medical x-rays he had undergone since October 13, 1965, failed to reveal a critical injury—the loss of his dear friend left a hole in his heart.

As soon as he was stateside, Jim was only afforded a brief time to reconnect with his family who had spent tense weeks praying for his safe return. Unable to suppress the deluge of national and international press seeking all the details about his harrowing experience, journalists and curious locals were incessant in their quest for breaking news. The McConnell AFB Office of Information made a valiant effort to keep a reasonable schedule for interviews, but briefings for high-ranking Air Force officials and Congressmen's requests for interviews took precedence over everyone, even Jim's family.

Good natured as well as photogenic, Jim obliged the public and smiled through chronic pain. He made an effort to hide the extent of his injuries from Mary Ann and his children, too. Thankful to have survived the ordeal over North Vietnam, Jim did not complain, but it was clear that McConnell's medical facility could not provide the necessary therapy to ensure his full recovery. After a few incredibly difficult weeks, Headquarters decided to transfer him to Luke AFB in Arizona where he received the required physical therapy and pain management that the highly skilled medical corps on base could provide. The Air Force had lost a valuable airplane, but a fighter pilot as skilled, dedicated, and experienced as Jim was irreplaceable. The military was determined to get him back in the cockpit as soon as possible. That was Jim's unspoken goal, too.

Mary Ann and the children stayed in Kansas while Jim convalesced from November 1965 until January 1966 in Arizona…another Christmas apart. Since Jim was deemed medically qualified to return to flight status in January 1966, he was sent to Eglin AFB in Florida on a 6-month TDY, flying the test program for the anti-surface-to-air missile equipment being installed in the F-105. Finally, in June 1966, Jim returned to McConnell AFB and his family in Wichita, Kansas. Due to all the national and international focus on Jim after his rescue over North Vietnam, the public continued to show an interest in his story. TAC general officers were watching, too.

On August 23, 1966, when USAF Headquarters announced the initial re-organization of the TAC Fighter Weapons Center at Nellis AFB with General Ralph G. Taylor taking command, Jim received orders that he was being re-assigned to Nellis. He was selected to be the Operations Officer in charge of conducting the operational and suitability testing of the F-111 prior to the aircraft being accepted into the Air Force's inventory. He was fortunate in that his Wing Commander at McConnell arranged for Jim to check out in the F-111 before his re-assignment, so he was well prepared to assume command upon his arrival in Las Vegas. There was no doubt about the respect his commanding officer held for Jim.

It was a scramble setting up the move on such short notice, but it was also important to get the children registered for the upcoming school year in Nevada. Mary Ann had loved Las Vegas, so she was happy to be returning even though moving a family of six was a logistical challenge. There were a lot of decisions to make before the moving van arrived. Meanwhile, Jim was hoping the change of station would quell the undercurrent of tension in their marriage over his wife's smoking. She had managed to give up cigarettes each time she was pregnant, but she no longer made empty promises to kick the habit. Jim worried not only about her health but also his children's health as well as his own. The latest statistics on secondhand smoke were unsettling. After watching his father's lungs fail and the haunting years of his dad's suffering, Jim could no longer ignore his concerns. Something would have to change.

Once the dust settled from the frantic effort to relocate and re-organize the Randall family at Nellis, Jim was back on a familiar flight line, and he was clearly in charge of Base Operations as he assumed his responsibility. Consequently, his commander General Taylor showed confidence in him immediately and relied on his judgment. *Esprit de corps* in the 4525th Fighter Weapons Wing was evident from the onset. The pilots and crews were the cream of the crop, and brightly colored 100-mission patches abounded on flight suits. Jim had not completed 100 missions over North Vietnam, but his remarkable rescue and his admirable reputation preceded him. Jim had spent his career working assiduously to excel at the highest level he could attain. He lived the credo emphasized throughout his youth by his mother Ora, and it continued to serve him well. Some things you can never really prepare for, though.

Within his first few weeks of heading up Base Ops, Jim realized the importance of purchasing a motor scooter. General Taylor called frequently, and when he summoned Jim, it was usually an emergency. His first experience with the gory aftermath of a plane crash began with his commander's terse explanation. He would never forget it. "We have lost an F-111 out on the gunnery range. I want you to go up there and just look around. See what you can find out. Come back and let me know."

Since the Air Force set up official investigative boards to assess all the factors attributing to an aircraft crashing, Jim was both surprised and confused to be asked to make a preliminary assessment, but he suppressed the urge to ask questions. Instead, he secured an L-20 for the flight, engaged a military photographer, and headed for the gunnery range at nearby Indian Springs. Landing at the edge of the crash site, Jim could feel his stomach churning upon seeing body parts—not just of the aircraft but of former colleagues.

Witnessing vital and highly trained men reduced to a far-flung scene of appendages and viscera was simply overwhelming. Reality hit him hard. These were the remains of loved ones—fathers, sons, brothers.

Some things remain etched in memory, never to be forgotten. Jim lifted his mobile phone and called his commander. "General, would you call the hospital please and have the hospital commander to get his people out here to police up this area? Sir, I am sorry but I just cannot go out to the site. There is too much carnage lying away from the site area."

After the hospital crew completed their mission and left, Jim located the main fuselage in one area and the right wing of the airplane in another. Since the huge wing carry-through box—where the right wing had once been attached—was now exposed, Jim noted flaws in the metal where the wing was molded. Curious, he instructed the photographer to take pictures of both sites—the wing carry-through box and the wing itself, where the wing had broken off from the wing carry-through box.

Jim knew the F-111 crew was on a dive-bombing run, and it appeared the wing separated from the airplane when they pulled off from the bombing run. F-111 pilots do not wear individual parachutes. Instead, there is a semi-detonate cord around the cockpit area, and when the pilot squeezes the trigger—the ejection handle—the cord is electrically triggered so that the entire cockpit area separates from the main part of the fuselage. Chutes are attached to the capsule to slow it down, and there is a huge chute attached to the fuselage to lower it to the ground.

In order to determine what might have occurred, Jim walked back and forth across the crash site, studying the detritus of what was once a sleek F-111 and its crew. By comparing those details to his knowledge about executing bombing runs and triggering the ejection process, he drew an informed conclusion. He decided that the flaw in the metal within the wing carry-through box resulted in the wing detaching as the pilot pulled out of the bombing run. The attitude of the aircraft was probably at a 45-degree left angle as the pilot triggered the handle, and he quite likely tried to eject the escape capsule away from the F-111 when his instrument panel alerted him of an emergency. Tragically, due to the plane's low altitude as it pulled out of the bombing run and its trajectory as well as its speed, the capsule fired into the ground.

Returning to Nellis, Jim instructed the photographer to develop his pictures as soon as possible and submit them to the general. Then he hurried over to Headquarters to brief General Taylor, his commanding officer, about what he thought had happened.

A few weeks later the Air Force investigative team determined that the inception of the problem occurred at the factory during the pouring of the steel, which resulted in a faulty wing carry-through box. Of course, this led to the question—Was this an isolated, one-time imperfection or was it prevalent in other airplanes in the fleet? General Taylor arranged for Jim to fly an F-111 to the General Dynamics factory in Forth Worth, Texas, to discuss the situation with engineers, and as a result, all the F-111s were grounded for an entire year.

Sitting in the cockpit of an F-111, Jim considers all the factors that caused the F-111 crash at Nellis AFB's gunnery range. A USAF investigative team verifies his conclusion, and it leads to the solution to the problem—a year-long grounding of the F-111 to inspect every aircraft and to address issues related to the manufacture of the aircraft's wing carry-through box as well as the wing. (Photo courtesy of Regional History & Genealogy, Pikes Peak Library DIstrict, Image #412-116)

F-105s picked up the slack during the 12-month period that the wings of each F-111 were removed and x-rayed to guarantee there were no imperfections. No notation was ever made acknowledging Jim's significance to the investigation, but from that point on, General Taylor called Jim first whenever there was a serious issue with an aircraft. He trusted him implicitly throughout the entirety of his tour.

Late one Friday afternoon Jim was sweating heavily under the Nevada sun but determined to finish mowing his lawn when his mobile phone rang. He carried it with him at all times, and it rested on the nightstand beside the bed when he slept. He was not surprised to hear the general say, "Come to my office right away. I need to talk to you." Jim tried to explain that he was mowing his lawn so he'd need to shower first, but the general growled, "Did you hear what I said?" Jim raced into his quarters, ran a cold washrag over his face and arms, combed his hair, and sped directly to headquarters on his motor scooter. The staff in the front office looked askance when Jim rushed in. Still sweating and wearing Bermuda shorts with a torn T-shirt, he faced the general who, as usual, was in a freshly pressed uniform. Mortified, Jim realized there was still dirt under his fingernails; the general's nails were notably clean.

General Taylor jumped right into the issue at hand. It was distressing. Two F-111s had gone down within days of each other over Vietnam. Not only did the general want to know why, but he also instructed Jim to organize a flight of four F-111s to take off Tuesday morning for Thailand; he was to deliver two of the F-111s as replacements. Considering Jim had to organize the mission over the weekend, he called his maintenance officer immediately after leaving the general's office, and he explained the circumstances. He needed to have four F-111s ready to taxi out onto the runway and ready to go on a mission to Thailand by 10 o'clock Tuesday morning...per General Taylor's orders.

Checking out all the possibilities, Jim called three of the most highly qualified pilots in the unit to "fly the airplanes and to go ride on a tanker." Without hesitation, every pilot that he contacted eagerly accepted the mission. Jim further instructed the crew that he would be meeting with them at 2 p.m. on Monday in his office to brief them on the status of his request and to determine whether anything had changed. He, in turn, expected to be briefed about the status of all the arrangements that they were responsible for and to be notified of anything that had been overlooked. He finished with, "At 10 o'clock Tuesday morning I want to start engines. Everybody understand that?" They did.

Next on his itemized list Jim called the Food Service Officer and explained he needed food for four F-111 flight crews by 6 a.m. Tuesday morning. Departure for Thailand would be 10 o'clock so Food Service would need to prepare accordingly. Finally, he mapped out all the details for the impending flight of over 8200 miles. He pinpointed the general area where refueling would be required and arranged for the scheduling of tankers.

On Tuesday morning, four F-111s took off from Nellis AFB with Jim in the lead. They reached the tankers at the rendezvous point just as Jim had scheduled and headed to Hawaii where they spent the night. Up at the crack of dawn the next day they stopped enroute at Guam—a tiny dot on the map surrounded by the vast Pacific—where they spent the night before taking off for the final leg of their journey—destination Thailand.

The mission unfolded in the designated phases without a glitch, and Jim's 4-ship handed over the two replacement F-111s to the flight personnel and their commander at Takhli after verifying that there had not been one single write-up or discrepancy on the flight over. The crew was inoculated, as required prior to their re-entering the United States and then they boarded the flight Jim had pre-arranged for the trip back to Las Vegas.

The F-111s had performed beautifully on the flight to Southeast Asia, so Jim was looking forward to de-briefing the general upon his return…only to learn that the F-111 he had flown without incident had crashed on a mission the following night. In total shock, Jim mentally re-traced his entire flight across the Pacific, trying to remember the tiniest detail that might give a clue as to what had happened. To think that the plane had crashed after he had verified it was flight-ready haunted him. Had he missed something?

Since Jim was part of a small detachment of pilots who flew and tested the F-111 regularly, he usually designated one specific aspect of a flight to scrutinize how the aircraft performed and to determine whether it met the Air Force's toughest requirements. Still puzzling over why the F-111 he had ferried across the Pacific had crashed the following night, Jim climbed into the cockpit of an F-111 with his Wizzo (the weapons systems officer or WSO) and flew straight to the bombing range. The mission for the day was to evaluate the aircraft's weapons release system. After carefully recording how the weapons reacted and how close the bombs landed to the intended target, Jim headed back to Nellis. Upon takeoff, he had been aware he did not have a full load of ordnance or fuel, which would have been over 31,000 pounds of JP4 (a mixture of kerosene and gasoline). Surprised upon completion of the mission that he still had fuel remaining, Jim made a snap decision. He directed the Wizzo to enter the coordinates of Scottish Castle into the navigation system.

Scottish Castle is in the north end of Death Valley, and though elevated above the valley floor, it is 238' below sea level at its nadir. The Wizzo was curious but silent as he put in the coordinates. Then Jim asked him to enter the coordinates for Bad Water as he turned south toward the lowest part of Death Valley. He also advised his navigator to set the Clearance Plane Setting at 100' so that the aircraft would maintain an altitude of 100' above the terrain as they descended enroute to Bad Water. Jim did not notice the anomaly at first, but there was a sand dune in the midst of the terrain and though they cleared the dune and dropped down on the other side, Jim did not think they had cleared the dune at the height he expected. However, the F-111 did remain a steady 100' above the terrain until they reached Bad Water.

Jim was still pondering how the Clearance Plane Setting had functioned when he joined the usual de-briefing with the representative from General Dynamics who had followed the test flight. First, Jim covered the findings from the bombing mission, which was the primary purpose for the flight, and then he launched into how the airplane reacted on the impromptu flight down Death Valley. He described the sand dune they encountered and explained that he didn't think the airplane centered that sand dune by 100'. Concerned, he requested that one of the factory pilots replicate the scenario he had experienced to see if the F-111 would react the same way.

Instead of going to Death Valley, General Dynamics decided to have a set of factory pilots take an F-111 up to the North Rim of the Grand Canyon, where there are towering evergreens, and they flew at the designated Clearance Plane Setting over a thicket of tall trees and snow-covered ground. They were surprised to find that the plane did not react in accordance to their expectations. They continued to fly in various areas with heavily forested patches of tall trees that necessitated different Clearance Plane Settings, and once again the F-111 did not react in accordance with the requested ground clearance that was placed into the F-111's system. It appeared that, as the F-111 was flying over certain types of terrain, some of the radar was being absorbed by material over which it was passing rather than bouncing back to the airplane.

Jim's suspicions were confirmed, and so he decided to approach General Taylor with his theory that the F-111s we were losing over or near Thailand might be as a result of this variable that seemed to impact the accuracy of the Clearance Plane Setting. He pointed out that the planes he had flown over to Southeast Asia as replacements were now flying at night over immense stretches of jungle peppered with tall trees. General Taylor could see the logic in Jim's deductive reasoning, and he apparently contacted Inspector General Joe Moore who was forming a military group to go over to Thailand. The mission was to interview the pilots and their mission profile to determine why aircraft were mysteriously being lost, particularly at night and in rainy weather.

Once again General Taylor called Jim into his office to inform him that he would be returning to Thailand as part of Inspector General Moore's investigative team. Although it was a quick turn-around, Jim joined Moore's team and interviewed numerous pilots in Thailand, discussing the climatic conditions on the particular day or night when they were flying with airplanes that were lost. He wrote copious notes, shared his observations, and detailed his personal experience, which led to General Dynamics working on the accuracy of the F-111's Clearance Plane Setting as well as this one peculiar discrepancy. He also noted that he had flown one of the replacement F-111s from Nellis AFB over the Pacific to Takhli, Thailand, without incident…only to have it crash the following night.

When Jim returned to duty at Nellis, he immersed himself in maintaining his high achieving unit on the flight line while going home at night and giving his entire attention to his family. He never discussed all the pressures of his job once he walked in the door of his quarters and hugged his kids and wife. As expected, he never saw the results of the F-111 investigation either, but General Dynamics doggedly pursued the fine-tuning of the Clearance Plane Setting to an infinitesimal degree and corrected the issue Jim had brought to their attention. Perhaps it was hopeful thinking, but the crash rate of the F-111, especially in Thailand, seemed to dissipate somewhat.

A General Dynamics engineer shakes Jim's hand in appreciation for his assistance in solving a critical problem. As a test pilot, Jim is keenly observant, always mentally noting anomalies and linking disparate factors together to determine why an aircraft crashes. Analyzing a recent crash, Jim theorized that a sand dune seemed to cause an F-111's Clearance Plane Setting to respond inaccurately. General Dynamics pilots tested Jim's theory; they learned he was correct. (Photo courtesy of Regional History & Genealogy, Pikes Peak Library DIstrict, Image #412-117}

From the first day he reached Nellis AFB, Jim was well aware of the enormous responsibility he was expected to shoulder, and he was confident that he was up to the task. What he hadn't considered was that their quarters on base would become less accommodating for a family of six—three of them teenagers. His older daughters, Roberta and Louise, deserved more privacy, and Billy, his only son, complained that he was outnumbered on school mornings when it came to getting into the bathroom. Patricia was only in elementary school, but she needed her space, too.

Moving off base would mean Jim would be away from home much longer each day because his job demanded that the general would always have immediate access to him in emergencies, but perhaps Mary Ann would be happier and return his concern about his family by quitting or at least cutting back on her smoking. He was looking for a reasonable compromise. Since Jim had little time for house hunting, Mary Ann was given the perfect opportunity to find the home of her dreams. It would be a fresh start, hopefully the answer to mending an increasingly troubled marriage.

As Operations Officer at Nellis, Jim continued to be deeply involved with General Dynamics each time an F-111 malfunctioned or an accident resulted in the death of the crew. Every accident was heavily investigated and the detailed reports as to cause led to General Dynamics' continued efforts to resolve issues. Some situations were simply isolated incidents. For example, on one occasion an F-111 on a training flight out of Nellis crashed due to a wind deficient windshield that bulged down from the top of the canopy bow and instantly crazed and fractured. Each anomaly required extensive and time-consuming investigation, which usually led to exorbitantly expensive solutions. Still, the loss of even one pilot was not acceptable. After crew members died due to a wind deficient windshield, General Dynamics replaced fifty F-111 windshields in 1969. A year later it was 93 more that had to be re-installed. On yet another occasion when an F-111 crashed and was irretrievably damaged, a control system failure was deemed the culprit, but thankfully the crew ejected safely.

Then there were the incidents where the circumstances were so incredibly ironic that it was almost unbearable. Jim often thought back to that fateful January day in 1967, when his commanding officer called to tell him he was to fly to Edwards AFB to pick up Colonel Don McCance, the Wizzo accompanying Major Foster Brightwell on an F-111 flight to California. Upon landing just slightly short of the runway due to improper wing sweep setting, the aircraft reacted erratically, but Brightwell miraculously brought the plane to a stop and jumped out. Unable to unbuckle his lap belt, Colonel McCance was still struggling to escape when Brightwell raced around to the Wizzo's side of the plane to help him.

Tragically, Brightwell stood in a pool of JP4, which ignited and burned the heroic pilot over 80% of his body. He was immediately air evacuated to the burn unit at Brooke General hospital at Fort Sam Houston in San Antonio, Texas. When Jim arrived at Edwards AFB to escort McCance back to Nellis, he spoke to the Operations Officer and flight line crew at Base Operations who had raced out and witnessed the entire incident. They explained how McCance had managed to escape with his life, but he had received burns, too. He was at the Edwards AFB hospital.

Jim hurried over to the base hospital to check on McCance, and the minute he walked into the hospital room, he realized the burns to his friend's face would probably unalterably transform his appearance. Trying to mask his shock at seeing McCance's disfigured features, he promised the injured navigator that he would check with the attending physician to get a medical release so that he could fly McCance back home to Nellis. If that was not feasible, he would make arrangements for him to return to Nellis and his family as soon as possible. After visiting long enough to learn McCance's account of what had happened, Jim spoke to the attending physician who agreed to sign the navigator out of the hospital after a few days. Jim contacted his commander about the turn of events and made arrangements to stay at the BOQ until McCance was released to him.

Although Jim had hoped to have a quick turn-around, the extra time would afford him the chance to make a more thorough investigation of the situation. He headed back to the flight line to learn more about the incident. The group at Base Ops explained that fire crews and emergency personnel had raced out to the site immediately and that they had managed to prevent a major conflagration by relentlessly hosing down the fire. Even when they had it under control, they continued watching for erratically spiking hotspots and drenching them. They had remained on duty, working in long shifts and spelling each other through the night. Somehow, they got ahead of the fire and spared the flight line.

Several days later Jim returned to Nellis with McCance. Sadly, Foster Brightwell had succumbed to his injuries prior to their return, but Jim brought back a few sentimental mementos for Brightwell's wife and three children—his wallet and a metal ring of keys. The bizarre juxtaposition of family and fated flights created ongoing stress for Jim, but he remained upbeat and attentive whenever he returned home to his family. He avoided expressing the deep-seated emotional anguish he was experiencing as he continued to lose admired colleagues and personal friends.

Fortunately, there were occasional highpoints that offset the pall of tragedies. When Nevada Senator Howard Cannon arrived on October 28, 1967, for a formal briefing in the F-111, General Taylor called upon Jim to take charge. In addition to being an important member of Congress, Cannon was also a Major General in the Air Force Reserves. However, there was a unique bond the two men shared. Like Jim, Cannon had survived being shot down during combat. Jim guided the senator through a thorough pre-flight briefing and a 90-minute flight in the F-111 to demonstrate the aircraft's capability. Upon his return to Congress, Senator Cannon wrote an extensive analysis of the F-111 in his article, "The F-111—A Pilot's Report." Cannon began his article with, "A whole flock of these $6 million dollar flying machines are nesting at Nellis Air Force Base where U.S. Air Force pilots are taught the complexities of this bird." After covering his experience flying the F-111, Cannon surmised, "I discovered for myself that what the F-111 can do is fly further, faster, with a bigger payload and with greater accuracy than any other combat plane." General Taylor was pleased. For Jim, it was mission accomplished.

Jim reviews topography on maps with Senator Howard W. Cannon, a Major General in the Air Force Reserves, in a detailed briefing prior to their flight in the F-111. The senator is interested in making his own assessment of the F-111's performance in order to give a thorough analysis of the aircraft to Congress.

Jim guides Senator Cannon through a simulator session. Jim often takes dignitaries through this process. Movie star and Brigadier General Jimmy Stewart attended one of these detailed briefings. (Photo courtesy of Regional History & Genealogy, Pikes Peak Library District, Image #412-143)

Lt. Colonel Randall congratulates Senator Cannon following their flight in the F-111 as Wing Commander General Ralph "Zack" Taylor joins them on the flight line at Nellis AFB. (Photo courtesy Howard Cannon Collection, October 28, 1967, PH-00192 Special Collections and Archives, University Library, UNLV, Las Vegas, Nevada)

Meanwhile, Mary Ann was excited about several appealing pieces of real estate on the golf course in Las Vegas. She had been so focused on house hunting that she didn't appreciate the magnitude of her husband's responsibilities and stress. From the outside looking in, Jim was flying high. There had been a literal spotlight on his remarkable career from the moment he arrived at Nellis. When *Ebony* magazine discovered there was a Black American hero in their midst out in Las Vegas, they came calling in full force with reporters and photographers to capture the essence of Jim's exploits. They created a photo profile of the remarkable test pilot living on Nellis AFB with his four spirited children and outgoing wife. Captions on the spread of the attractive Randall family showed a picture of Jim playing chess with Billy. Another snapshot caught Mary Ann listening to records with Roberta and Louise while cute little Patricia looked on. Mary Ann was quoted as saying, "I wouldn't trade my place with anybody in the world," implying that her family had achieved the American dream.

It was rumored that renowned Black artist Roy LaGrone, who was a Tuskegee Airman himself, was commissioned to paint Jim's image as a fighter pilot for the cover of *Ebony* magazine—the May 1968 issue. Nellis AFB was abuzz about the whole thing.

By the spring of 1968, Jim was scheduled to lead a 5-ship flight of F-111s to Hawaii to provide air-to-ground cover for a U.S. Army unit on maneuvers. Since he had previously organized similar missions, he completely immersed himself in making all the arrangements, beginning with the flight over the Pacific to Hawaii to link up with military counterparts in the army. By working late at night and also shifting his tight schedule to accommodate *Ebony's* numerous photo shoots and interviews, he had managed to stay on top of his military responsibilities while simultaneously fulfilling his commitment to *Ebony*. The magazine's crew had left Las Vegas thrilled with the spread they were about to publish.

However, Jim's priority was the mission. As he lifted off the steaming desert runway with the 5-ship flight that he was leading, he no longer gave a second thought to *Ebony's* intention of making him the lead story for their May issue. He was just relieved that his commander was pleased with the outcome of his interaction with the magazine's staff. The military had grown cautious where the media was concerned. Factions of the American public—who vehemently opposed the country's role in Southeast Asia—were receiving wide coverage from the press even as war raged on in Vietnam, and the commanders at Nellis were especially sensitive to public opinion. The remarkable Thunderbirds, the USAF aero demonstration team, were also based at Nellis and public relations was a major component of their mission. Being above reproach was paramount, and so the team had changed its policy and only accepted pilots who had flown combat in Vietnam.

Likewise, Jim's sole concern at the moment was supporting the military mission and exercises such as the upcoming event in Hawaii. Thanks to Jim's organizational skills, the 5-ship flight of F-111s lifted off right on time on April 4th and headed for California. Although Jim had not previously met his navigator, there was already tension between the two men because the Wizzo lit up a cigarette as soon as they were airborne. Jim firmly addressed the issue and expected that to be the end of it. Nothing more was said, but Jim was troubled by the incident.

As they reached the California border and completed refueling in preparation for the long flight to Hawaii, Jim received an ominous transmission over the airwaves. The tanker pilot asked him if he could tune in to the local radio station in Los Angeles. Curious about such an unprecedented request, Jim reached the designated frequency just as he launched his F-111 off California's shores and into the darkening sky above the vast Pacific. Turning up the volume, Jim could feel his heart beating faster, and he trembled with shock as he listened intently to the breaking news. The words pierced his heart. "Dr. Martin Luther King, Jr…assassination…in Memphis, Tennessee." Sitting in disbelief and consumed with sorrow, Jim choked back sobs as his body stiffened and he stared into space. He could not conceive that such a thing could happen again. It had only been 5 years since an assassin took the life of President John F. Kennedy and now Dr. King was gone, too. It seemed as though America had lost its very soul and the world was ending.

The Wizzo apparently quelled his nerves by smoking because he immediately lit up first one cigarette and then another and another, in spite of the strict rule regarding no smoking in the cockpit. The navigator's lack of respect for his vaunted and grieving pilot was enraging, but Jim remained stone silent. Flying through ebony heavens that thinly veiled the ocean below, Jim endured his chain-smoking colleague for interminable hours until they finally reached Hawaii. Upon landing, Jim summarily dismissed the Wizzo, leaving the insensitive fellow to reassess the future of his career. Then he tracked down one of his other pilots and traded Wizzos with him for the duration of the mission. Composing himself and lifting his head high, Jim walked into the scheduled briefing.

Considering the enormity of the tragedy everyone was experiencing, the intensity in the briefing room was palpable prior to the beginning of the joint military exercise. There was no idle chatter or the occasional moment of laughter at a witty remark after elements of the presentation. Each military member was razor-focused on the mission and determined to perform at the highest level of proficiency. The depth of pervading sadness among the troops manifested itself in professionalism and love of country. Once maneuvers were underway, spirits soared and the combined forces surpassed expectations.

Each night when Jim returned to the barracks, which housed all the TDY personnel, he dealt with the enormity of Dr. King's death. He grieved for the country he had fought for and served in three wars for—from the inception of the Army Air Force to the powerful United States Air Force. Yet he felt just as powerless as his fellow countrymen about how to restore hope once again. He desperately wanted to do something, anything to express his feelings. Then he had an idea…a small gesture to honor Dr. King.

Upon the completion of the combined forces' maneuvers, Jim tweaked his flight plan so that he and his colleagues would appear in the cerulean skies above Nellis precisely on schedule . . . down to the millisecond. On the approach for landing, the 5-ship flight of F-111s would execute a "fly by" and then circle back for the landing. Usually, the whole flight line and some of the commanders would come out to welcome returning pilots after an important mission, so he knew that a display of power by the flight of F-111s upon their return would lift spirits. Once, he had done something similar at McConnell. The Thunderbirds were the only pilots at Nellis who ever executed aerial maneuvers for those on the flight line when they returned home after performing airshows across the country. No one on the flight line would expect the 5-ship flight of F-111s to make an aerial statement, but knowing Jim was leading the flight, they would quickly realize it was a tribute to Dr. King.

When Jim informed his flight of pilots of his intention, he noted their somber but supportive reaction as he explained that he might have to keep making minor adjustments once they were stateside in order to have split-second timing on entry into Nellis's airspace. Each pilot agreed it was a great idea, and everything happened just as Jim had planned. Roaring down the flight line after touchdown, he could hear the cheers of the larger-than-usual assembled crowd the minute the canopy of his plane lifted. He had achieved his goal of reassuring everyone that during their time of grief, "You can count on the fighter pilots of the U.S. Air Force."

Once Jim reached base housing and had a chance to hug his kids, he sat down to hear about the special house Mary Ann had found. She went into great detail about the wonderful location, the generous square footage, the beautiful landscaping, and how the size and floor plan suited the family perfectly. She wondered if Jim could find time to go look at it. He merely asked, "Is it what you've been looking for?" When Mary Ann nodded her head, she was stunned by his reaction. "Then let's buy it. Set up an appointment with the realtor." It was as though Jim had completely changed somehow, but she was thrilled as she rushed over to pick up the phone.

Mary Ann had no way of knowing how much everything was about to change. During the arduous flight over the Pacific with a chain smoker, Jim had realized that the whole scenario in the cockpit was like a synopsis of his marriage. He had reached his limit and could no longer tolerate Mary Ann's constant smoking. Unless she sought professional help to break the habit, he wanted out. However, he loved his family dearly so he made several major decisions. He planned to move his family into a lovely home in a neighborhood where they would be happy, safe, and secure. Perhaps in the setting that Mary Ann had always longed for, she would finally stick to her promise to give up smoking. If not…

Soon Mary Ann was once again totally engaged in all the familiar intricacies of setting up a move, and she woke up every morning delighted to take on the challenges of the day. As April faded into May, the Randalls were happily ensconced in their new home. It was the first house they had ever owned. *Ebony's* editor still published the impressive story of Jim's accomplishments in its entirety, but instead of a dramatic LaGrone portrait of Jim, the May 1968 cover honored Dr. Martin Luther King, Jr. Of course, it was undeniably the right decision. The juxtaposition of a story honoring a Black American pilot as a patriot contrasted dramatically with the assassination of the most famous Black American civil rights activist in the country. It posed a severe test of America's ability to remain unified.

The one bright spot in his life midst all the turmoil was the friendship he enjoyed with Colonel Chester Van Etten. As a commander on base, Van Etten had interacted almost daily with Jim, and while returning from a cross-country test flight in the F-111 together, he had let it slip that Jim was on the Colonel's list. It was exciting but poignant because things at home were not going as Jim had prayed they would.

Colonel Chester L. Van Etten and Colonel Randall return from an F-111 flight and meet to discuss the aircraft's performance with a General Dynamics engineer. They are joined by a General Dynamics personnel member.

Jim cannot suppress a smile as Colonel Chester Van Etten pins silver eagles on the lapel of newly promoted Colonel James E.P. Randall.

Newly promoted Colonel James Randall experiences a bittersweet moment—he has achieved his career goals, but he is uncertain about the rest of his career and the life-changing decisions he is making in his marriage. It is time for reflection as he heads to his upcoming assignment.

Although Jim had hoped for the best, Mary Ann settled back into old patterns and was smoking heavily again, which led to time worn arguments late at night. When the situation finally reached the breaking point and divorce seemed inevitable, Jim was torn by conflicting emotions. He took leave and booked a flight back East to share the heartrending news with Ora. What would she think? She had been so proud of all his successes. He was chagrined, but he had to tell her personally that he had failed in his marriage.

By the time he was assigned to Nahkon Phanom Air Base in Thailand where he was to be the Vice Commander of Task Force Alpha, his marriage had essentially ended, but he requested a delay in his departure for Southeast Asia so that he could attend the high school graduation of his daughter Louise. It was the last major event he attended with the Randall family intact, a touching experience full of gut-wrenching emotions that he managed to conceal from his beloved children.

CHAPTER 26

RETURN TO THAILAND

Jim boarded the military transport thinking of how different the return to Thailand would be this time. The irony of completing a combat tour 6 years after he was shot down in 1965 did not escape him. Puzzled, he had received a non-flying assignment, which was an unwelcome aspect of his new position even though he would be a Vice Commander. His new job was shrouded in secrecy, not to be discussed with anyone, and so he felt as though he was entering a wormhole as an entirely different human being—a soon-to-be officially divorced father of four who proudly wore the shiny silver eagle of a new colonel. He was a seasoned test pilot who would no longer be hopping into the cockpit of an F-111 every day.

How many times had he led a fleet of silver birds across the Pacific—F-105s and F-111s. From the California shoreline dotted with surfers to the war-torn jungles of Thailand, Jim had a mental image of the entire route just like an atlas cartographer. He had once flown round trip to Southeast Asia and back on two occasions within a ten-day period, and he was so exhausted that the hair on his head and even his eyebrows hurt. USAF wanted to know whether or not the camouflage paint on the F-111s might affect their combat performance, and so Jim led a flight across the Pacific and meticulously recorded every single aspect of his camouflaged plane's reactions in comparison to the unpainted birds accompanying him. It was a major undertaking but the outcome was reassuring. The camouflage paint job had little if any bearing on the F-111's performance. It might have seemed logical to come to that conclusion without all the time and expense involved, but on combat flights, minor discrepancies could mean the difference between life and death.

Jim had logged an impressive number of flying hours during his tour at Nellis. He had proven his expertise in analyzing and determining the reasons for serious accidents that occurred during flight, and he had also established his superiority as a test pilot assessing the performance of the latest aircraft being introduced into the USAF inventory. His reputation was impeccable, and he was usually the first person his commanders called upon in a crisis. He had arrived at Nellis as a major and was departing five years later as a full colonel, so he was surprised to be selected for a non-flying role in Thailand, even though he would have a significant mission. Was the U.S. Air Force planning to phase him out of the cockpit, he wondered? He was 45 years old with the aches and pains that can result from a compromised ejection from the cockpit during combat, but he avoided making an issue of it. Flight surgeons held inordinate power over pilots—they possessed medical knowledge that can lead to grounding.

Jim's mind raced from one scenario to another…like watching a movie of his life. So much had happened. Usually, he nodded off after an hour or so on these military transport flights, but not this time. He was coming to grips with what a drastic turn of events he had experienced over the final months at Nellis. He fully appreciated the mission of his flights during the day but he struggled through the difficult conversations with Mary Ann late at night. "Irreconcilable differences" would probably be the words on the final divorce decree, but that hardly captured the complexity of his marriage. He had always made a practice of leaving the demands of his job on the flight line behind when he opened the door to his home each evening, and instead, he focused on his children and their interests. His family really had no idea about what his job entailed or the level of stress he dealt with every day, and that was by design. Jim did not want his children to grow up with the fear of his imminent death—something that had haunted him throughout his own childhood.

What had been the turning point, though? The point of no return in his marriage?

Certainly, April 4th, 1968, was a pivotal point in U.S. history at the very moment Dr. Martin Luther King, Jr. dropped to the floor of a motel balcony in Memphis, Tennessee, and his heart stopped beating at the hands of an assassin. The world's greatest Superpower hit the nadir of life, and grief spread across the country. In rethinking that whole dramatic twist of fate, Jim remembered vividly how he had reacted as he sat in a smoke-filled cockpit with an inconsiderate Wizzo and listened in disbelief to a journalist's description of Dr. King's untimely death. It had been surreal but life-changing. That was when he set unstated deadlines in his marriage.

Jim was jolted out of his trance as he heard the wheels of the military transport touch down. Could they really have reached Hawaii already? Usually, the flight across the vast Pacific droned on for hours. As a pilot, he was accustomed to being in control and following his carefully honed flight plan, but time had become amorphous, without parameters these days. Hawaii would be a brief stopover and then off to Clark AFB in the Philippines for an overnighter before the final leg into Bangkok.

Airborne once again after everything checked out in Hawaii, Jim slipped back into thought, reviewing his life once again. He was glad he had taken leave before this reassignment to Thailand. Traveling back to the East Coast to visit with Ora and discuss his upcoming separation and inevitable divorce from Mary Ann had been torturous, but it was the right thing to do. He had always tried to be an honorable son—maintaining his monthly allotment to his mother, welcoming her to each of his latest assignments for a visit, and corresponding with her on a regular basis. Ora had rarely been solicitous toward him, but he had hoped for words of guidance or empathy. At least he had shown his mother the utmost respect by speaking to her personally.

Rushing back to Las Vegas, Jim had arrived in time to attend Louise's high school graduation ceremony with the family, just as he had with Roberta. Billy would be on deck in another two years, and he planned to be stateside again for that. Patricia was far younger so she would be the only one of the four to remain in the Las Vegas school system from elementary school through high school graduation. He hoped the stability would be to her advantage. Born in Germany, she had lived in South Carolina, Kansas, and Nevada by the time she was five.

To create a sense of being rooted midst constant mobility, military families often referred to "home" as the family itself because the children sometimes never returned to their birthplace, especially if it were overseas. That was one of the many reasons why he had decided to buy a house in an especially nice neighborhood in Las Vegas for Mary Ann and his children. They had spent more years at Nellis than any other base. Las Vegas held more memories for them than anywhere else.

At least his family was settled and safe, which was more than Jim could say for himself. For the first time in his life, he was at loose ends and looking at an uncertain future. He had always been very intentional in his goals. Suddenly, it seemed as though he had none, other than to provide for his family to the best of his ability and to continue giving his all to the U.S. Air Force.

The flight from Hawaii to the Philippines was more than twice the distance of the first leg of the trip, and Jim thought of all the times he had determined his position for refueling mid-air over the Pacific by sighting the blinking light on the wing of a KC-135 tanker. He could use a guiding light in life now. How he wished his father had lived long enough to know all Jim had learned how to do. He would have been fascinated to sit on the front porch of the family home in Gainsboro and listen to his son's airborne feats. Sam would have been interested in every detail of how fighter jets are re-fueled mid-air over the Pacific or how many times Jim had flown over the Mariana Trench, a gaping maw at a depth of 35,876 feet on the floor of the Pacific near Guam.

Ora had moved away from Roanoke long ago, but if Sam had lived, Jim was sure they would have kept the family home because he would have helped pay for it. Jim could hardly believe his father had been gone for 30 years. Even though Jim was in his 40s, he still missed Sam as much as that heartbroken 15-year-old teenager who struggled to be the man of the family when his father passed—the darkest day of Jim's life. If Mary Ann had experienced what Jim went through, would she have kept her promises and quit smoking?

Looking out the plane's window at the tangle of islands below, Jim anticipated that he would soon be landing in the Philippines. There would be the usual processing ritual and probably a military vehicle waiting for him on the other side. He knew the routine. He was emotionally exhausted, and all he was interested in was a hot shower, a good meal, and a comfortable bed in the VOQ. Then he would switch mental gears the next morning and board a military transport to Thailand and whatever awaited him there.

Upon landing and disembarking with an endless stream of uniformed passengers, everything went just as he had expected until he finished processing through and thought he heard someone yell his name, but that was impossible. He didn't know anyone in the Philippines. Then he heard, "Jim!" again and he couldn't believe his eyes as a familiar figure from his past rushed through the crowd toward him. Leonard Johnson had been his flight surgeon in Germany! He hadn't seen him in almost a decade, a lifetime ago. What were the odds that their paths would cross in the Philippines at this uncertain moment in Jim's life when he could use a friend.

Chattering a mile a minute, Leonard explained that, from the moment he learned Jim would be processing through the Philippines, he planned to be on board when his friend arrived. Hustling Jim into his car, Leonard drove straight to the VOQ to make sure he had overnight accommodations and then the talkative physician headed to the Officers' Club to treat his friend to dinner. Jim was jet lagged and bleary eyed, but Leonard's enthusiasm and eagerness to resume an old friendship was invigorating. The conversation over dinner was non-stop. Leonard and Jim swapped nearly 9 years' worth of stories, pausing only long enough to take another bite of dinner in between moments of laughter. Nothing conquers loneliness quite like sharing memories and amusingly embellished experiences with a friend from the past.

Finally, Jim begged Leonard for mercy and the chance to get some sleep, but he thanked him wholeheartedly for his timing as a friend. The evening had been pure therapy for Jim. He had never revealed so much to anyone in his whole life. Leonard reminded Jim that he would soon be returning to the Philippines for Jungle Training, so he had a surprise for him. His parting words were, "There's someone I want you to meet. A great lady, a librarian. I knew her in Germany. She's on vacation in Japan at the moment." Jim tried to explain that he wasn't interested, but Leonard just smiled and took off, leaving Jim sweltering in the humidity and climbing the steps of the VOQ to the throbbing beat of the jungle.

Touching down in Bangkok after a lengthy stint in another military transport plane, Jim was swept up in a whirlwind of briefings and quick hops in and out of Thai bases—Udorn, Ubon, Takhli and Nakhon Phanom. With only a few weeks to assert himself as a commanding officer, he was soon back on the ground in the Philippines and processing through to meet with Leonard for a quick dinner before he began Jungle Training the following day. When he finally spotted the flight surgeon frantically waving his arms above the bustling crowd of weary travelers perfumed with sweat, Jim hurried toward him. "She's here!" is all his friend said as he grabbed Jim's arm and dragged him toward two women standing at the edge of the crowd and checking the tags on a stand of luggage.

After a few whispered words, Jim and the excited flight surgeon walked up behind the pair of stylishly dressed women and Leonard said, "Let us gentlemen help you."

The taller of the two attractive women spun around, and she laughed upon recognizing Leonard. Meanwhile, Jim tucked the smaller suitcase under his arm and hefted a larger piece of luggage with his free hand. "Essie, I would like for you to meet the close friend I have been telling you about. This is Colonel James Randall."

Jim quickly put down the suitcases and extended his hand as Leonard announced, "This is the military's outstanding Head Librarian for Southeast Asia, Jim. I'd like to introduce you to Essie Aldrich."

The die was cast.

CHAPTER 27

THE LIBRARIAN

Leonard Johnson raised an eyebrow and suppressed a knowing smile as Jim suggested that he and Leonard would be delighted to take Miss Aldrich and her friend out to lunch, but Essie graciously declined. As Jim stood speechless, Leonard quickly stepped in. He pointed out that he had not been exaggerating about Essie's importance to the military just to tease Jim, a notable tease himself. Instead, the animated flight surgeon explained the extent of Essie Aldrich's importance to the 13th Air Force. She actually was the Head Librarian for the military in Southeast Asia, and she was at the airport to pick up the librarian standing beside her. Essie was responsible for briefing the diminutive young woman about her new position and what it entailed as well as familiarizing her with the facilities on base. The most pressing issue at the moment, though, was that there was a celebration being held back at the library for members of the staff who had received a promotion. As their supervisor, Essie needed to return as quickly as possible with her new protégé in hand. Essie smiled at Leonard's thorough accounting of her responsibilities.

Jim was quite impressed by Essie's composure and willingness to visit for a moment considering the circumstances, but he had certainly spent enough time in the Gainsboro Library as a youngster to know that Essie displayed qualities typical of a librarian's nature. He remembered that his favorite librarian was highly educated, well-informed on a wide-range of topics, and interested in helping him find answers to his questions. Surprised by the unexpected opportunity to make a new friend, Jim pressed the issue and asked if Essie would be available later in the evening, perhaps for dinner or a drink. He casually mentioned that he would be off to the jungle for training within two days, hoping that would allay any concerns that he was being too forward or flippant. Essie Aldrich was clearly a self-assured professional woman, and Jim didn't want to offend her. His deference toward her was rewarded.

Later that evening Jim and Essie connected at the cocktail lounge in the building where she and other staff members were quartered. The two chatted amiably for a while as Jim tried to conceal his fascination with Essie's knowledge of current affairs and the military's role in Southeast Asia. As the Head Librarian in charge of the Library Service Center on Clark AFB, she ordered and processed books for 13th Air Force, which included Thailand and Taiwan as well as the Philippines. An avid reader from childhood, Essie was constantly reviewing material that would be of interest as well as informative for those military members stationed abroad. She had held the position working for 13th Air Force Headquarters for 3 ½ years and loved the opportunity to travel and learn about all the intriguing sights, history, and cultures on the other side of the world.

Jim was mesmerized by Essie's charming demeanor and intelligence. She also had a quick wit, which took him by surprise when he realized she was sometimes kidding. He could have sat for hours enjoying her company, but he wanted to show her that he was a considerate person. Instead of regaling her with all his exploits, he noted that Essie had experienced quite a hectic day. He suggested that she join him for dinner the following night at the Officers' Club so that they could continue their conversation. Smiling with delight that he was so perceptive, she accepted his invitation, admitting that she was a bit tired. As she shifted to get up, Jim rushed over to pull out the chair for her. Again, she smiled at the gentlemanly gesture, thanked him for his thoughtfulness, and turned to leave.

Watching the stately librarian as she headed for the elevator to her quarters, Jim was pleased that he had made the right move. He had been so depressed over the failure of his marriage that he never anticipated in his wildest dreams that he would ever meet such an engaging woman as Essie Aldrich. He hated to admit it, but Leonard Johnson had been right. Thanks to Leonard, a chance meeting at an airport in the Philippines might turn into a year of conversations and a growing appreciation for one another's companionship…or maybe something more.

The following evening Jim came well prepared after doing a little research about South Carolina where Essie said she was born. He would wait to tell her about his experience of landing in Mr. Oates wheat field—somewhere between Shelby and Kings Mountain, North Carolina—until she knew him better. First impressions are potent, and he hoped to make a good one. He didn't want to come across as the Hollywood version of a jet jockey. Essie had probably brushed aside her share of those types. No, he was going for Ora's frequent description of what a gentleman was.

As a sumptuous seafood dinner was served, Jim considered his options. He couldn't discuss his military mission in Southeast Asia. Besides, he didn't want to appear too self-centered, and so out of curiosity he asked about Essie's family and her childhood. How did she end up in such an all-encompassing job in the Far East? Bingo! He picked the perfect topic.

Essie relaxed. She was impressed that a fighter pilot was interested in learning more about her rather than trying to impress her with all he had accomplished. As it turned out, Essie had grown up in a Black community like Jim, but it was in rural South Carolina, a village called McBee. Unlike Jim's childhood in Gainsboro, a bustling urban subdivision of Roanoke, Virginia, with most of the amenities of a city, Essie lived on a farm. The Aldrich family only had access to a small grocery store, a drugstore, and a post office in the nearby village, but the family's vegetable garden was always lush with fresh produce during the warm months. By the end of summer, her mother canned enough vegetables to carry the family through the winter. A handful of constantly clucking chickens and a docile cow provided enough eggs and milk for the family of ten, so they were fairly self-sustaining and generously shared the bounty from their garden with less fortunate neighbors.

As Essie described her youth, Jim could envision the Aldrich homestead and garden, and thought back to how he managed to bring food home from Hotel Roanoke every night when he waited tables. After his father's death, Ora could scarcely make ends meet. There were times when sympathetic friends and neighbors would even bring over blocks of cheese and other essentials to help out. Jim wondered if Martha and Bernice had masked their nearly impoverished circumstances and presented themselves as "city" girls when they were away at college. Growing up in an urban area was often worn as a badge of success in the South, but clearly rural girls were better fed and equally well educated… especially if they had parents like Richard and Nancy McFarland Aldrich. As he listened to Essie talk on, Jim was touched by her candidness as he continued to mentally compare the contrast in their upbringing.

Momentarily distracted by his thoughts, Jim tuned back in to Essie's recollections about her family.

Although he was not a wealthy man, her father Richard Aldrich was a good manager and he provided well for his family. Essie's eyes lighted up as she depicted the beautiful wood panels on the side of the station wagon he brought home one afternoon. It was the first one she had ever seen, and it had three rows of seats so that it could accommodate the entire Aldrich family. Occasionally Essie's father loaded his daughters in the car, and they traveled to nearby rural communities for necessities—Hartsville for clothing and Bethune for other supplies. Her brother Richard, Jr. usually opted to stay home to watch over his frail mother who, in addition to having 8 children, had also miscarried two other dear ones.

Fascinated, Jim listened without interrupting until Essie casually mentioned that she had six sisters—Nancy, Hester, Rebecca, Greta, Precious, and Lugenia, whom the family affectionately called Jeannie. Her older brother Richard was the only boy in the family. Jim immediately tried to imagine the Aldrich family dynamics. Having to share one bathroom with his two younger sisters, Martha and Bernice, had been an unending source of discord for the three of them. How had her brother Richard survived seven sisters? He wanted to meet the stalwart soul.

Essie explained that her father had been the overseer of a peach farm, a demanding job that involved his hiring as well as firing workers. He also managed the payroll. Jim began to realize Essie had been a precocious youngster who excelled in math when she described doing the calculations and helping her father maintain the payroll records. She pointed out that her father always cross-checked her work. Then as an afterthought, she hesitantly added that only once had her father indicated she made a mistake. When he realized she was actually correct, he commended her but no apology was forthcoming. She didn't protest. Instead, she said that she made a note of how she would treat people under similar circumstances when she was an adult. Jim understood her reticence to confront her father. He had grown up with the Ten Commandments, too. "Honor thy father and mother" was only superseded by one.

Visualizing what seemed like Essie's idyllic childhood, compared to his own, was thought-provoking. It reminded Jim of the joyous summer he spent with his Aunt Lily and Uncle Henry. He could share that experience with her. It had been one of the happiest times of his youth. Late each night on Uncle Henry's farm after everyone was tucked under Aunt Lily's handmade quilts, it was so quiet that Jim could hear the night song of a cricket chorus as he fell asleep. It was the first time he realized how heartbreaking the situation was back home. Each night when he looked out his dormer window at the stars, he would say a prayer for his father. Then he would crawl into bed and put a pillow over his head to block out the death rattle of his father's intermittent gasps for air throughout the night. Jim wondered how Essie would react to hearing about Sam's illness and the pall that hung over Jim's youth. Should he share something that personal? Her reaction might be a mirror to reflect the truth. He'd never really had a confidante. Maybe in time…

Alternately listening to Essie's animated accounts of her upbringing and drifting in and out of his own memories, Jim couldn't help but make painful comparisons. Nurtured by loving parents and closely nestled midst all the diverse personalities and talents of her siblings—especially Jeannie who Essie emphasized was 18 months and 7 days younger than she, but as dear to her as a twin—Essie Aldrich had grown to be a mature, empathetic, intelligent and confident woman. In spite of the brevity of childhood, those years indelibly imprinted her entire life. It was reassuring just listening to the mellow tempo of her voice and the occasional laughter that her memories evoked for her. She was also a generous listener, fully attentive to whatever Jim shared.

He didn't want the conversation to end, but Jungle Survival Training awaited him at the break of dawn so after dinner he walked Essie back to her nearby quarters. He was heartened when she invited him up for a quick night cap before he headed back to the VOQ. Essie was the consummate hostess. She shared a cocktail with Jim and wished him well as he stood to leave. Instinctively, Jim took off his watch and handed it to Essie along with his briefcase, keys, and camera and asked her to keep them until he returned. Startled at first, Essie agreed to secure his few valuables in the heavy black trunk where she kept her own.

She admitted that during her very first week in the Philippines, her brand new camera disappeared from her quarters after the maids completed their cleaning duties for the day. Rampant thievery was the dark side of the economy in the Philippines. Essie understood why Jim didn't want to leave anything valuable behind, so she locked everything in her trunk for safekeeping, joined him in the elevator as he was leaving, and wished Jim good luck. This time he took a chance and kissed her on the cheek before he slipped off into the heat of the night and headed to the VOQ for a few winks of sleep.

Jolted awake only a few hours later by his buzzing alarm clock, Jim stumbled out of bed, stepped in and out of a cold shower, and donned his fatigues. Fortunately, he had packed his gear the previous afternoon. There was only time for a quick breakfast before joining the two-dozen other military guys being transported by bus across Luzon Island for Jungle Survival School or "Snake School" as some previous graduates nicknamed it.

Jim had been through similar training at Stead AFB in Reno, Nevada, in 1965 before he arrived in Vietnam as the war suddenly escalated. What had previously been referred to as the Vietnam Conflict—with U.S. involvement labeled as a "police action"— blew up into an undeclared full scale war when President Lyndon Johnson ordered troops to Vietnam to stabilize a collapsing government in the South. It was his intention to preserve democracy in South Vietnam by halting the encroaching communist government in the North. Huge numbers of American military were nearly circumnavigating the globe to stem the tide of Hanoi's insurgency. Spirits were high among the troops, but U.S. involvement in the conflict between the North and South Vietnamese had vocal detractors as well as supporters at home in America, especially as the war raged on for years.

Returning to Southeast Asia in 1971 to complete his previous tour, which was interrupted when he was shot down over the outskirts of Hanoi, Jim continued to observe how much had changed. President Richard Nixon was working to bring U.S. troops back home. Pacific Air Forces (PACAF) Jungle Training was still critical, though. The United States Air Force had learned harsh lessons that led to an intense onsite course at Luzon focused on SERE—Survival, Evasion, Resistance, Escape. Some of the tactics taught were based on input from downed pilots who were rescued as well as POWs when they were released…a sore reminder to Jim. He was still waiting for word about Pogreba, who seemed to have vanished off the surface of the earth, and Fred Cherry, still languishing as a POW in Hanoi.

Able to compartmentalize the various aspects of his life and focus accordingly, Jim was especially interested, now that he was back in Thailand, on the impact of a substance being used for defoliation to minimize the enemy's cover in the jungle. Knowing the irreparable damage to his father's lungs from all the chemicals Sam ingested as he repaired train engines, Jim wondered if our troops, as well as the enemy, would be impacted by chemicals used to precipitate defoliation. Several years later, he would learn the answer to his question in a disturbing report on Agent Orange.

When Jim returned at dusk after two weeks of jungle training, he rushed right over to Essie's quarters and called for her to come down and join him. He wanted to retrieve his belongings, ask her out to dinner, and pick up where they had left off with their conversation about their families.

Essie had just returned from the library and was still dressed in a short-sleeved white linen suit with a crimson silk blouse. Always so stylish and attractive, she looked like she was ready to pose for the cover of Vogue magazine instead of returning home from a busy day at work. She smiled but then broke into laughter when Jim explained that he had just come back from the jungle training course, and he would like to take her out to dinner. His fatigues looked like they hadn't been washed for a week, his boots were caked with patches of mud, and there was no sign that he had access to deodorant during his training. He realized what he must look like when she responded, "Yes, I'd like to join you . . . after you shower."

Half an hour later, Jim arrived in his freshly pressed uniform with the silver eagle pinned above his left breast pocket. He cut a handsome figure, but one look at Essie as she stepped out of the elevator of her building took his breath away. She wore a pastel flowered dress of voile that fell in flowing folds below her knee. A simple gold cross hung from the delicate gold chain around her neck. Poised and understated, she looked elegant. He couldn't wait to resume their conversation.

Over dinner Jim learned that Essie's family was as focused on the education of their children as his mother Ora was. Neither Richard nor Nancy Aldrich was a high school graduate, but Essie's father was very knowledgeable and intellectually curious. Richard Aldrich drove to Bethune once a week to teach night classes about agriculture, and though there was no time for him to seek higher education himself, he was determined that all his children would graduate from college. The public schools in McBee accepted students from "primer" or pre-school through 10th grade. Then the family had to drive them to Mather

Academy in Camden, South Carolina, for 11th and 12th grade. Mather, a Methodist-sponsored private school, was a 54-mile round trip distance from McBee, and so the children lived in dormitories on campus throughout the school year, returning home only for Christmas, Easter, and summer vacation. Richard made sure his progeny were not spoiled, though. Soon after they returned home, they were back in the fields working the crops.

Essie was sixth in the pecking order of the children and when she graduated from high school, she was offered a scholarship to the University of South Carolina in Columbia. Instead, she turned it down to attend Bennett College in Greensboro, North Carolina, because it was farther away, almost to the Virginia border. She dreamed of traveling and this was the first step.

Remembering how hard it had been for Ora to send her three youngsters to college, Jim marveled at Richard Aldrich's unflinching commitment to his eight children…especially his seven daughters. Essie described the love she felt for her father when he came home late one afternoon and shared a conversation he had with the owner of the McBee grocery store, a White man. He suggested Mr. Aldrich was wasting his money sending girls off to college and advised him to invest more heavily in his son. Essie spoke with pride and deep appreciation about her father's visionary attitude regarding women. He wanted his daughters to be educated and self-sufficient.

Jim was also surprised to learn that Essie went to Bennett College and in checking on birthdays, he noted that his younger sister Bernice probably was at Bennett at the same time as some of the Aldrich sisters. Essie confirmed that not only Bernice but also Martha had attended Bennett when she was there, but one year Essie's father could only afford to fund three of his children's higher education so he decided to let Nancy, who was 12 years older than Essie, decide which daughter would sit out for a year. As the eldest, Nancy decided Essie would be the one, reasoning that she was the most avid student among the daughters and would not lose interest in earning her degree even if she had to drop out of college for a year. Nancy had been right, but Essie felt punished instead of being rewarded for her dedication to becoming a librarian, a decision she made as a young girl when she first fell in love with books.

By the end of the evening Jim felt like he knew Essie to her heart, and he didn't want to lose her, but where were they headed? As friends or maybe more? He was scheduled to fly to Nakhon Phanom AB (Air Base) in Thailand in the morning. Of course, he could call her frequently through the military communication system, but that wasn't like actually being with someone. He felt such a strong connection with her and wondered if she felt it, too. Then he remembered Leonard Johnson's comment about one aspect of Essie's job. As the military's Head Librarian, she traveled to each of the libraries on military bases across Southeast Asia.

Before parting he asked how to get in touch with her by phone and also if she would be traveling the circuit between all the military libraries any time soon. Would Thailand be on the route? He could not conceal his feelings when she responded, "I will be at Nakhon Phanom in two months.

"I'll be waiting," he said.

In spite of their demanding careers, Essie and Jim share matching smiles as their friendship offers moments of happiness in war-torn Southeast Asia.

CHAPTER 28

CROSSROADS AT NAKHON PHANOM

It was late in the afternoon at NKP (Nakhon Phanom AB) in northeastern Thailand. A heavy rain had made its daily impact and the intense heat had relinquished somewhat, but everyone outside would soon be sweating again. It was a moment of respite to relish, though. The air was fresh and the jungle near the perimeter of the base glistened.

It had been two months since Jim had seen Essie, but he had made good use of the time apart by calling her every night for at least a brief conversation. During the day he kept a sheet of paper folded in his breast pocket, and he frequently pulled it out to pen an anecdote or make an observation that he thought might intrigue her. Sending a letter full of questions to be answered had become an almost daily ritual for him. His hope was that if he provided enough incentive, Essie would respond.

Back in the Philippines, Essie was too busy reading reviews of books, magazines and newspapers to be as prolific a letter writer as Jim, who rivaled Victorian lovers known for their intensity as correspondents. Since Essie was the consummate professional, she penned only short notes at first, but eventually she trusted Jim enough to share some of the challenges she faced in her job.

Essie was a quiet but strong leader who loved living abroad. Still, cultural differences sometimes presented frustrating situations, and she had recently learned some disturbing information. One of her male assistants, a native Filipino who was an entrenched staff member at the Library Center on Clark AFB, was advising various librarians not to be quite so conscientious. Otherwise, he pointed out, their efforts might indicate that more work could be accomplished by fewer people, and that could put their position as well as the jobs of others at risk.

He was quite heavy-handed in dealing with the female staff members and insisted that everything had to be approved by him, a hierarchy that he had covertly established. When one of the young librarians finally revealed what was going on, Essie was disappointed in his lack of ethics and made it clear that she was in charge. Inspiring deserving staff members was her preferred style of leadership, but she was quite capable of admonishing manipulators, regardless of tenure or titles. Jim was duly impressed. After two months of correspondence, he was eager to see her.

Excited as he headed to the flight line to await Essie's arrival, Colonel James Randall was deep in thought. He had worked very hard to establish himself as a talent in the cockpit, but he was also a team player; his rapid rise to full colonel was the result. At each new assignment, he attained the respect of his commanders for his analytical approach to solving problems, as well as for his expertise as a pilot. Jim exuded a level of confidence that made him stand out among his colleagues. He had reached the point that he no longer noticed whether or not there were any other Black aviators in his unit. It didn't matter because he felt equal to every pilot with whom he worked, and he was proud of what he had accomplished.

Even so, when he considered the faith the U.S. Air Force had placed in Essie, he was deeply moved by what a young Black woman from McBee, South Carolina, had achieved. It was obvious how much her position as the Head Librarian for the military in Southeast Asia meant to her. It was a crowning achievement, and yet he was beginning to realize how important she had become to him, too. Was it selfish to even consider asking her to give up her career for him? He had planned never to marry again, but he had to admit that he couldn't imagine life without her. What a quandary.

As the military transport landed, Jim waited with the gathered crowd on the flight line for the passengers to disembark. Spotting Essie dressed in a pastel blue linen suit and carrying a leather briefcase at her side, he smiled at how she stood out like a glimpse of home in the midst of a sea of uniformed men. Suddenly, when a young fellow in a neatly pressed blue shirt and trousers made a beeline toward her, Jim realized he was either the head librarian from the NKP Library and Education Center or more likely a staff member assigned to meet his superior, so Jim hurried to catch up with him. As the two men reached Essie, the young fellow nervously welcomed her and explained that he had reserved overnight facilities for her at the VOQ but had forgotten to pick up a key so he would accompany her on the NKP base bus to see that she was settled before her meetings the next morning.

That's when Jim stepped in and assured the younger fellow that he had dropped by the VOQ, picked up a key, and had a car waiting to take Miss Aldrich to her quarters. Flummoxed and uncertain what to do but noting that a USAF colonel was addressing him, the young man looked desperately toward the Head Librarian for 13th Air Force. Essie smiled and graciously thanked him for coming out to welcome her. She reassured him that she looked forward to working with the library staff the following day but that she had plans for the evening. Relieved, the young librarian mumbled a few words of appreciation, looked curiously at Jim, and without further question he hustled over to join the newly arrived passengers boarding the bus idling at the edge of the flight line.

As a uniformed driver rushed to take her briefcase and baggage, Jim hugged Essie and led her to the military vehicle at his disposal. Dropping by the VOQ so she could check in and freshen up before they grabbed a quick lunch together, Jim reassured her that he had everything under control. He revealed that he had special plans for the evening as he returned her to the VOQ afterward, but he purposely left her wondering what he meant. This could be a turning point in their relationship, and he hoped to create a little mystery, a foreshadowing of their future.

When Jim arrived to pick up Essie for dinner later that evening, she was dressed more formally in a lovely floral-patterned gown that reached to the top of her white patent leather heels. He felt so light-hearted that it was as though they were youngsters headed for the prom until a burst of firepower, that was far too close, shattered the magic…an intrusive reminder of the war's proximity. North Vietnam and the demilitarized zone that traced the 17th parallel were only 75 miles or so away and the guerrilla forces of the Pathet Lao just across the Mekong River in neighboring Laos were unpredictable. Although Thailand was not officially a part of the ongoing military aggression in that area of the world, sapper attacks from small enemy cells were always a possibility. Essie was well aware of impending danger, but she never flinched as Jim escorted her to the car. She had courage.

Once they arrived at the Officers' Club, Jim led Essie to a separate dining room reserved for colonels and generals, and as he proudly entered the double doors with Essie on his arm, he announced, "Gentlemen!" Suddenly all the high-ranking officers, seated at candle-lit dinner tables covered with white tablecloths, jumped to their feet and, noting the presence of a lady, they stood in place until Jim seated Essie at the only table adorned with a special bouquet of tropical flowers. The delightful look of surprise on Essie's face as she reached to squeeze his hand in appreciation simply made Jim's night.

Since he had given the Officers' Club staff specific directions about what and how everything was to be served throughout the evening, Jim and Essie enjoyed an exquisite Thai meal without interruption, and the other diners respected their privacy. Essie had once expressed her desire to travel to Australia, but she was full of excitement when Jim revealed he was arranging a trip to Singapore for the two of them, once they could match their schedules. Neither of them wanted the evening to end, but Essie had commitments to fulfill the following two days, and so Jim dutifully returned her to the VOQ before midnight. It felt as though his feet hardly touched the ground as he walked back to the car.

Just as he had hoped, Jim was able to spend the next two evenings with Essie in a more secluded setting where he broached the subject of his circumstances. From the beginning he had been honest not only about the failure of his marriage but also the importance of his family. He had implied he did not intend to marry again, and Essie admitted she was happily married to her job, but what began as friendship had developed into something much more meaningful to Jim. She was a beloved companion.

Prior to Essie's arrival at NKP, Jim had spent late nights looking at the logistics—not in his career but in his life. No matter what happened, he would not waiver in his commitment to the monthly allotment for his mother and soon he would be accepting both legal and appropriate financial arrangements for Mary Ann and his children. These were his priorities. It was a point of honor. He was taking a risk, but he wanted to be straightforward with Essie, especially if she was interested in pursuing a relationship with him.

There weren't many options for privacy on NKP, especially since he and Essie were high profile figures, but he picked up a catered picnic dinner from the Officers' Club and took Essie to a quiet niche on NKP that was public enough not to be considered clandestine. Essie seemed happy with the change of pace. Though she loved traveling, it had its hectic moments and she enjoyed sharing what had happened throughout the day, beginning with her briefing with the base commander.

Jim was genuinely interested but apparently Essie could tell he had something on his mind, and she actually provided the segue for his expressing his thoughts. The mood shifted as Jim explained all the complications of pursuing a relationship, but he concluded with his hope that she was interested in sharing a future with him. It was not a marriage proposal. He posed more questions than promises really.

Essie had listened intently without interrupting so Jim had no idea where he stood, but after an interminably long moment of silence, she smiled and placed his hand in hers. She expressed her depth of respect for the way he valued his family and affirmed that she supported his determination to continue to be the bulwark he had always been for them—both emotionally and financially. She would have expected nothing less, she assured him.

Her compassion opened the floodgates, and Jim felt tears pooling in his eyes as he shared the grief of losing his father…listening to Sam struggling just to breathe…watching his father work hard among healthier men so that he could support his family…being unable to shake the unbearable loneliness of Sam's passing. As Essie consoled him and pointed out that his loss at 15 years old was unimaginable, Jim tried to explain why Mary Ann's inability to quit smoking had become such a wedge between them. Essie was deeply moved by such pain and listened with an empathetic heart…valuing his suffering.

Sharing his deepest feelings so openly and honestly was cathartic for Jim, and Essie seemed more at ease than usual as they laughed and traded stories the following afternoon. When Jim escorted Essie to the flight line to catch the military transport back to the Philippines, he felt as though they had become a couple. The sun was already shining with intensity, mirroring Jim's sense of hope. After years of hiding his broken heart, he felt the relief of having someone share his pain. When he kissed Essie farewell on the cheek, her strong, supportive hug goodbye was the one he had desperately needed as a grief-stricken 15-year-old boy. It was the healing gift of loving kindness.

After a day of attending briefings, writing assessments, and dealing with paperwork regarding his position as Vice Commander of Task Force Alpha, Jim takes a moment to reflect on Essie's visit to Nakon Phanom. (Photo courtesy of Regional History & Genealogy, Pikes Peak Library District, Image #412-140)

CHAPTER 29

HONORING A LEAP OF FAITH

Jim had not entered one single minute of flight time in the cockpit on his pilot's log throughout his entire tour at Nakhon Phanom, a nightmare for a seasoned fighter pilot, but he had accomplished something more significant. While returning to Thailand to complete his action-packed tour in 1965 that was cut short over the western outskirts of Hanoi, he had found a partner. Essie Aldrich was one of the biggest surprises of his life, and meeting her was all thanks to Leonard Johnson, his intuitive friend and previous flight surgeon.

Since Jim continued to correspond daily and make phone calls to Essie each night, the conversations had heightened their understanding of one another, but he was due to return to the States in April 1972 and time was running out. He had a lot of life-changing decisions to make. It was already rumored that he would be going to Eglin AFB, which was an exciting possibility. Eglin was situated in the panhandle of northwest Florida near Panama City and Pensacola, and the vast 464,000-acre base had a lengthy history as an important proving ground for the development and testing of weaponry and aircraft as well as a training ground for covert missions. Doolittle's Raiders had practiced there in the 1940s in preparation for the legendary attack on Japan. More recently in 1970, Army Colonel Arthur "Bull" Simons trained with a select Special Forces unit from August to September prior to deploying to Thailand in November. His mission—lead an attempt to rescue POWS from the notorious Son Tay prison camp in North Vietnam.

At any other point in his life, especially when he was young, Jim would have jumped at the chance, but he had decided he wanted to spend the rest of his life with Essie. Faced with a situation somewhat like the characters in O'Henry's poignant *Gift of the Magi*, Jim was willing to make a sacrifice equal to Essie's giving up her dream job in the Philippines. He had not anticipated that he and Essie might experience a similar outcome to the one in the classic O'Henry tale. He just wanted to be honorable.

Lawyers and the court system would figure out the legal aspects of his divorce and make arrangements for his financial responsibility in ensuring the future of Mary Ann and the children. He wanted the best for them, and he planned to comply without question. His military allotment for his mother Ora would continue as it had for decades, but what about Essie?

He knew she had researched openings for librarians on U.S. Air Force bases across the country and had found two possibilities in Colorado Springs, one at Ent AFB and the other at the Chidlaw Building. If he could get his assignment to Eglin AFB changed to the Chidlaw Building, he and Essie could marry and also continue their careers together. Essie would certainly be the top candidate for any head librarian's job in Colorado Springs, though he realized that a stateside position would not compare to accommodating the military across the entirety of Southeast Asia. Likewise, Jim's mission at the Chidlaw Building would not be as thrilling as leading a flight of F-105s across the Pacific or being an F-111 test pilot. Instead, he would be head of Operations at Chidlaw, but he would have access to nearby military bases and the opportunity to fly again. It was a compromise.

Adjusting to a different approach to his career, Jim read everything he could find at the NKP library about the Chidlaw Building. It served as the headquarters for ADC (Aerospace Defense Command). Located near Ent AFB in the heart of Colorado Springs and leased by the U.S. Air Force, the Chidlaw Building featured three floors, one of which was purposely built underground, and since there were no windows, other than at the entrance, it was designed to be a self-contained fortress, a miniature version of a military base within a massive 300,000 square foot concrete building. For added security there was a civilian guard force. Jim was intrigued and actually looking forward to a tour of Chidlaw and the first briefing about his position there.

Colorado Springs was also home to NORAD (North American Aerospace Defense Command), an elaborate communications nerve center that was created in agreement with Canada for the protection of the North American continent against the increasing threat of Soviet aggression. Designed to be developed within the granite walls inside of Cheyenne Mountain to make it virtually impenetrable, it had taken years to blast through solid granite in order to create a gigantic cave-like open space suitable for the military's visionary purpose—a multi-service unified command capable of decisive and immediate interaction between Army, Navy, and Air Force units. It was originally dubbed CONAD (Continental Air Defense Command).

NORAD was a state-of-the-art facility that was closely guarded and inaccessible to literally everyone except those who worked "in the mountain." Rumors circulated about military technicians who sat monitoring the atmosphere and the entire world on gigantic screens like those in movie theatres. The truth was that NORAD was far more remarkable and futuristic than even the most imaginative mind could conceive at that point in history.

Colorado Springs was a beautiful place to settle down. Jim was certain that Essie would love it. Pikes Peak hovered protectively over the city and created magnificent views from every angle. There were multiple military installations—Fort Carson Army Post, Ent AFB, Peterson AFB, and also the U.S. Air Force Academy. Each installation would accept the Randalls' ID cards and permit use of their facilities. Everything was falling into place. It would be good to be back in the States again.

Jim alerted Essie to his plans weeks before his departure date, but he decided to wait until he found a suitable home in Colorado Springs before asking her to marry him. Since Leonard had been the reason Jim met Essie in the first place, Jim took the flight surgeon into his confidence but swore him to secrecy. Leonard advised, "A woman likes to know," regarding his friend's decision to wait until the last minute to pop the question, but Jim was determined to make his intentions a big surprise.

In late April of 1972, Leonard and Essie arrived at the airport in the Philippines to wish Jim well and see him off. Jim was full of excitement over his big secret and eager to finish all his elaborate arrangements in Colorado Springs. He didn't realize Essie was experiencing mixed emotions. She was sad to see Jim depart for the States and hoped his seeming lack of regret over leaving her behind was due to the relief of finishing his tour in war-torn Southeast Asia. Leonard, on the other hand, was curious about how everything was going to turn out. He worried that Jim's secrecy would create a Shakespearean comedy of errors. Jim was juggling a lot of balls.

As soon as he boarded the military transport back to the States, Jim thought of all the things he wished he had said before he left so he pulled out a sheet of paper from his breast pocket and began writing; it was second nature to him now. When he finally reached Colorado Springs, he called Essie without even checking the difference in time zones.

The first weeks after reporting to duty at Chidlaw, he was inundated with tours, briefings, and evenings filled with studying manuals, but he made a point of checking in with two local realtors—Bill Jackson and Charlie Couch, a former pilot he'd known in Las Vegas. He dispatched the pair to search for a suitable house for his future bride. It was a friendly competition between the two, but Charlie came up with the winning piece of real estate. Without being asked, they continued to help Jim out in preparation for Essie's arrival, and in appreciation for their continued assistance, he asked both men to act as witnesses at the wedding.

Everyone at the Chidlaw Building knew Jim was soon to be married. The only person who didn't know was Essie! Finally, Jim had all phases of his plans either in process or fully completed, and so he sat down on the chair-less carpet in the living room of his new house to make his usual Saturday morning call to the Philippines. When Essie answered the phone, he nervously teased her and asked about the latest news from Southeast Asia and listened patiently as she filled him in on all that had happened that week.

The minute there was a slight lull in the conversation, he slowly began with, "Essie, I love you and—"

"Oh! You said it! You actually said it!" she exclaimed, and Jim proposed over the phone.

Leonard was right. Words matter. Women want to know.

The wheels were in motion for the wedding to take place on September 13th. Consequently, all future phone calls and letters focused on Essie's input about the details. She wanted formal dining room furniture by Henredon, so she sent a catalog from the furniture manufacturer in North Carolina to Jim and marked her choice. He placed the order immediately. Once she knew Jim's position at the Chidlaw Building was official, she sent her resume to Ent AFB as well as the Chidlaw Building since both libraries had suitable openings. There was so much to do, that months flew by like days, but the excited bride-to-be arrived in Colorado Springs the first week of September.

In a ceremony held at St. John's Church in the heart of Colorado Springs, Reverend Milton Proby officiated while the rival realtors, Bill and Charlie, stood at each side of the couple as witnesses. Essie, wearing a long, pale green dress, smiled at Jim in his dark suit and mouthed *I love you* with a smile as the minister asked them to repeat their vows to each other. By the time the couple exchanged wedding rings and Reverend Proby proclaimed them to be "man and wife," it had begun raining outside. The wedding party hoisted umbrellas as they left the church, and Jim told Essie, "Lift your dress," so the hem wouldn't drag through the mud puddles. Charlie couldn't resist the urge to tease Jim one last time and he called out, "Can't you wait until you get to the hotel?" In spite of the ominous clouds overhead, the Randalls marriage began with laughter.

Since Jim was 46 years old and Essie only three years younger, they were both eager to be settled in their new home. For the first time in his life, Jim had purchased a house for his family in Las Vegas before he left for Thailand. Prior to that, Jim and his family had either rented or lived in base housing, but this was the first time Essie had ever bought a home, so she and Jim were both excited about creating a place of their own.

As soon as Jim informed Ora of his marriage, she rushed to Bernice's house to check out Essie in her daughter's yearbook from Bennett. Ora had already advised Jim that she planned to come for a visit within the next few weeks, which he fully expected, and over the weekend he was busy putting in the maze of a sprinkler system and laying sod in the back yard in preparation for Mother Randall's scrutiny. For years he had lived up to the expectations about yard maintenance on bases across the globe, and he was always "mower-ready" to groom the landscape around his quarters. Colorado's arid climate, after living midst the thick foliage of Asia's jungles, was proving to be a challenge, but the friendliness of his next-door neighbors, Martha and Jerry, made up for it. One afternoon Jerry leaned over the back fence at the end of Jim's latest tussle with sod and sprinkler systems and handed him two huge pots of flaming red geraniums. That was the beginning of many over-the-back yard fence conversations between the two.

Martha and Jerry had two teenage sons, but the most outspoken member of the family turned out to be their precocious 3-year-old daughter, Laura, who adopted Essie and Jim immediately. Each day when her older brothers were supposed to be monitoring her latest antics, Laura would traipse over to the neighbors, stretch high enough to ring the doorbell, and ask, "Can Mister Colonel Randall come out to play?" Bemused by the boldness of such a little girl, Jim would often go outside and spend time with her by including her in yard work or a game.

Laura included Essie in her plans when she was bored and Jim was not available. She was remarkably observant and always interested in her good-natured neighbor's stylish outfits, especially when one day she saw Essie sitting on her deck and enjoying a sugar-rimmed glass of ice tea. She was wearing an exotic caftan splashed with brightly colored tropical flowers. Laura, who had been kicking a ball in the back yard, was full of questions. What kind of dress is that? Where did you get it? What is Thailand? Where is it? Essie responded that she'd tell Laura all about it after she finished preparing lunch, and she went back into the house to finish slicing strawberries and pitting cherries for a fruit salad. A few minutes later there was a knock at the front door. Pushing the bowl full of fresh fruit aside on the counter, Essie walked down the hall to the front door, opened it, and looked down. There was Laura, waiting for answers. She quickly learned Essie would spend all day with her if she asked enough questions, and sometimes she'd even share her lunch.

Jim and Essie had decided to buy one room of furniture at a time, and so when Ora arrived sooner than expected, their new home was not yet fully furnished. The back yard was beginning to flourish and the formal Henredon furniture graced the dining room, but Essie had just begun designing the style of furniture and color scheme that she wanted for the living room. "Mother Randall," as the family had always called her, immediately asserted herself when Essie took her new mother-in-law shopping with her.

At the grocery story, Essie pleasantly considered all Ora's strong opinions about each and every product while Essie quietly purchased what she had planned to buy in the first place without Ora noticing. The shopping trip to a high-end furniture store to check out their inventory of living room furniture was a different story. Essie was especially interested in finding a specific style of upholstered chairs when Ora immediately pointed to a white couch and loveseat as the best choice in her opinion. With her usual poise, Essie firmly explained that she had a different color scheme in mind that would tie in with the accent colors in the carpet she and Jim had purchased.

Meanwhile, Jim was beginning to get worried. His wife and mother had been gone much longer than expected. When the two returned home chatting amiably about all the decisions they had made, he was pleasantly surprised and curious about what had happened. Clearly, Ora accepted her new daughter-in-law as an equal. Essie had won her first major challenge and avoided a possibly life-long roadblock. When Jim asked how she had pulled off such an unexpected *coup d'etat,* Essie wisely avoided making an issue of Ora's sometimes frustrating personality traits and simply explained, "I just treated her with the same respect I show my mother." Jim breathed a sigh of relief.

Unfortunately, there was no simple answer for an unexpected challenge that could have changed the dynamic of their marriage. They had planned everything so meticulously that they never saw it coming.

Although Essie was overqualified for the librarian position at both the Chidlaw Building and Ent AFB, she was denied the job. The reason? She was married to an officer who held a major role regarding both installations. Essie was stunned. Her career had been the focus of her life, and though she was happily married, the thought of not being able to support herself independently, should hardship befall them, was inconceivable to her. Jim was equally shocked by the military's stance, but he reassured Essie that he was fully capable of handling all his financial commitments and that she would never have to be concerned. "I will always take care of you. You don't have to worry," he said. "I promise." At the time Essie had no way of knowing they would spend 47 years of adventures together, but she took a leap of faith and believed in Jim.

Life continued to fall into place for the couple like a track meet…one hurdle after another. Next up was a trip to Las Vegas. The last time Jim had been with his family was at Louise's graduation so he was apprehensive, but Essie was looking forward to meeting Mary Ann and the children. Essie had grown up in a large, loving family that abided by the Golden Rule, and she still followed its wisdom. She planned to treat Jim's family with the same love and respect she had always enjoyed. When Essie and Jim arrived in Las Vegas, they registered at a hotel, unpacked their luggage, and changed into more comfortable attire. Then Jim turned to Essie and explained that he planned to go visit Mary Ann and the children.

"What are you going to do?" he asked.

"I'm going with you," she answered. Essie entwined her arm in his and as he closed the hotel room door, he smiled with pride at her confidence and courage.

The visit went well. Essie arrived with a gift and a heart full of compassion. After getting to know Essie's kind nature, Mary Ann simplified their relationship. She always introduced Essie as "the wife of the father of my children." For children, of course, divorce is never that simple.

Jim thrived at the Chidlaw Building. Being an experienced combat pilot and a former test pilot with exceptional problem-solving skills, he was a major asset to the command, so that kept him on the move constantly. He was checked out in numerous aircraft and also familiar with many of the engineers still with General Dynamics as well as figures in Congress like Howard Cannon, who shared Jim's experience of having been shot down.

One of the most exciting moments in his life, though, happened in 1975 when an officer whom he had admired greatly throughout his entire career became the incoming Commander in Chief of ADC, newly promoted General Daniel "Chappie" James himself! To serve under the renowned pilot, the first African American 4-star general, was not

Sitting atop his desk, legendary General Daniel "Chappie" James, Jr. becomes Commander in Chief of North American Aerospace Defense Command in Colorado Springs, and receives his 4th star in September 1975. (Photo courtesy Regional History & Genealogy, Pikes Peak Library District, Image #342-449)

something Jim had ever anticipated, and here he was not only serving under Chappie but also attending briefings the general directed frequently.

Throughout the majority of his career, Jim had worked in base operations because he wanted to be where the action was and where he felt he could be of the greatest use. Time was of the essence on the flight line, especially when he was called upon to organize major missions. As a result, Jim checked his watch constantly. It had become a conditioned response type of reflex, and he no longer was even aware of how frequently he lifted his wrist to note the time.

One morning when the staff assembled for an early briefing, apparently Chappie had been detained and was running a bit late. As the general rushed into the designated room to begin the briefing, Jim instinctively lifted his wrist and noted the time. The ever-observant general caught the slight movement in his peripheral vision, and as he strode to the front of the room, he made an acerbic remark to let Jim know he was displeased. No one in the room seemed to notice, but the minute was frozen in time for Jim as he looked at his wrist still mid-air and knew instantly that the barb was intended for him.

Chagrined, Jim pondered how to ameliorate his situation, but Ora had always taught him to take responsibility for his actions rather than make matters worse by trying to explain himself out of an awkward situation. Miserable and distracted throughout the briefing, Jim tried to be very attentive and waited until he filed out of the room with all the other officers at the conclusion of the meeting. "Sorry, sir," he mumbled as he walked past Chappie, who acknowledged with a nod.

Nothing more was ever said, but Jim knew he could not afford another slip. He would be considered insubordinate and nothing could be farther from the truth. He had always been deeply respectful of his superiors, but he knew he probably could not break such an entrenched habit. There was only one solution. Every day when he was to attend a briefing with his imposing 6'4" commanding general, Jim removed his watch and slipped it into his pocket, where it remained for the duration of Chappie's comments.

Jim was well aware that he would be in his 50s by the end of his tour at Chidlaw. Time was catching up with him. Like all fighter pilots, his days in the cockpit were numbered and the pain of spinal injuries endured in his unintended parachute landing near Hanoi were becoming chronic. Thankfully, Essie was understanding. That helped.

Essie was also adjusting to a very different life style. She joined the Officers' Wives' Club and volunteered for many committees that kept her busy interacting with important figures in Colorado Springs who appreciated her expertise. Her focus in life never veered from supporting Jim in his endeavors, though. He was her priority. She felt fortunate that Mary Ann trusted her to welcome Patricia, the youngest of Jim's children, to their home in Colorado every summer, and of course, there was always Laura, their delightfully inquisitive and ever-present little neighbor. Essie thought of her own mother often and tried to treat all the youngsters in her life with the understanding and love that she had enjoyed as a child.

Sadly, Laura's family was hit with an irreversible tragedy. Laura's father Jerry experienced a devastating stroke which left him unable to speak other than letting loose a swear word or two out of sheer frustration. When Laura's mother Martha worked to get her real estate license to help support the family, Laura's brothers were charged with more responsibility for Laura. Essie and Jim tried to be even more solicitous toward the child, but she was usually a step or two ahead of them and always figuring out how to be even more independent. Early one morning Essie answered the phone and it was Laura asking, "Miz Colonel Randall, can I come over?" When Essie asked Laura how she got her phone number, Laura quickly replied, "Mother wrote it on the book by the phone."

Amazed by Laura's resourcefulness, both Essie and Jim fell in love with the tiny tyke. She always left them wondering what she would come up with next. It seldom took very long to find out. One late summer afternoon Jim was out in the back yard digging a trench deep enough to plant several flowering golden potentilla to create a bank of shrubs across the back fence. Laura was busy planting a pansy in a flowerpot he had given her so she could take it home to her family. Watching all the activity in the back yard through the kitchen window and realizing how hot Jim and his little apprentice must be, Essie made a big pitcher of icy lemonade and had just set it on the patio table with two glasses when Jim called over to his industrious little sidekick, "Laura, will you get me a glass of lemonade, please?" Both he and Essie nearly convulsed with laughter when Laura stood up and with her hands on her hips she defiantly responded, "Mister Colonel Randall, I'm not your wife, and I'm not your servant either!"

Jim never asked a favor of little Laura again, but he sure hoped the Montesorri School she was to begin attending in the fall wouldn't dampen that outrageously independent spirit of hers. As far as he was concerned, she was born to be a fighter pilot!

CHAPTER 30

TAKING COMMAND

After four compelling years at the Chidlaw building, Jim felt he had played a significant role in Aerospace Defense Command's visionary preparation for a drastically changing future. He was reassured about the security of the country, but personally, he was a bit concerned about his own. He was approaching his 50th birthday in November and nearing the end of his career; future assignments would reflect that.

Consequently, Jim was surprised when he received the news about his next tour of duty. Moving to coastal north Florida was definitely going to be an adjustment, but it would be an honor to assume command of Tyndall AFB as the base commander. Perhaps his commanding general had his thumbprint on the decision. It was rumored there were issues at the base, and Jim's position at Aerospace Defense Command made him the logical choice to step in and suss things out.

On the drive home to tell Essie about the unanticipated turn of events, he reminisced over being sent TDY to Tyndall from Dover AFB for All Weather Training back in 1954. He had been only 28 years old at the time, but he was a seasoned pilot who had flown 75 combat missions over Korea. Even so, once he arrived at Tyndall for training, which would prepare him to ferry aircraft from Dover AFB to Europe, he avoided going into Panama City and other nearby southern towns adjacent to Tyndall. He intended to avert becoming entangled in any racial incidents.

Jim remembered all those weekends he stayed on base and studied instead of joining his fellow students to enjoy the good times in Panama City. It had been lonely, but it was the right decision and it resulted in his achieving the top flying grades in his class. He left Tyndall with a copy of his performance record inscribed with his commanding officer's glowing comments and a newly found confidence. He had proven to himself that he could compete at the highest level and excel, regardless of the competition. Still, it had been a lonely patch of time.

Somehow it seemed like divine justice that 22 years later he was returning to be Tyndall's base commander. Local economies—heavily dependent on the base both for commerce and help in major emergencies—would welcome Jim as an important leader and if there were any racial incidents to deal with, his opinion would count. The irony did not escape him. However, he had earned his status in the U.S. Air Force by being positive, hard-working, analytical, and a problem solver, so his goal was to continue as he always had—expect the best but be prepared for whatever might happen.

As Jim pulled into his driveway, he stared up at the magnificent view of Pikes Peak. He would miss the Rocky Mountains that sheltered Colorado Springs and produced more temperate winters within the heart of the city than in the suburbs. Cheyenne Mountain to the south of Colorado Springs concealed the arsenal of protection hidden within its belly under its soaring granite peak. NORAD was not in full view, but it was there, and its military occupants were ever watchful. Soon he and Essie would be leaving the rarefied atmosphere of life at over 6,000 feet in Colorado Springs to live near the sandy, sea-level shores of Florida's Gulf Coast.

Every military move requires extensive pre-planning, and each one presents unique challenges. Jim and Essie had enjoyed owning their home, buying new furniture, and adding decor to reflect their taste and their travels abroad, but in Florida, Jim and Essie would be expected to move into quarters designated specifically for the family of Tyndall's base commander. Since Jim knew he ultimately wanted to retire in Colorado Springs, he decided to rent their own home to a military commander at Fort Carson, the U.S. Army post south of Colorado Springs, before he set up the logistics of the move.

Meanwhile Essie, as Jim's designated navigator for the trip, researched the most interesting route to their destination. Neither of them had driven across the scenic southern part of America before, and she circled spots that were of significance on the state maps that she spread out across the dining room table. Jim planned to drive, of course, but there was a lot of interesting American history to be seen between Colorado and Florida, and neither she nor Jim wanted to miss anything as they wended their way back to the Southeast. Other than an important stopover at Maxwell AFB in Montgomery, Alabama, which Jim had scheduled, the couple was free to sightsee across the South for two weeks.

Midst the maelstrom of movers, farewell parties, final reports, and research about the Deep South, Jim and Essie finally left the dry climate and cool nights of Colorado and headed toward the heat and humidity of northwestern Florida. Both Jim and Essie had grown up in the South, and they were looking forward to having fresh seafood, oranges straight from a grove, avocados, and all the delicious cuisine available on the Gulf Coast of Florida.

When Colonel James E.P. Randall arrived at Tyndall AFB to assume his command, it was 1976, the 200th Anniversary of America's Declaration of Independence. Prior to his arrival, the local newspapers printed a definitive article about Jim's career, causing the tide of opinion among many residents to surge with approval. There was a hero in their midst, and they held a parade in his honor. Under a cloudless ultramarine blue sky in early June and with windows open wide, Jim and Essie sat in a black Cadillac, both car and driver compliments of the local dealership in Panama City, and they waved to the crowd with genuine appreciation.

Although they noticed that a few people, midst the throng of cheering supporters, seemed surprised and stopped waving as the car passed them, the couple laughed, assuming not everyone had seen the photo accompanying the article on the front page of the newspaper. Jim was the first Black officer to be selected as Tyndall's base commander, and the welcoming event was very meaningful to the Randalls.

Wishing his father Sam had lived to see the day his son was welcomed by such an enthusiastic crowd of Floridians, Jim was happy and relaxed until they arrived at their aging residence on base. The previous base commander had left for a two-week vacation rather than setting up the move to his new assignment, and so the house was not accessible to the Randalls yet, but they had decided to drive over and at least check out the grounds. The minute Jim and Essie stepped outside the car and peered through the windows of the wood-shingled residence, their first image of the aging abode was a skittering crew of squatters that had taken over the interior during the previous commander's absence. Quickly escorting his distressed wife back to the car, Jim immediately drove to the VOQ and reserved a suite where he and Essie could stay until a fumigating crew could rid the quarters of its unwelcome intruders—hordes of roaches!

Once Jim's predecessor finally returned and facilitated his move, the fumigating crew continued to decontaminate the house and entire property until their new commander deemed his quarters inhabitable. Movers appeared on the scene and Essie directed the placement of their furniture in the four-tiered quarters while Jim set about meeting all the personnel on base and listening to briefings. He knew many of the officers by name, rank, and responsibility since he interacted with the Southeast Sector at Chidlaw for four years, and this gave him an advantage. Still, he was keenly aware that his first days on the job would make a lasting impression about his leadership. Dealing with the sad state of the base commander's quarters was a strong indication that he needed to start by setting standards. By the end of Jim's first week at Tyndall, there was no doubt who was in charge!

The mission at Tyndall—the security of the Southeast Sector of the United States—was critical, and Jim was intent upon getting all the base facilities functioning at a high level to enhance the lives of those assigned to the base. Hurricane Eloise had hammered the area the previous year and repairs were still underway. Jim immediately set benchmarks and timelines for completion of major projects so that everyone was on the same page and interacting efficiently to achieve and even supersede objectives. Jim had always been goal-oriented and the example he set as he went about creating pride on the base was more effective than the usual motivational speeches.

Jim had personally benefited from the commanders who had written positive comments about his leadership qualities when he was a young officer, and he knew the fine line between critiquing rather than criticizing. He was quick to commend and encourage as well as advise how to meet expectations more effectively. He also wrote a column for the base newspaper to stay in communication with all personnel. At Chidlaw he had been an integral part of a high functioning team and he wanted to create that same environment at Tyndall.

In conversations with city officials in Panama City he realized that being a base commander was essentially akin to being the mayor of a city, but as a military officer in command he actually had more power to effect change, and he used his position judiciously. With his ready smile and quick wit, he was soon asked to speak at many local functions in Panama City and neighboring communities. Due to the demands of his position on base he was not always able to comply. On one occasion a civilian woman's group, who had been unable to book Jim as a guest speaker, asked him if his wife could be their speaker instead. Much to Jim's surprise, when he checked with Essie, she told him she was not available. He quickly learned that she did not plan to "fill in" for him. She fully supported him, but she had a demanding position of her own and did not plan to be a "second choice." Jim wisely dropped by a florist before returning home that evening.

During their four years in Colorado Springs, Essie had gotten to know the wives of several commanders, and she knew what she wanted to accomplish during their tour at Tyndall. She accepted the role of advisor to both the Officers' Wives' Club and the NCO Wives' Club at Tyndall, not to set her agenda but to offer guidance and support, which was a welcome approach to the wives on base.

Once Essie unpacked all their belongings, arranged their furniture in the various rooms of the sprawling residence, and highlighted the décor of each area with artifacts, art and mementoes from their travels across the world, she set about creating an inviting atmosphere for entertaining. Following Jim's requests, she planned to open their home to a broader cross section of people on base. Also, since she and Jim were finally back east of the Mississippi and in the South, they hoped family members would join them for a visit.

Jim and Essie hosted many small dinner parties during their first months at Tyndall and entertained primarily commanders and their wives as well as visiting dignitaries. Essie was an excellent cook and she immediately won over dinner guests with her culinary talents. With the fall holidays approaching, she wanted to set a precedent and open their home to a large cross section of the base.

Although Essie had never entertained huge numbers of people before, she and her sisters had helped their mother prepare meals for a family of ten on a daily basis, and she had learned the importance of organization in the kitchen as well as having access to numerous helping hands. She was confident that she was ready to stage a big party. When the list reached 85 guests for the first Christmas celebration at Tyndall, she realized she would have to serve heavy *hors d'ouevres* rather than a formal dinner. She devised an especially creative menu featuring both seafood and international cuisine, and at the last minute she took a risk by including marinated Brussels sprouts.

Jim planned to hire a bartender from the Officers' Club, but Essie's housekeeper mentioned that bartending was her husband's trade and that she would provide her services free of charge for the evening to assist Essie in any way she was needed. It was a deal too good to pass up, and the Randalls were delighted when the young couple arrived several hours before their guests. Wearing a form-fitting, designer dress and hair beautifully coifed, Essie's housekeeper had transformed overnight into a beautiful social butterfly who flitted among the guests while casually emptying ashtrays, refilling trays of food, and surreptitiously mixing in with the women who remained at the bar enjoying cocktails served by her husband…who was the spitting image of Robert Redford.

Essie smiled as she realized her housekeeper's generosity was no doubt based on ulterior motives. She was also amused that one of the guests, who originally turned up his nose when offered marinated Brussels sprouts, always seemed to have another one on his plate when he frequently sneaked back into the kitchen for extra helpings of everything on the menu.

Soon the Randalls became noted for their Southern hospitality, and civilians as well as military members looked forward to receiving an invitation to the next gathering at the base commander's residence. Essie had developed quite the reputation for the delicious meals she served. One of their neighbors, a unit commander on base, facetiously complained that their dog Marcie seldom returned when they let her out in the morning. They discovered that the miniature silver poodle usually spent an hour or so in Essie's lap eating treats at her leisure before she returned home. When the couple ended up being assigned to Norway, which enforced a lengthy quarantine for animals prior to entry, the commander's family reluctantly gave Marcie to the Randalls, claiming their beloved pet had adopted Essie any way.

Just as Jim and Essie had hoped, family members accepted their open invitation to come for an extended visit. Not only was their 4-level home suitable for accommodating numerous overnight guests, but there was also a guest house on the property that featured a sitting room, bedroom, and bath. Oddly, it was also where the laundry room was located, a peculiarity that was handy for visitors but a quandary for Essie and her housekeeper.

Ora was the first to arrive, as expected, and at 78 years old she was as robust and opinionated as ever, but she was finally in awe of how her daughter-in-law had enhanced her son's life, and she thoroughly enjoyed her stay. Essie was pleased to have Ora's approval, but she was even more thrilled when her widowed mother Nancy traveled from Connecticut, where she was living with Essie's sister Jeannie, and upon her arrival she agreed to an extended stay.

Marcie, the former neighbors' poodle, had become entrenched as Essie's faithful shadow, but she quickly changed loyalties when Essie's mother arrived and petted her frequently. The following evening when Nancy meandered into the kitchen for a small dish of butter pecan ice cream, the poodle ignored Essie and whined for Nancy to take her for a walk. Instead, Essie's mother merely picked her up, and continued to stroll through the Randall's quarters, admiring their stylishly furnished home.

Nancy had never lived near the coast back home in McBee, South Carolina, and when she walked into the Randall's glassed-in Florida room, she stood spellbound and watched the fluorescent orange and blue sunset melt into the Gulf of Mexico. Waking up early the next morning, she decided to follow the urge to walk to the water's edge just beyond the field that extended from the Florida room to the beach. Once she wandered out into the early morning sun with Marcie by her side, she headed across the grass to embrace the grandeur of the mighty gulf and the marina that she could see in the distance. The scenery was breath-taking...except for one thing.

When Nancy returned home with Marcie, she rang the doorbell, which Essie thought was odd, but when she opened the door, she understood why. There stood a tail-wagging but sheepish Marcie, her curly fur embedded with sandspurs. A distressed Nancy, whose slacks were equally covered with the prickly stickers, apologized profusely to her daughter for the outcome of her impromptu adventure. Essie was not about to let either her mother or Marcie into the house at that point. Instead, she marched the two culprits out to the laundry room, which was in a small adjoining building, and handed a pair of leather gloves to her mom as she donned a pair herself. Both mother and daughter picked off endless sandspurs for the rest of the morning.

By the time Jim came home for lunch, Nancy and Marcie were finally permitted back into the house! Jim and Essie had restored their residence to its former glory, but the field extending from the Florida room to the shore was still thick with Florida's intrepid sandspurs. Nancy assured her daughter that they would eventually be laughing about the whole episode…as soon as the poisonous little barbs that remained under their skin stopped hurting.

An equally memorable but more touching moment was when Ora's beautiful sister Thelma and her husband Earl arrived for a visit. Thelma had not been blessed with a child, and so from Jim's birth she pampered him as her own. He had many memories of their times together, especially when she introduced him to the wonders of Washington D.C. and gave him a detailed tour of the U.S. Mint, where she worked. Essie and Jim prepared the guest house for them as though they were dignitaries, and since the Randalls were hosting a formal event at their residence for the holiday, Jim rented a tuxedo for his uncle, a modest man who was humbly grateful.

Like most events at the Randalls, the evening was a stellar experience for everyone, especially Jim's aunt and uncle. Thelma looked elegant in her softly draped white gown and her husband Earl was handsome in his tux. Throughout the evening both Jim and Essie would glance over to make sure their cherished relatives were enjoying themselves. Occasionally, they stopped to introduce the couple to various dignitaries or share a family memory with each of them.

At the end of the party after the last guest had departed, Jim was about to ask the couple if they'd had a good time. Instead, his uncle hugged him in appreciation, joyously spun around with his arms outstretched, and claimed, "I felt like I *was* somebody tonight!" Jim and Essie blinked away their tears at the poignancy of his happiness.

Both Jim and Essie deeply respected how hard their elders had worked and sacrificed so that their children could thrive. How they wished Jim's father Sam and Essie's father Richard could have lived to see what they had accomplished. The two men had literally worked themselves to death to make sure their children had their chance in life…an immeasurable gift a son and daughter could only repay with integrity.

Throughout the tour at Tyndall, Jim had continued to keep track of Chappie James and was so proud when his former commander was assigned to be Special Assistant to the Chief of Staff of the U.S. Air Force in December 1977. Only two months later Jim was shocked to learn that the towering figure of a man that he so admired was retiring in February due to serious issues with his health, specifically his heart. No one was prepared, though, when newspapers across the country carried front page headlines about General Daniel Chappie James' death on February 25, 1978, just two weeks after his 58th birthday in Colorado Springs. Chappie had given his all for his country and was buried as a patriot and a hero at Arlington.

Along with the rest of the international community, both Jim and Essie were grief-stricken by Chappie's passing. He was a bigger than life figure with such a heart full of love for his country. He often gave impassioned speeches about America that resonated with Jim, who felt the same way. The newspapers were full of remembrances and passages of Chappie's speeches that deeply moved Jim…one in particular.

I've fought in three wars and three more wouldn't be too many to defend my country. I love America and as she has weaknesses or ills, I'll hold her hand.

Jim already knew that he would be returning to the Chidlaw building to be Chief of Safety in June. He could not believe that Chappie was gone. After his own recent physical, it was a wake-up call for him.

CHAPTER 31

PIECING TOGETHER THE PUZZLE

Jim's remaining months at Tyndall were rewarding. He embraced his responsibilities with fervor and experienced the impact a leader can have beyond his talent as a military pilot committed to national security. He had spent glorious hours in the rarefied airways above the bright blue marble we call Earth—an image captured by astronauts' photographs from beyond the grasp of gravity. As a base commander, however, Jim witnessed the myriads of interactions that happen on a military installation on a daily basis, not only among the military members but also their families. After all his years on the flight line, he now witnessed the entirety of life in the military.

Looking in retrospect he marveled at the decades of peace Allied leaders had achieved from the moment he first left Tuskegee to attend college classes at Hampton Institute. Achieving his goal to enter the sacred brotherhood of aviators, he kept up with world events and was relieved that world leaders—both winners and losers—made a concerted effort to establish some form of civility between disparate factions. The result was the Cold War, but it had certainly been better than the real thing.

As a fledgling fighter pilot, young husband, and new father, Jim had survived 75 combat flights over North Korea, but he was just beginning to put the puzzle pieces of life together. By the time he was the commander of the Alert facility at Spangdahlem in post-World War II Germany—a country nearly dismembered by the actions of a maniacal Axis leader bent on scapegoating an ethnic group into oblivion—Jim witnessed the fragility of world peace. It became personal when U.S. backed Cuban exiles tried to overthrow Fidel Castro's communist regime. The devastating consequences of President John F. Kennedy's Bay of Pigs debacle led to the Cuban Missile Crisis.

The USSR's retaliatory action of placing ballistic missiles in Cuba pointed at the Southeast Sector of the United States with the intent of arming them with nuclear warheads, left the world teetering on the precipice of war. As commander of the Alert Facility in Spangdahlem, Jim had a front row seat to the epic confrontation.

He flew combat training missions over Africa in preparation for a showdown between Superpowers.

He sensed how close the world was to the unthinkable—a nuclear attack in the Western hemisphere. For an intense 13 days in October 1962, just two weeks after the family celebrated baby Patricia's first birthday, the world prayed that frantic efforts at diplomacy and reason would prevail. The possibility of a nuclear holocaust was terrifying. Fortunately, meeting strength with greater strength proved to be successful long enough for the United States and Russia to come to better conclusions. Proof of the U.S. military's superior capability was enough of a deterrent to quell the international game of "chicken" and who blinks first.

The ultimate challenge of how to maintain world peace was clear, and Jim fully understood his part in the puzzle. He never forgot how it felt to be watching from afar as his beloved country faced real peril. How must Tyndall's base commander have felt during the Cuban Missile Crisis? The burden of being responsible for the welfare of the people in the Southeast Sector must have been all consuming. A base commander would have seen the faces and heard the screams of those who would have disappeared in an instant in the poisoning clouds of nuclear dust…his own family included. Thoughts about how the story might have ended during the Cuban Missile Crisis were unsettling.

Over time there had become a tendency in society to avoid remembering history's lessons with the degree of intensity that those events demand, but not for Jim. He was painfully reminded in the skies over Hanoi as he drifted through space to enemies below. Chronic pain from injuries he experienced were daily reminders of the price of world peace. He would return to Chidlaw with a chess master's understanding of the pawns and the players. He realized he was still a vital member of the U.S. Air Force. He could now put together the puzzle pieces of his military experiences and see all the nuances in the big picture. He was looking forward to completing his tour at Tyndall with honor and going home…to Colorado Springs.

Planning for the move midst all the farewell events proved to be a challenge. Not only had both Jim and Essie made quite a few major purchases, but Essie had also acquired a veritable garden center of plants, which she didn't want to leave behind. She was especially fond of a stately Christmas cactus even though it had failed to produce flowers two Christmases in a row. Like their military friends, they knew the solution to their dilemma—U-Haul!

Since Jim had a truck with a camper attached, he installed the necessary equipment and hooked up the rented U-Haul. With the cautious touch of a florist, Essie filled it with her prized plants while Jim supervised the movers. The Randalls had also hired a cleaning crew. After the Randalls' dreadful experience upon their arrival, they intended to greet the new Tyndall base commander and his wife with a vacant and thoroughly cleaned residence, ready for occupancy!

It was June 1978, a great time to be leaving Florida for the cool summer evenings in Colorado Springs, but Jim had one request as Essie began mapping their route—they had to go through Denton, Texas, on the way back home. He explained that a Black officer he had befriended during their tour in Germany had promised Jim he would give him his coveted secret recipe for barbecue sauce, if he visited him in Denton, Texas. Jim intended to hold him to his promise. Besides, Denton was the halfway point on their journey…almost. Soon the Randalls pulled up stakes and headed west.

After two days of enjoying delicious meals in Denton, Texas, Essie had to agree the stopover had been well worth it. She had also learned about marinating wild meat to remove the "gamey" taste, which was a useful hint since Jim was an avid hunter.

As they headed northwest for the final leg of their journey to Colorado Springs, the couple reminisced about what an all-encompassing experience the tour in Florida had been for both of them. Jim was personally involved with everyone on the base—entire families, both NCOs and officers, all the commanders, base hospital personnel, and chaplains. Additionally, he was the face of the military to civilians in Panama City and neighboring towns—the people in city government, business owners, local organizations. He and Essie had even attended the AME church in Panama City each Sunday.

As a fighter pilot, Jim had faced danger on many occasions, but as a base commander he had experiences he never anticipated. Being very organized, he woke up every morning totally prepared for the demands of his position, but fortunately he was also resilient, especially when a man appeared in the Tyndall Base Hospital with a gun. Calling the military police and the OSI (Office of Special Investigations) immediately, Jim headed to the hospital to remain onsite until the situation was under control. Fortunately, no one was injured so he returned home for a late dinner.

On another occasion, a young Black lieutenant who was teaching a night class on base asked another Black officer's wife, who was attending the class, to go to a movie with him. Foolishly, she agreed, but when he later made more serious advances, she reported him. Jim had no recourse but to make a judgment in accordance with the severity of his actions, which ended what might have been a promising career. Military law is stringent.

Both Jim and Essie enjoyed friendships with many civilians, especially the Gulf Coast State College President. They were often invited to dinner parties in Panama City, some of which turned out to be thinly disguised political events. Jim was courteous, but also emphatic that as a military officer, he did not ascribe to involvement in local politics.

Jim received scrapbooks full of memories from units on base, and Essie received similar booklets from the two clubs she advised—the NCO Wives and the Officers' Wives. After hours of trading stories back and forth, they finally reached the Colorado state line just as Essie recalled the time she and Jim attended a special buffet dinner where serving tables were laden with seafood. Everyone knew that Essie loved shrimp, but for some reason she wasn't eating any. When a disappointed NCO wife asked her why, Essie meekly explained that she really didn't like to eat shrimp unless it was deveined. Then she lowered her voice in embarrassment and admitted that she did not like to peel and devein shrimp herself. The young woman looked surprised and disappeared. A few minutes later she returned with a plate of freshly peeled and deveined shrimp.

Everyone had a good laugh when Essie announced, "Anyone not willing to peel and devein their own shrimp doesn't deserve this!"

It was very late at night when Jim pulled into their driveway in Colorado Springs. He was exhausted and Essie was, too, so they decided to go straight to bed and tend to unloading everything the next day. Opening all the windows to let the cool breeze flow through the bedroom, they crawled under the covers for a well-deserved sleep only to be awakened a few hours later by the bright rays of the early morning sun. After a makeshift breakfast of what was left in the cooler in their camper, Jim unlocked the U-Haul and when he opened the doors, he stood back surprised and yelled for Essie. Worrying that something had happened to her plants, she rushed out and was as shocked as Jim. Knowing they would be traveling westward during the heat of summer, Essie had heavily watered all of her leafy beauties, which created a warm, humid environment in the unopened trailer. The result was quite spectacular. Essie's Christmas cactus was at long last in full bloom!

Returning to Chidlaw was more like a homecoming than a new assignment, but Chappie's absence was notable. There were no more big dinner parties at his house with Chappie holding court in his inimitable way. He had visited Tyndall several times while Jim was the base commander and with his love of seafood and dancing, Chappie's big personality filled the room. At Chidlaw, where staff members were accustomed to his powerful presence, his absence was palpable.

Jim decided to fill the gap by inviting groups from Chidlaw over for dinner and quickly learned that Essie had retired from her former position as hostess to an entire base. She reminded Jim that he now had the coveted barbecue recipe and if he grilled the main course, she would provide the vegetables and dessert. Much to her amazement he prepared the entire meal, graciously served it, and mingled among the guests throughout the night. Even more surprising was that after the party he insisted that Essie retire for the evening while he cleaned the kitchen. The following morning when she stepped into a spotless kitchen, she praised him for his hidden talents. He assured her that it was a one-time performance.

Meanwhile, Laura, the Randall's precocious little neighbor, had been somewhat tamed by public school and was now totally committed to becoming an ice skater. She practiced with her coach at the famous Broadmoor Hotel's ice rink, and Essie now attended her performances as a devoted fan, championing Laura's latest dream to become an Olympian.

With Jim's encouragement and his observation that Essie's experience as a military wife would be especially helpful to other military families in the process of moving to Colorado Springs—both U.S. Army and Air Force—Essie decided to return to the workforce. She had earned her real estate license before they moved to Tyndall, and so it was easy for her to step back into the role of realtor, but instead of doing so as a salesperson she pursued and obtained her broker's license. Since Jim traveled in his position as Aerospace Defense Command's Chief of Safety, Essie became ensconced in her new role in local real estate and unintentionally transitioned into life after the military. For Jim it was not so easy.

In 1980, retirement ceremonies for Jim lauded his 31.5 years of dedication to the U.S. Air Force. They acknowledged his service to his country in World War II, Korea, and Vietnam. That little boy who looked out his bedroom window in Virginia and dreamed of being a pilot had attained 7350 hours of flying time as he traversed the sometimes troubled skies above Earth's massive continents and oceans.

He led flights across the Atlantic 8 times as he ferried aircraft to America's Allies across Europe, and he led flights across the Pacific 8 times in F-111s and F-105s to support U.S. efforts in Southeast Asia. He was a Command Pilot and an Iron Eagle whose left breast pocket of his uniform was a rainbow of colorful ribbons acknowledging him as a patriot—the Legion of Merit, Distinguished Flying Cross, Bronze Star, Meritorious Service Medal, Air Medal, Purple Heart, and Congressional Gold Medal.

On November 9, 1980, Jim added the one final official document to the tattered oversized manila folder, which contained sacred documents—his individual flight records that confirmed every hour, every aircraft, every destination in his amazing career. Military pilots dread adding that final document to their records because it states the reason that they are no longer on flying status. For many fighter pilots, especially those who are medically retired, it is a painful transition, but in a life full of unexpected twists and turns, there were still quite a few more surprises awaiting Colonel James E. P. Randall.

For the first month or so after his retirement, Jim seemed to be adjusting to having his wings clipped, but his relaxed demeanor was deceptive. He had actually been working on how to approach Essie about his dream of buying an airplane. He had found a deal that he just could not pass up, he explained one night over dinner.

In spite of Essie's warning about the time-honored admonition that "If it seems too good to be true, it probably is," Jim was convinced that owning an airplane would be an adventure. They could take off on trips without all the hassle of boarding crowded commercial flights. They would have full control of their journey and be more flexible about their destinations. The aircraft he had in mind was a Commander—a 6-seater that the owner, a pilot himself, explained he planned to rent from Jim so that he could run a courier service. Jim figured that the cash flow from frequent rentals would offset his payments substantially, and they could enjoy taking friends and family on short trips when the aircraft wasn't being used for courier flights.

Of course, Jim had been in operations on the flight lines of bases across the world, and so he was familiar with the cost of fuel, which had begun to soar, but Essie pointed out that the military covered the cost of mechanics and maintenance, insurance, investigative teams in case of accidents, rent for storage facilities, etc. What would those monthly costs be? Besides, she added, if a courier business could offset all those expenses, why was the pilot selling his plane? Jim was the owner of the plane before he had answers for all Essie's insightful arguments.

The original owner made several courier flights and covered the cost, but after a few months he explained that circumstances had changed and he planned to move back East. Essie rolled her eyes at the flimsy explanation, but Jim had planned a special trip to see family over the Christmas holidays so Essie bided her time as she balanced the checkbook and made detailed monthly lists about the cost of the 6-seater Commander.

There was a memorable trip where the Randalls hosted a flight and took friends to Salida, Colorado, for breakfast and another one to Wyoming, but other activities began to take precedence over the Commander, which sat gathering dust in a hangar most weeks. At one point Jim asked Essie to join him as he practiced "touch and go" landings. Once airborne, he would drop down on the landing strip, taxi a short distance, and then take off to fly a loop across Colorado Springs again. After completing the sequence half a dozen times or more, Essie finally said, "Enough." It was at that point she decided to share her observations as well as her mathematical calculations about the actual cost of flying off to have breakfast in a nearby city or spend an afternoon "touching and going."

She didn't stop there, though. She had also researched the cost of taking a cruise to an exotic far off place, something Jim had never done. Choosing promotional flyers about Alaska because of its uniqueness, Essie was armed with enticing photos of Alaska's unimaginable beauty—breaching whales, snowcapped Denali glowing golden in an Alaskan sunset, glaciers extending down into the arctic water, polar bears with cubs on ice floes. Essie was so excited that Jim agreed to make Alaska their destination.

Since Essie's beloved sister Jeannie was finally retiring, they invited her to join them on the adventure. Traveling through the northwestern states to reach British Columbia, they embarked on a cruise ship and for the first time Jim marveled at all that was happening beneath him as he flew across the vast oceans of the world. Reaching Anchorage, they boarded a motor coach with two knowledgeable college students, one who served as the bus driver and the other as a tour guide. Destination: Fairbanks…361 miles!

Jim enjoys going on a cruise with Essie after finally relinquishing his airplane, the red and white Commander. He had to admit it is easier crossing the Pacific on a cruise ship. He has done it many times the hard way…in the cockpit of either an F-105 or an F-111.

The two young men had planned many activities, beginning with a Gold Diggers' breakfast early the next morning followed by panning for gold in Alaska's bone chilling, ice cold streams. A late afternoon dinner on a boat preceded boarding the train on a narrow-gauge railway to experience the summer explosion of blossoming fireweed that painted endless fields with ethereal pinks and purples blending like watercolors. At such a northerly latitude, the sunset seemed to be followed by a sunrise within just a few hours. The adventures were almost non-stop.

Low-hanging clouds concealed parts of the magnificent snow-shrouded Denali as the bus traveled through the park with its quarry of tourists, but a big surprise was right around the bend. Turning the motor off, the youthful driver let the vehicle quietly drift downhill until he was within sight of one of Mother Nature's wonders—a mother bear nudging her furry little cub to cross the road. Everyone fell silent, enchanted by the sight. Jim had to admit that Essie was right. Adventures on land can be compelling. Nature does not disappoint.

After the trio returned to Colorado Springs, Jim willingly parted with his red and white Commander when he realized how many cruises he and Essie could take if they sold it. Besides, you couldn't beat the spacious accommodations on a cruise ship in comparison to the Commander's cockpit and additional 4 seats for guests. It was the beginning of a wonderful series of trips abroad for the two world travelers.

CHAPTER 32

THE REST OF THE STORY

It was Essie's 67th birthday and she had taken a flight back to Columbia, South Carolina, to be with her older sister Nancy, a yearly tradition since the two sisters shared the same birthday. When you grow up in a family of 8 children, celebrations are a major event, and Nancy, being 12 years older than Essie, was usually the focus of attention, but to Essie it was always magical because their birthday fell on the winter equinox, December 21st. This time, though, Nancy was in the hospital recovering from a stroke, and Essie was determined to lighten her older sister's spirits.

Accustomed to daily phone conversations with her favorite younger sister, Essie persuaded Jeannie to fly down from Norwalk, Connecticut, to be part of the celebration. Booking her flight weeks in advance, Essie begged Jim to accompany her, but he wanted to drive instead…one last big adventure on the road for an aging fighter pilot who had reached his 70th birthday in November. He made advance arrangements at the guest cottages on post at Fort Jackson in Columbia, though, so that Essie and Jeannie would have comfortable accommodations as soon as they arrived.

After only a few hours of rattling around in an empty house and missing Essie's cooking, Jim soon regretted his decision, and so he decided to drive back east sooner than he had planned. Instead, he could arrive just in time to surprise his wife several days before her birthday, but first he had to maneuver around a roadblock. His doctor.

Over the years Jim had developed some troubling issues with his heart, and his primary care physician had made it clear that lifestyle changes were in order for the former fighter pilot. Driving cross-country alone presented risks, he warned, so Jim checked with his cardiologist Dr. David Greenberg and eventually negotiated a compromise with the equally concerned heart surgeon. By agreeing to take a copy of his medical records and promising to seek medical attention if he experienced any worrisome symptoms, Jim made a convincing argument, and his doctor reluctantly sanctioned the impromptu trip.

Following his physician's advice, Jim picked up his medical file, alerted a neighbor of his plans, and joined myriads of holiday travelers on the highway. In spite of brisk temperatures, the sun highlighted the cerulean blue of the December sky. It was perfect weather for flying, but a road trip across the country would have to suffice. Reaching Tennessee, Jim stayed overnight, but by the break of dawn, he was on the road again and reached Columbia, South Carolina, late the next afternoon.

Delighted about making the journey without incident, Jim stopped long enough for a beer and a burger before checking in at the Fort Jackson VOQ to make himself presentable. When he arrived on the doorstep of the Randalls' guest cottage on the army post before dusk, Essie's wide-eyed look of surprise when she saw her husband captured the moment he was looking for. Mission accomplished.

Never anticipating that Jim would be in town, Essie and Jeannie had already planned an all-day shopping spree in Columbia for the following morning. Since Jim had no interest whatsoever in that venture, he took off for an auto parts store, instead.

After checking out much of the inventory, he bought just a few items—a protective shield to go across the front of his radiator, a bottle of cleaning compound, and a can of wax. When the attentive young clerk at the counter rang up the total and bagged the purchase, he was unusually courteous and asked if Jim would like help out to his car. Stunned, Jim pointed out that he only had three items, but the clerk continued to stare at his customer and hesitated for a moment before shrugging his shoulders and handing over the small bag. He didn't push the issue, but he seemed to be inexplicably troubled by something. Perplexed, Jim thought it odd but hurried off to get busy working on his red Lincoln Navigator. He liked to keep it in tip-top shape.

After stopping briefly for the guard at Fort Jackson's gate, Jim glanced over at the huge hospital complex near the post's entrance and then drove straight to the guest cottage to change into some old clothes. Always happy when working on his car, he was intent on restoring the hood, which bore the carnage of insects and grime accumulated on his cross-country trip.

He was about halfway finished with the surface of the hood, when he doubled over in pain. It felt as though something had hit him in the chest, and suddenly he was not feeling very good at all. Cautiously, he ambled over to a big oak tree close by, leaned his back against the bark of the trunk and slid down to the ground.

After 10 minutes or so of resting, he felt totally fine again so he hurried back to his car. The sun beat down on the metal as he worked the cleaning compound into the hood, and soon he surfaced a shine when he rubbed off the film of cleaner. Standing back to admire his work, he was surprised by another jolt in his chest. This time when he sat down, the discomfort continued, and Jim couldn't ignore the fact that he might be in trouble. Real trouble.

Remembering the promise to his cardiologist, he decided he better go to the hospital. He knew where it was. He had passed it each time he had entered and exited the gate, and so he got behind the wheel and headed toward help. As he reached the facility, he saw a huge Emergency sign and turned into the parking lot where he noticed an Army captain standing on the corner chatting away with a guy in civilian clothing.

Searching for the emergency room entrance and feeling weaker by the minute, Jim was unaware that he was becoming somewhat disoriented, too. He didn't know that he had circled the medical facility until he saw he was approaching the captain and his friend once again. Realizing he needed assistance, Jim slowed to a stop, lowered his window, and asked directions to the emergency room entrance.

The friendly young officer walked out to the car to be helpful, but after taking one look at the confused driver, he noted that Jim didn't look well and perhaps shouldn't be behind the wheel of a car. Offering to drive Jim to the emergency room, check him in, and park his car, the captain took charge of the situation. By now Jim was in such pain and so alarmed, he was grateful for help. He handed over his keys to the total stranger.

Moments later, the captain left the car idling in front of the building and rushed to the passenger's door to assist the ailing older man. Holding Jim up by grabbing him around the waist, the concerned officer draped Jim's arm around the young man's neck. Seconds later, the two men entered the doors of the emergency room.

Suddenly doctors appeared from every direction as hospital attendants placed Jim on a sheet-covered gurney. One of the physicians leaned over and asked Jim how he was feeling. More relaxed, knowing that he was in the protective care of trained medics, and being concerned that his family had no idea where he was, Jim lied. He insisted he was much better and could probably return to the guest quarters to rest. Then that electrifying jolt slammed him in the chest again and there was no hiding the pain.

Trying not to alarm his patient, the physician firmly explained that he would not be releasing Jim. Instead, he planned to air-evac his new patient to the hospital in Augusta, Georgia, a facility that he felt was better equipped to deal with the situation. But when Jim experienced yet another excruciating spasm, the doctor quickly changed his mind. It was obvious that Jim was in serious distress. He wasn't going anywhere. There wasn't time.

Pain became constant and blotted out Jim's ability to speak intelligibly. Soon reality dissolved into the realm of the surreal as medical personnel hooked him up to tubes dangling from aerial bottles, secured to mobile posts. Caught up in the whirlwind of synchronized trauma care specialists, Jim was whisked away by the concerned medical staff while the captain who had rescued him faded into the background. Random thoughts burst across Jim's mind without form or sequence. He didn't even know the name of the officer who had helped him, but the determined young captain had certainly been Jim's guardian angel.

Strapped to a gurney that was now being rolled down a hallway toward some mysterious destination, Jim watched the lights in the ceiling fly by as he tried to hold on to consciousness. Mind-numbing anesthetics dripped into his veins, easing his pain but making it difficult to focus his thoughts. *Essie. Essie doesn't know where I am. Have to reach her. Let her know. Essie doesn't....*

Drifting in and out of feverish dreams with no sense of time or place, Jim slowly emerged from the fog of sedation. Aware of a presence by his side, he opened his eyes. He was in a hospital room with two men dressed in olive drab scrubs. The younger one stood in respectful silence when the older man stepped closer and announced that Jim's condition was going to require immediate attention. It became obvious that he was the attending physician when he explained that he would be performing Jim's surgery in the morning. Then the surgeon whispered something to the younger man and walked out of the room, leaving Jim with dozens of unanswered questions and increasing anxiety.

Thinking that the young man who had remained by his side was probably an orderly or medic, Jim didn't ask him questions about the impending surgery that crowded his troubled mind. But feeling alone and facing frightening prospects, Jim was grateful for sympathetic company.

The doctor was in and out and checking on Jim several times during the next few hours. Finally, after reviewing test results and assessing exactly what Jim's surgery would entail, the military doctor explained what the staff had arranged. Early the following morning, Jim would be transported by ambulance to the university hospital in Columbia for cardiac surgery.

Having no control over his situation, Jim was under such duress that he couldn't go to sleep. Cardiac surgery? What did that mean? Cardiac surgery had advanced to the point that surgeons were even removing hearts and replacing them with artificial devices. Jim feared the worst and the seasoned veteran broke into tears. He would drift off for a few minutes, but soon awaken. Fear about the approaching surgery gnawed away at him.

Meanwhile, personnel at Fort Jackson had somehow located Essie. She and Jim were to have had dinner that evening with Norris Rubenstein, a civilian engineer Jim had known at the Chidlaw Building, but after their foray into Columbia to go shopping, the two sisters impulsively stopped by a nursing home for an unscheduled visit to see Lulu B. Bryan, a superintendent of a school the Aldrich girls had once attended. They were running late by the time they returned to the guest cottage. Essie was worried that Jim would be concerned about her. Instead, Jim was nowhere to be found. He had simply disappeared.

Essie was seldom unnerved, but she was frantic over what might have happened to him, and as soon as she and her sister Jeannie received word of his whereabouts, they rushed to the hospital on Fort Jackson. They visited with Jim throughout the evening to comfort him, but in his heavily medicated state he was hallucinating and certain that surgeons were going to remove his heart and replace it with an artificial one. He remembered articles he had read about it, he insisted, and he began pulling out all the IV tubes dripping both nutrients and sedation into his body. With the help of the attending nurse who restrained Jim, Essie continued to reassure him that such a complex procedure only happened in extreme situations. Unconvinced, Jim was fixated on his fears, but he was too weak to fight the inevitable and calmed down. Of course, Essie and Jeannie could not stay the night, and so eventually they went back to the guest cottage to get some rest before the vigil at Richland Memorial Hospital the following day. Once again Jim was alone, except for the faithful young medical staff member who never left the room.

Jim slipped in and out of consciousness throughout the night and each time he awakened, Jim learned a little more about his companion. He seemed like a youngster, but it turned out he was actually a registered nurse, who tried to ease Jim's fears by engaging him in casual conversation. At one point Jim asked where the attending nurse was from, and the young man laughed as he named two small towns rarely, if ever, mentioned in the news. He added, "You probably don't have the slightest idea where they are." He was stunned when Jim could literally give the coordinates for the area, and so the curious male nurse asked, "How did you know where Shelby and Kings Mountain are?"

The young man stared in shock when his patient responded, "Because I landed an airplane between those two towns."

"Are you a pilot?" the younger man persisted. When Jim answered that he was, the nurse's face lit up. "Well, we had a pilot land in my grandfather's wheat field one time." The young man went on to describe how he and his friends grew up with the legend of the Black pilot who had fallen from the sky and ended up touching down in the midst of the family's property. A field of winter wheat, to be exact.

He explained that it had happened long before he was born, but he and all his friends often scoured the fields to retrieve bits and pieces of metal, traces of the plane left in the soil after the pilot's fateful landing. He described how every discovery of the tiniest bit of evidence was an historic relic to young Black boys set on adventure and proving the legend true. The boys saved their dirt-encrusted treasures, considering each one a talisman that might bring good luck. Looking at Jim, the amazed nurse sputtered, "Then you must be—"

"I was that pilot," Jim finished. Speechless, his wide-eyed young companion put his hand to his gaping mouth and nodded his head in amazement.

The room fell silent for a moment as both men were transported to a place of wonder, realizing how incredulous it was that their lives crossed paths at this particular moment in time.

Jim remembered the kindness of the Black farmer who had taken off his overcoat and draped it over Jim's shoulders to comfort the young pilot, shivering with the cold and in shock. That was back in December 1953. Now as Jim faced the trauma of surgery, an especially compassionate Black nurse comforted and calmed him. First a farmer and 47 years later, his grandson appeared by Jim's side when he most needed a friend. It was something far more than coincidence. It was a miracle, truly one of life's blessings.

Finally, Jim fell into a deep sleep. When he awakened, he was in the recovery room of Richland Memorial Hospital. His surgery had been successful. Although his watchful night nurse was no longer with him, a bond—never to be broken—had been forged between Jim and his young companion. Nurse Douglas Oates and Jim remained friends for a lifetime.

And that's the rest of the story…

CHAPTER 33

THE COLORS OF PATRIOTISM

When Jim was well enough to leave the hospital in downtown Columbia, South Carolina, and return to Colorado Springs, he was reminded that there are good people everywhere. He was grateful for the outstanding and compassionate medical care he received in a state that once rejected his children. Life can come full circle if that is society's intention.

Once back home, Jim paid a visit to his distressed cardiologist who advised him to slow down and accordingly set him on a regimen to regain his strength. Since travel was temporarily out of the question, Jim engaged himself in meaningful activities to express his appreciation for life itself. He was a lifelong member of Payne Chapel AME Church and was involved with several civic organizations, but nothing quite compared to the camaraderie he experienced with a group of spirited fellows who served in WWII as Tuskegee Airmen.

As a photographer who documents many Tuskegee Airmen events with his camera, Mike Kaplan becomes good friends with Colonel Randall. (Photographs in this book capturing Jim as a Tuskegee Airman are courtesy of Mike Kaplan)

Standing line abreast: Superintendent Lt. General Michelle Johnson, Colonel James Stewart and Tuskegee Airmen James Randall, Randy Edwards, Franklin Macon and seated Marion Rodgers.

As the youngest member of the Tuskegee Airmen Hubert L. "Hooks" Jones Chapter, Jim joined with colleagues Franklin Macon, Clarence Shivers, Sam Hunter, Randy Edwards, Lowell Bell, Marion Rodgers, and Loran Smith to visit youth in public and private schools to share the Tuskegee Airmen's role in history. Dressed in identifying red jackets adorned with medals acknowledging their exploits, the group sought to inspire their very young audiences to pursue a good education as the foundation for achieving their dreams. In 2007, President George Bush recognized all Tuskegee Airmen with the Congressional Gold Medal for a "unique record that inspired revolutionary reform in the Armed Forces" so youngsters were thrilled to meet a few of them.

Colonel James Randall places a wreath at the Tuskegee Airman sculpture, which is featured on the Terrazzo at the U.S. Air Force Academy. The sculpture is by Tuskegee Airman Clarence Shivers.

Jim loved the cadence of a classroom…the buzz of excitement upon the elderly pilots' entrance and the immediate silence when the teacher introduced each guest. The youngest children usually sat cross-legged on the floor and smiled broadly in anticipation of what they were about to learn. Every visit with wide-eyed and curious youngsters invigorated Jim, and the students sat mesmerized as he shared some of his adventures. Being in the company of innocent and questing minds and answering their sincere questions with both wisdom and humor, Jim thought of the nurturing environment teachers and librarians had provided for him, and he tried to repay the debt. He always returned home in good spirits and with renewed hope for the future after spending a morning in the midst of vibrant youngsters.

Left: William Randall, Louise Lawler, Roberta Rollins and Patricia Rotenburg.
Right: Mary Ann Bell Randall.
The Randall family, though living in different states, gathers for special occasions.

Jim's own children were scattered across the country. After graduating from UNLV, Billy received his law degree at UCLA and returned home to become a Las Vegas lawyer, addressed as William. Louise graduated from UNLV with a degree in physical education. As a United Airlines flight attendant when the tragedy on 9/11 shocked the nation, Louise left the airlines and earned her master's degree. She joined the school system in Atlanta, Georgia, as a physical education teacher. Both Roberta and Patricia found positions with insurance companies and focused on health insurance, Roberta in Colorado and Patricia in Austin, Texas. Jim was proud of his children, but he realized that his demanding career had often prevented his sharing whimsical moments with them, reflections that he now enjoyed recounting in Colorado Springs' classrooms. Duty, honor, country exacted a price. Consequently, the one thing Jim relished in retirement was the possibility of spontaneity and holidays with family.

Ora Randall, Martha Hunter, Jim, and Bernice Marshall. Each time Jim is assigned overseas, he makes a point to travel back East to visit with his mother and sisters.

Ora is a frequent visitor each time Jim receives a new stateside assignment. She remains a strong and capable woman until her death at 101 years old.

One Sunday morning when Essie's mother Nancy was in Colorado Springs for a lengthy visit, the Randalls took her to the Protestant church service in the magnificent cathedral at the U.S. Air Force Academy. It was always a special experience when the morning sun shone down through the mosaic of colored glass tracing each of the spires that created the roof of the sanctuary. The subtle kaleidoscope of colors danced unpredictably above parishioners as clouds controlled when each color would shine, a celestial rainbow.

With the huge silver propeller-like cross suspended in space above the clergy at the front of the cathedral and the rich chords of a pipe organ accompanying the choir in the loft behind the congregation, the service had touched Essie's mother deeply. After the service, though, there were at least a dozen concrete steps to climb down to reach Jim's car and at an altitude of over 7,000 feet, Nancy was winded.

Jim was helping Nancy as she struggled to get into his awaiting automobile, when a Black cadet rushed down the cathedral steps. Dressed in his bright blue uniform with silver braid adorning the epaulets on each shoulder, the handsome young man raced to the Randall's car to offer his assistance. It was a serendipitous moment for both the Randalls and the thoughtful young man, who became a part of their life.

The Air Force Academy had a program that permitted civilian families to sponsor cadets during their tenure at the college, but it was voluntary and the number of sponsors fluctuated. Cadets were enterprising, though, and once Jim and Essie rewarded the young man with an invitation to join them for dinner, he didn't wait to be issued a sponsor. He adopted the Randalls.

Word about Jim quickly got out among the cadets on campus. They were very excited to learn that there was a distinguished retired Black fighter pilot in their midst! It was the beginning of a deeply rewarding relationship between Jim, Essie, and their burgeoning "family" of Air Force Academy cadets who could not believe their good fortune. Jim was a living legend, and his advice was based on his personal experience as a seasoned fighter pilot. He had flown a combined total of 119 combat missions over North Korea and North Vietnam. He had survived being shot down. He had credibility.

Of course, another major reason the Randalls drew a crowd of cadets to their home was equally important. Essie was a good-natured hostess and a great cook, with emphasis on the latter. Like the cadets, Essie had lived at boarding schools since she was in 10th grade, and she truly empathized with the loneliness of being away from home. For homesick Black cadets, the Randalls were more than sponsors. They welcomed cadets not only into their home but also into their hearts. They became family, a relationship the aspiring officers maintained long after hats were flung high and Thunderbirds roared overhead at the Air Force Academy graduation.

As it turned out, Jim's bond with students even extended across the Atlantic Ocean. He was truly overwhelmed when he received a very special invitation in the mail one afternoon. The envelope adorned with foreign stamps was postmarked France, and it was clearly addressed to him so there was no mistake. Perplexed, he quickly opened it and was stunned when he realized that it was from his first class of students at Craig AFB, the Class of 1951—Michael Durand, Claude Roumilhac, and Claude Bonson! How in the world had they located him after more than half a century.

Jim was overcome with sentiment and deeply humbled as he read that his former students from villages across France were planning a reunion, and they wanted to honor him as their instructor when they were hopeful young pilots learning to fly the P-51 at Craig AFB in Selma, Alabama. To be fondly remembered after such a long time moved Jim to tears. He had held himself to a high standard throughout his life and valued everyone who crossed his path, but he had never realized what an indelible impression he had made on others. Such a loving act of kindness and appreciation was a gift beyond anything he had ever imagined in life. He felt blessed.

Essie suggested that flying over to France for the reunion might be the perfect opportunity to catch a rail to Germany and take a sentimental journey across the country since they had both been assigned there, though at different times. Jim agreed and he immediately responded to his former students, accepting their invitation to the reunion and notifying them of his plans to travel first to Germany to sightsee with his wife Essie and then meet them in France. He briefly described his experience as commander of the Spangdahlem Alert Facility and the dramatic point in history he experienced there as his reason for the side trip. The Frenchmen were ecstatic that Jim and Essie planned to join them in France afterwards. According to their travel plans, Jim shared the day and approximate time they expected to reach Paris, and his hosts designated the meeting place—the base of the Eiffel Tower.

The reunion in France unfolded like scenes from a movie. Everyone had grown older, but the affectionate Frenchmen embraced Jim and warmly welcomed Essie in Paris with the same exuberance they had shown as young men. They had planned every aspect of the Randall's 10-day visit as meticulously as though it were a military mission. They arranged for everything—lodging, transportation, visits to historic sites, dinners at special restaurants as well as exceptional meals in each of their homes. Even more importantly, they set aside time each evening to reminisce with one another for hours about all that had happened in their lives. It was a joyous experience for Jim, seeing the country through the eyes of his students. It broadened his perspective of France in contrast with the impressions he formed in 1959 at Etain during America's confrontation with de Gaulle. He felt great pride in the people his former students had become.

Returning to the States after the reunion, Jim pondered having surgery on his back. You don't eject from an F-105 at mind-numbing speeds without paying a price, especially by the time you are in your seventies. Jim had ferried aircraft across the Atlantic 8 times without incident, but one round trip to Paris and back on a commercial airliner had been painful. Convinced that skilled surgeons at the Air Force Academy could alleviate the gnawing pain and discomfort in his neck and back, he finally agreed to an operation.

Following the surgery, Jim was in pain but optimistic as he returned home for a week or so of rest before beginning rehab. After the first few days he was still feeling fragile so he decided to retire earlier than usual one evening. He was just beginning to drift off to sleep when the phone rang. He could hear part of Essie's muffled answer as he rolled over on his good ear.

"Jim," she called softly as she shook him on the shoulder and handed him the phone. "There is someone from Lincoln, Nebraska, who would like to speak to you." Sitting up and putting his hand over the receiver Jim mouthed, *I don't know anyone from Lincoln, Nebraska,* but Essie urged him to take the call so he responded. The man at the other end of the line wanted to know if Jim was the James Randall who had been a fighter pilot in Southeast Asia.

Jim acknowledged that he was, and the caller asked, "Were you flying F-105s with the 562nd TAC Fighter Squadron?" Again, Jim acknowledged affirmatively.

"Well, I have some good news for you."

"What is it?" Jim asked. He was now fully awake.

Without answering the question, the man said, "You were shot down over there, weren't you?"

Growing suspicious, Jim answered, "Yes, I was."

"Well, I know where your helmet is."

"You WHAT?"

"I know where your helmet is," the man repeated.

"How do you know it's MY helmet?" Jim asked in disbelief.

"Because there's the squadron designation, the stencil on the side of the helmet, and your name is on the helmet. I have been over to Cambodia several times because I have a friend over there who makes knives. He's the one who has your helmet."

Stunned, Jim asked, "How did he get my helmet?"

"From what I understand he was in Ho Chi Minh City walking down the street one day and passed a flea market. He saw this helmet hanging there and he said, 'That looks like an American helmet.'"

"Well, okay. Where are you now?" Jim was surprised to learn that the fellow was within a mile, as the crow flies, from where Jim and Essie lived. He had traveled down from Nebraska and was visiting his son in Monument, a small community nestled at the edge of the mountains north of Colorado Springs.

After a brief discussion, Jim learned that the stranger, Gary "Paco" Gregg, was a retired stone mason and a Vietnam veteran who lived in Lincoln, Nebraska. The friend he mentioned was Dominque Eluere, actually a renowned Samurai sword and knife maker in Phenom Penh, Cambodia. Once Paco learned of the helmet, he set about trying to locate the pilot. His attempts to receive assistance from the U.S. Air Force were met with a strange reaction. The military would not give him any information whatsoever. It was as if they had never heard of James Randall. The U.S. Air Force implied that he was not one of their pilots.

More curious than ever and unwilling to give up on the search, Paco placed an ad in various military-related news services requesting information about a pilot named Randall who was possibly shot down over North Vietnam during the war. Much to his delight he received an answer from a retired pilot, who claimed that there was a Jim Randall in Colorado Springs who was shot down in North Vietnam in 1965. Paco scheduled a trip to see his son in Monument, and upon arrival he began calling each Randall in the phone book, and BINGO! Essie answered the phone.

"I would like to come over and see you," Jim said. He was tuned in now, wide awake and full of questions. Paco gave him directions to his son's house and welcomed Jim to join him the following day. Hanging up the phone, Jim was initially shocked the military did not confirm that he was the owner of the helmet and that officials offered no help, but in thinking back to that era of military history, he recalled that the missions he and his colleagues were flying were not officially acknowledged by McNamara and his crew at the Department of Defense. Was that section of his records sealed? He was a patriot, and he did not want to cause a stir, but he wanted his helmet. It was personal.

Jim was so full of anticipation that he tossed and turned midst snatches of sleep until the Colorado sun finally slipped above the horizon. Showering and getting dressed as quietly as possible, he planned to leave, but Essie insisted that he sit still long enough to relax a bit and have breakfast with her first. Soon he was off to pick up freshly baked donuts at the store and head to his meeting with Paco. He was so excited that he hardly noticed the occasional twinges of pain in his back.

Paco was waiting with a fresh-brewed pot of coffee when Jim arrived, and the two sat at the kitchen table munching donuts and hashing over the events that led to their finally connecting. As it turned out Dominque Eluere had bought the helmet some years ago, thinking that it should be returned to its rightful owner, but he didn't know where to begin the search. When he mentioned his concerns to Paco, the veteran immediately accepted the quest.

"Do you have the e-mail address for this individual who has my helmet?" Jim asked.

When Paco said that he did, Jim continued, "Do you have time for us to e-mail him and get a reply? Could he send a picture of it so I can make a positive identification?"

Paco agreed that was a good idea, and he immediately sent an e-mail explaining that he was sitting with the helmet's owner. Could they get a picture of the helmet? Since Paco was a veteran himself, the two men fell deep into discussion about the military and had lost track of time when less than an hour later, Eluere responded to the e-mail. He included a photo of the white plastic helmet with a familiar blue stripe extending down the middle. Jim read the words above the visor, "Maj. Randall." With tears of joy he declared, "No doubt about it. That's my helmet!"

Almost 48 years had passed since Jim's gloves and watch were stripped from his arms during the incredibly forceful ejection from his F-105. His only mementoes from the dramatic experience were chronic pain in his neck and back…until now. Staring at the photo of his helmet was like seeing a beloved friend that you thought had been lost forever. The only thing better would be to see a photo proving Pogreba was still alive.

Once Jim confirmed the helmet was his, Paco and Eluere arranged to have it shipped back to the States. Since Jim and Essie planned to attend the 42nd National Convention of Tuskegee Airmen, "Bridge to the Past—Gateway to the Future," in St. Louis from July 31st to August 3rd, Jim suggested that returning the helmet at that time would be a significant experience for all the elderly pilots attending the event. Eluere agreed but his schedule was too tight to make the trip. Instead, he made plans to mail the helmet to Paco so that he could make the presentation in St. Louis. Out of gratitude Jim insisted on covering all the expenses for Paco and his wife to attend the Tuskegee Airmen's Convention as his guest.

On a memorable August 1st in St. Louis, Missouri, Paco walked to the podium at the center of the head table for the formal Heritage Luncheon and looked out at the sea of elderly pilots attired in distinguishing red jackets adorned with insignia and medals. Touched by the sight of the colors of patriotism, the veteran gave an eloquent speech describing the personal mission that led him to be with such an honorable group. With the venerable Colonel James E.P. Randall at his side, Paco concluded his remarks by lifting the white linen cloth on the table and revealing a familiar white helmet with a blue stripe tracing the middle from front to back.

Gasps of reverence and awe rippled through the air as long-ago memories of each aging pilot filled the room with emotion. The significance of the moment inspired everyone to jump to their feet and applaud. Swallowing hard, Jim said, "The good Lord was with me that day," as he stood before his brethren in arms overwhelmed, uplifted by the uniting power of true patriotism. A white plastic helmet symbolized their sacred and unflinching commitment.

Duty. Honor. Country.

A year after the Tuskegee Airmen reunion Jim receives a surprise visitor from Cambodia, Dominique Eluere, who discovered Jim's helmet in Hanoi. Dominique travels to the United States to meet Jim personally. Jim, Gary "Paco" Gregg, and Dominique pose by the enshrined helmet for a photo.

Jim sits in his home office after returning from a Tuskegee Airman celebration on the Terrazzo at the United States Air Force Academy. Surrounded by framed citations and medals, he smiles as he reflects upon the remarkable circumstances that led to the return of his long-lost helmet.

Wearing his bright red Tuskegee Airman jacket adorned with medals, Colonel (ret.) James E.P. Randall stands beside his pilot's helmet with the oxygen mask still attached despite his being ejected into space from his F-105 Thunderchief hurtling toward destruction at over 575 mph.

CHAPTER 34

RIGHTEOUS RESOLUTIONS

After returning to Colorado Springs with the long-lost helmet, Jim and Essie relaxed, thinking that was the end of all the excitement, but that was just the beginning. The following day they received a phone call from another gentleman. While visiting his daughter's family, he had read the initial article about the missing helmet in Colorado Springs' newspaper. He was fascinated and had instinctively sketched a design for a wood-framed glass display case for the helmet. He wondered if the Randalls would mind if he came over to take measurements of the helmet so he could embark on the project.

Touched by such kindness, Jim and Essie welcomed him to their home and learned he simply wanted to do his part in honoring a patriot. He explained that he planned to return to visit with his daughter's family at Christmas and hoped to finish the project by then. In the ensuing months they did not hear from him, but as Christmas approached they received another phone call. He had waited to put the glass panels in place until after he reached his daughter's house, but everything was assembled now.

Reunited with the compassionate stranger, Jim was amazed by his craftsmanship. The wood had been carefully chosen and the result was stunning. Not only had he created the glass display case but also a small modular table to place it upon. Lifting the helmet into its new resting place, he thanked his friend and remarked that it looked like a museum display. Essie agreed and pondered that thought.

Paco had accomplished his mission of returning the helmet, and an amazing friendship was his reward. The two veterans continued to correspond. However, to have a total stranger share his talent and expend so much effort out of regard for an aging fighter pilot was deeply touching. Jim and Essie took him to breakfast as a gesture of appreciation, but he turned down Essie's efforts to reimburse him. He insisted, "It was my privilege. A lot of people would've loved to have the opportunity to honor Colonel Randall. Thank you for your service, Sir."

After such an indescribable experience Jim did not expect that yet another surprise lay ahead. Checking the return addresses on the letters in his hand as he walked back from the mailbox one afternoon he puzzled over an unfamiliar name, Randall Owens. Opening the letter, he realized that it was an introduction from a student at the University of South Carolina. Apparently, the young man, Randall George Owens, was a PhD candidate, and he hoped Jim would agree to an interview. Jim was quite confused about why a total stranger would want to interview him until he read the topic of the young man's thesis—

G.I. JOE V. JIM CROW: LEGAL BATTLES OVER OFF-BASE SCHOOL SEGREGATION OF MILITARY CHILDREN IN THE AMERICAN SOUTH, 1962-1964

After all these years, had there finally been a resolution to the lawsuit he waged on behalf of the Shaw Fourteen? It was 2013. He began doing the mental math and realized that 50 years had passed since he and his family were first assigned to Shaw AFB and encountered the untenable circumstances of school segregation. What was the outcome of the court proceedings? Once he left Shaw AFB in South Carolina for his re-assignment to McConnell AFB in Kansas, he never heard anything more about the case.

Then his life took such a dramatic turn on October 13, 1965, when he was shot down over North Vietnam, that he forgot all about his effort to receive justice for his children and all the other children denied the right to attend school with their peers—both White and Black.

Jim hurried to the desk in his office and began composing a letter to Mr. Owens on his computer. Glancing over at his helmet, perfectly positioned in its protective glass case, he could not stop smiling. He never imagined that anything more amazing than getting his helmet back could ever happen, but fighting for justice for children was one of the most audacious decisions of his life. He couldn't wait to find out what had transpired. He carefully edited as he enthusiastically replied to the doctoral student's request. Satisfied with what he had written, he printed out the letter and drove to the nearest branch post office to send his response by certified mail. He was anxious to get answers to all his questions. Within a few days Jim received a call from Randall Owens, who asked Jim if he would consent to a telephone interview.

Jim had done some preliminary research and learned Randall Owens was an impressive man. He was a graduate of Florida State University and had already accomplished several advanced degrees—a Master of Arts from the University of South Carolina, a Master of Science from Troy University, a Master of Military Operational Art and Science from the USAF Air Command and Staff College in Montgomery, Alabama, and a Master of Liberal

Studies at the University of Oklahoma. Jim was quite certain that his mother Ora would have loved to meet this fellow. She had lived to be 101 years old and was keenly interested in everything that involved her son, but unfortunately, she died in 1999 before he was acknowledged by all these surprising accolades. Mary Ann had passed away in 1990. He regretted that she did not live to learn the outcome of their lawsuit.

Connecting for the telephone interview with Randall in October, Jim explained that he was eager to be of assistance and would gladly provide the contact information for Roberta, Louise, and Billy who had experienced the trauma of being separated racially from their peers. First, though, he wanted to know what the verdict was. Did they win the lawsuit?

Jim was amazed by Randall's detailed answer, but the astonishing result of the lawsuit was that all schools in South Carolina were fully integrated. After hearing the Sumter School District's legal stance, Judge Hemphill called their arguments in favor of segregation "irrelevant and invidious," and he "invoked precedent and the U.S. Constitution's Fourteenth Amendment to dismiss the district's claim."

On August 8, 1964, Judge Hemphill ruled in favor of the plaintiffs, the Shaw Fourteen. Children in Sumter County School District, South Carolina, including all the children from Shaw AFB, both Black and White, boarded school buses headed to the same school in September 1964. Listening intently, Jim realized that was when his own children once again attended integrated schools…in Kansas. Wow! What a victory! He was overwhelmed with gratitude. Children had been attending integrated schools in the Sumter County District of South Carolina for five decades, and he did not even know it! His belief in "liberty and justice for all" was vindicated.

Randall completed his interviews with Jim and members of his family, but the two had developed a friendship, and once he was awarded the Degree of Doctor of Philosophy from the University of South Carolina in 2016 for his efforts, Randall sent Jim a copy of "*Chapter 6: Shaw Air Force Base and Sumter County, South Carolina.*" Jim read every word with great pride. Sam and Ora would have been so proud. Watching their son racing his red tricycle across his grandmother's back yard, they never would have guessed the impact he would make in support of his country.

There was still one more surprise to be revealed, though.

In all their conversations Randall Owens harbored a secret that he never spoke about to the elderly fighter pilot that he had come to admire, but he had a mission of his own. It took several years to accomplish, but on February 13, 2019, Shaw AFB held a formal ceremony to install an official South Carolina historic marker on base acknowledging Jim personally and the Shaw Fourteen for their successful effort to open the doors of Sumter County District Schools in South Carolina to all children.

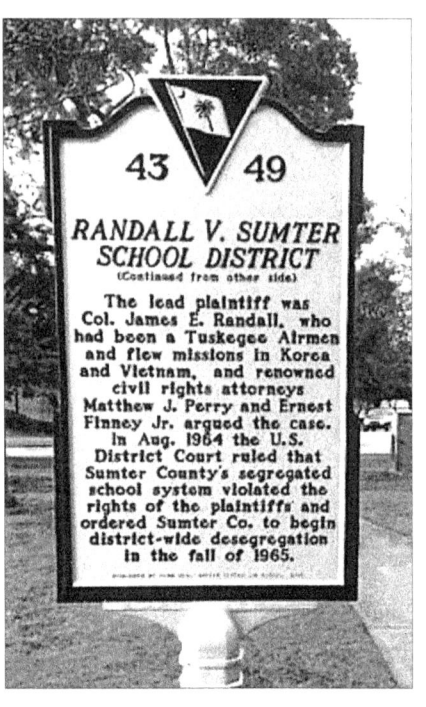

Colonel Derek O'Malley hosts the celebration to honor Jim and the Shaw Fourteen. He presents a photo of the F-51 Mustang for William Randall to give to his father. (Photo courtesy of Staff Sgt. William Banton)

William inspects the historic marker that recognizes the accomplishments of the Shaw Fourteen, led by Jim, in their quest to ensure the rights of children to attend school together. (Photo courtesy of Staff Sgt. William Banton)

Jim was in fragile health so he was unable to attend the ceremony, but his son William flew to South Carolina to represent his father at the festivities. Meanwhile, Mark Dickerson, President of the Hubert "Hooks" Jones Chapter of Tuskegee Airmen in Colorado Springs, worked in conjunction with Shaw's communication experts, and they provided live coverage of the event through a videoconference so that Jim could watch the entire ceremony and be able to speak to all the military members assembled in his honor.

Jim sat at his dining room table intently watching the whole spectacle on his computer with Essie, his daughter Roberta, her husband Mack, and Mark Dickerson seated behind him. He was transfixed as he watched the attentive and uniformed younger generation stand at attention as the ceremony began. In his heart he was right there with them, and he sat up straighter when Colonel Derek O'Malley, the 20th Fighter Wing Commander set the tone for the ceremony. Enrapt, Jim smiled as he listened to the senior officer emphasize the importance of stepping forward, even when your stand may not be welcome, but it is the right one. Nodding in agreement, Jim thought of all the times he had been inspired by one of his commanders. He had followed their example when he became a commander himself, and he never missed taking advantage of the teachable moment. Colonel O'Malley emphasized the reason they had assembled to honor Jim and his colleagues in uniform, The Shaw Fourteen.

We can never accept that the status quo is good enough. We can always be better, and just because a decision is hard, we can't just walk by it; we can't not make decisions because they are hard. That kind of perseverance is something Colonel Randall taught us so well. That we make hard decisions no matter what.

Dr. Randall Owens—whose dedicated research and determination to honor Jim and the Shaw Fourteen led to the state historic marker—shared the second stanza of the U.S. Air Force Airmen's Creed. Jim held the sides of his computer and he leaned closer to the screen as Dr. Owens began to read the stirring passage.

I am an American Airman. My mission is to Fly, Fight and Win. I am faithful to a Proud Heritage; A Tradition of Honor and a Legacy of Valor.

He continued by pointing out that Jim and his colleagues chose to heed that call to action and they pursued their stand against injustice regardless of the consequences.

Captivated by the somberness and dignity of the dedication of the historic marker, Jim was thrilled to see his son William participate in the ceremony. O'Malley also recognized the widow of one Jim's Shaw Fourteen colleagues who was in attendance. It had been a lifetime ago since he had last seen her.

Then Jim was invited to say a few words. The once virile and confident fighter pilot was now a diminutive and weather-beaten version of his former self, but his dark brown eyes sparkled with gratitude as he spoke. "Thank you so much for being here with me…to help me be here for the presentation of this plaque. Hope it remains there as a reminder for those in attendance as to what took place to get [it] there, and I hope it is there for a long, long time." It was his last hurrah.

For nearly four years Jim had been spending Tuesdays with his biographer to record all his memories, and now he knew how his story was going to end. He had reached that state of grace that transcends all understanding. At 93 years old and with Essie, Roberta and her husband Mack at his bedside, James Edward Preston Randall "slipped the surly bonds of earth" on December 9, 2019. He was truly an American Patriot, and the contrails of his life left the world a better place.

Watching the ceremony at Shaw AFB honoring him for his past efforts along with the Shaw Fourteen, Jim is reassured that the younger generation of the military will "carry on." Sharing the moment with him are Essie, Mack and Roberta Rollins, and Mark Dickerson, President of the Tuskegee Airmen Hubert L. "Hooks" Chapter. Addressing the troops one last time, Jim passes the torch of commitment to duty, honor, country. He can finally rest easy. Mission accomplished.

DE-BRIEFING: AN EPILOGUE

It might seem superfluous to add an epilogue to such an action-packed story, but like all the unexpected twists and turns in James Randall's amazing life, there was one more surprise awaiting the public. Essie and Jim had spoken at length about his end-of-life wishes, and following his passing, Essie made an effort to carry them out…beginning with the fate of his helmet.

When Dominique Eluere discovered Colonel Randall's helmet decades after his being shot down over North Vietnam, Gary "Paco" Gregg succeeded in locating Jim and returning it to him nearly half a century later. As a result of the helmet's circuitous journey across the world, Jim felt the storied helmet deserved a rightful place in the Smithsonian, and Essie pursued that goal. Much to the Randall family's delight, the Smithsonian agreed. In the summer of 2025, a white helmet with a prominent blue stripe tracing down the middle became part of a new exhibit honoring Colonel Randall at the Smithsonian's African American Museum of History and Culture.

Being acknowledged by the Smithsonian is the height of recognition, but I would like to offer my appreciation to some special people myself. First of all, I am grateful for Colonel Randall's commitment to his biography. It touched my heart when he handed his flight records over to me for research purposes. To a fighter pilot, nothing is quite so precious or carefully guarded as flight records. They list all imaginable aspects of each and every minute a pilot is airborne. For example, Colonel Randall's combat flights over North Korea were subtly denoted with a mere asterisk, but otherwise, the records were extensively annotated and signed only by authorized personnel. The flight records were the most reliable source of information available to me. They covered time lines, date of each flight and destination, type of aircraft, status of pilot (from student pilot to command pilot), pilot's rank, assigned Wing, etc. Discrepancies were always noted and amended; hours were meticulously entered and cross-checked. By the time Colonel Randall completed 31.5 years of service to the U.S. Air Force as a fighter pilot, his flight records were worn but fully intact, an irrefutable source of his accomplishments.

After completing the first draft of the manuscript, I began to search for readers. I hoped to find a military pilot or someone with an extensive military background. Tom Finneran, a former aviator himself, put me in touch with his good friend and former classmate at the Air Force Academy, Colonel (ret.) Samuel G. White III. Following graduation from the Academy with a BS in Aeronautical Engineering, Sam served 25 years in the U.S. Air Force. He commanded a B-2A bomber squadron as well as an operations group where he led B-52, B-1, B-2, KC-135, F-16, and RQ-4 squadrons. Currently, a 757/767 Captain and flight instructor for Delta Airlines, Sam also achieved an MS in Mechanical Engineering from Fresno State. He is a Command Pilot and Airline Transport Pilot with over 7000 hours of flight to his credit. When I learned that Sam also serves on the Red Tail Academy's Board of Directors, I could not believe my good fortune. Considering what a demanding life he leads, I am grateful that Sam found time to read the manuscript for Colonel Randall's biography. His insights, suggestions, and critiques were priceless. I deeply appreciate Sam's dedication to training American youth to be the future of flight. I count him as a friend. Thank you, Sam.

As an educator, I share treasured memories with many former colleagues, but I am especially indebted to Patti Marx, a former math teacher and dear friend. At my request, Patti filled yellow legal pad pages with her corrections, questions, and suggestions when she read Colonel Randall's manuscript. She was meticulous as she perused every page, recording her candid but honest reactions. Not only does she have an incisive analytical mind, but Patti grew up in an Air Force family so she was familiar with military life and its singular demands. Consequently, Patti had a sensitivity for Colonel Randall and his family. Like the Randall children, she lived abroad when her father, as a U.S. Air Force pilot, was assigned to NATO in Turkey, and she could appreciate how stark the transitions can be between moves—different educational systems, different languages or local colloquialisms and cultures. For family members, especially the children, there is always the demand to adjust quickly and be resilient even when uprooted without a choice in the matter. Patti had also experienced the impact war's drama can have on a military member, which can affect the family dynamic. Although Patti was not born until after World War II, she still has a copy of the Pilot's Statement that her father, 1st Lt. Morris Pitts, wrote after bailing out of his P 51-K over China during World War II. It began, "My engine failed about 30 minutes from the target area at 1135, 9 June 1945, while returning from a rocket and strafing mission on the Tainpu Railroad. I was forced to bail out at approximately 33 degrees 45'N – 115 degrees 12' E near a small Chinese village."

In great detail, 1st Lt. Pitts described Chinese villagers rescuing him and dressing him in Chinese civilian clothing before taking him to a small installation of Chinese soldiers who escorted him to Anping. They rode horses and gave the injured pilot a bicycle to travel the arduous journey. He remained under the supervision of Chinese soldiers four or five days and was interviewed by a General Wang who assured him that they would assist his rescue. Thus began a serpentine trek through small villages and military outposts. Arriving at a place pilots referred to as "Roger Two Sugar," 1st Lt. Pitts was joined by five Americans, POWs of the Japanese in Shanghai who had escaped. Chinese soldiers rode horses while 1st Lt. Pitts, nursing bruised thighs and a bruised shoulder, alternately rode or walked beside the mounted Chinese soldiers. The site at Pasture Field was too muddy due to torrential rains so the group continued to Valley Field where a transport awaited them. On 28 June, 1st Lt. Pitts returned to Ankang.

1st Lt. Pitts was relieved when he was returned to flight status soon after his ordeal. Patti's mother was even more grateful to learn that she could set aside the "Missing in Action" official papers she had received June 9, 1945. Thank you, Patti, for being so conscientious and helpful in the editing process of Colonel Randall's biography. I am glad to have the opportunity to share your father's story of courage and determination with the public.

Margaret Rivers, a friend who has joined me in many of my adventures to preserve stories about historic figures, also agreed to read the manuscript about Colonel Randall. She has always been active in the community and supportive of projects that enhance the culture of Colorado Springs. She has a generous spirit, a big heart, and a talent for bringing people together…partly because of her impressive culinary talents. Margaret has never been associated with military life personally, and so her reactions to Colonel Randall's manuscript were revealing. I was concerned about balancing the aspects of fighter pilots' missions and the terminology familiar to them that might not be readily understood by the general public. However, I also wanted Colonel Randall's story to be a tribute to the military, which meant writing some sections about the complexity of military missions in order to give appropriate credit to those in service. It was a conundrum.

I didn't hear from Margaret for a long time, and so I was afraid that I had failed the readability test that I was seeking. Finally, I picked up the phone to get the verdict. Margaret admitted that she had waded through lengthy passages about specific aircraft missions, accidents, and types of crises that she could not really envision. Then she added, "But I always knew there would be another good story coming up and that made it worth it." I really appreciated Margaret's candor. I hope readers feel the same way. Thank you, Margaret, for always being there for me.

I was equally concerned about the reactions of readers on the other end of the spectrum, those either on active duty or retired from military service as well as their families. I sent passages about combat flights to Colonel (ret.) Larry Burnette, my brother-in-law. Larry served two tours in Vietnam. His first tour was with the 6/15 Field Artillery Battalion, 1st Division (the Big Red One) from 1967-1968. The second tour was flying Cobra gunships with the 2/20 Aerial Field Artillery, 1st Cavalry Division from 1970-1971. Finally, he served on the Army General Staff in Desert Storm, February to August 1991. In retirement, Larry taught in a JROTC program in Bradenton, Florida, from 1993-2006. Thank you, Larry, for endorsing my efforts to portray Colonel Randall's military career with the respect he deserves. Also, thank you for serving with honor, both in military service and in your principled leadership of young men and women in JROTC.

Colonel Randall's wife, Essie, was a faithful supporter of my efforts from the first interview with her husband until publisher Rhyolite Press stepped in for the grand finale. Each time I completed a chapter, I read it to Essie so that she could offer her reflections and insights. She also listened patiently through all my revisions. Essie provided official military photos, pictures of past generations in the family, genealogical records, military records, medical records, letters, citations, and all manner of data that was helpful. She also shared all her memories, which enriched her husband's story. Over the years, Essie and I forged a friendship that will always be the most wonderful outcome of writing Colonel Randall's biography. Essie, I cannot thank you enough for always being my cheerleader.

Roberta Rollins, Colonel Randall's oldest daughter, readily shared treasured family photos, too, and she was always ready to step in and help. Thank you, Roberta. I was with Roberta and her thoughtful husband Mack on quite a few occasions, and their love and concern for Colonel Randall as well as Essie mirrored the closeness of my own family. It was painful to lose Colonel Randall and witness Roberta's grief. I could feel her love for him and the depth of her loss because I had felt the same way in 1965 when my father passed. It is such a personal connection. I hope you, Louise, William, and Patricia like your father's biography, Roberta. I know how much all of you loved him.

Thank you to Elynor "Dibba" Butler Hamilton, who sought information about the elusive Madora Thaxton Campbell Flood for me. To my sister, Dee Burnette, one of the kindest and most generous people I know, thank you for decades of championing my efforts to pursue meaningful projects. Finally, my sincere appreciation to Susie Schorsch, my editor, who remained dedicated to the task at hand until this book was worthy of Colonel James E.P. Randall, a true patriot.

NOTES

Chapter 1 All in Due Time   1

p. 1 The Gainsboro History Project, Chapter 3 "N&W Railway Becomes Source of African-American Jobs
https://gainsborohistoryproject.org/chapters/chapter-3

p. 2 "St. Paul's United Methodist Church"
https://gainsborohistoryproject.org/locations/churches-cemeteries/saintpauls-united-methodist-church

pp. 4-5 "Henry Street Business District"
https://www.hmdb.org/m.asp?m=134600

pp. 4-5 The Gainsboro History Project, Chapter 1 "Gainesborough: Roanoke's First Neighborhood"
https://gainsborohistoryproject.org/chapters/chapter-1

pp, 4-5 The Gainsboro History Project, Chapter 4 "Gainsboro Becomes Cultural and Business Center"
https://gainsborohistoryproject.org/chapters/chapter-4

p. 6 "St. Andrew's Roman Catholic Church"
https://gainsborohistoryproject.org/locations/churches-cemeteries/st-andrews-roman-catholic-church

Chapter 2 Wheels Before Wings
pp. 1-10 James Edward Preston Randall Family Tree and Pedigree Chart secured by Colonel

Randall through genealogical research in Roanoke, Virginia while in search of his mother Ora Evangeline Flood Randall's white grandfather—likely either the owner of the Thaxton plantation north of Roanoke or one of his 3 sons—who fathered her mulatto grandmother Madora Thaxton born in 1829. Madora's mother (Ora's great grandmother was the house maid for the white Thaxton family). Madora's Virginia birth certificate listed her as Madora Thaxton. Pauline and Wesley Campbell adopted Madora, and she became Madora Thaxton Campbell. Possibly, Pauline Campbell was the Thaxton house maid. Madora (b. 1845, Thaxton, VA) married Pleasant Flood (b. 1867, Bedford County, VA) and they had a son, Pleasant Preston Flood (b. 1872, Thaxton, VA)

Ora Evangeline Flood (Madora's granddaughter) married Samuel Edward Randall. Ora's mother was Martha Ellen Johnson (b. January 1878, Gretna, VA) and her father was Pleasant Preston Flood (b. 1872, Thaxton, VA.)

Genealogists, with whom Colonel Randall consulted, speculated that records about Madora Thaxton Campbell Flood's biological white father probably were destroyed.

Chapter 3   A Big Surprise in A Small Package   11
p. 11 Centers for Disease Control and Prevention 1933|CDC (gov)
Births Stillbirths, and Infant Mortality: 1933 p. 30
"Premature birth and congenital debility. The rates from premature birth and congenital debility show very slight variations from month to month, the highest rate from premature birth appearing for June and the highest from congenital debility appearing for October. As in previous years more deaths resulted from premature birth than any other cause, 27.2 percent of all deaths of infants having been attributed to this cause."
(Records do not indicate whether premature births delivered at home are included)
https://www.cdc.gov/nchs/data/vsushistorical/birthstat_1933.pdf

Chapter 4   A Few Broken Arms   17
pp. 17-18 The Gainsboro History Project, Chapter 6 "Neighborhood Schools Open Doors for African Americans"
https://gainsborohistoryproject.org/chapters/chapter-6

p. 18 Photographs from the Gainsboro Branch Library
http://www.virginiaroom.org/digital/exhibits/show/gainsboro-library-end-panels/gainsboro-library-images

Chapter 5   How the Other Half Lives   21

pp. 21-22 James Edward Preston Randall Family Tree and Pedigree Chart secured by Colonel Randall through genealogical research in Roanoke, Virginia.

Samuel Randall, Colonel Randall's father, had a sad childhood compared to his wife Ora. Samuel's father, James Daniel Randall was born in Fluvanna County, Virginia in May 1849. On November 14, 1878, when he was 29 years old, he married Anna Chandler who was born in Rockbridge County, Virginia, in 1862. She was only 16 years old when she became Mrs. Anna Randall. Her husband was 13 years older than she. Samuel and Anna had 3 children—Charles, Lily, and Samuel Edward Randall—Colonel Randall's father—who was born on June 15, 1881. Samuel was Anna's last child.

Tragically, Anna died sometime in 1883, when Samuel, her youngest child, was only a few years old. Samuel's father James Daniel Randall remarried a widow, Julia, who had 3 children—John, Lucian and Addie—and so little Samuel, Colonel Randall's father, was overwhelmed… lost in the crowd of 6 children. Samuel remained close to his sister Lily who married Henry Field. Visiting Aunt Lily and Uncle Henry's farm outside of Buena Vista was a very special occasion because, as an adult, Samuel (Sam), never had a vacation.

p. 24 "A Proud Legacy: History of Virginia Military Institute"
https://www.vmi.edu/about/history/

p. 24 VMI Archives
https://libguides.vmi.edu/fieldwork/early-years

Chapter 6. Decisions and Consequences   25

pp. 25-26 The Gainsboro Library
https://www.hmdb.org/m.asp?m=142998

pp. 25-26 Articles about Tuberculosis in the 1920s and 1930s, two focusing on Virginia. (Newtown, VA. Article about tuberculosis in the 1930s in the state)
https://newtownhistorycenter.org/pandemics-in-new-town/it-didnt-fade-mildred-lee-grove-and-tuber(culosis-1930s-late-twentieth-century/

Author: Laura Byrd Earle, Work Title: Pine Camp: From Tuberculosis Sanitorium to Community Center, Website: https://thevalentine.org
Published : November 7, 2024, Updated : November 18, 2024, Copyright : © 2025 The Valentine Museum

"A Gigantic Task: Treating and Paying for Tuberculosis in the Interwar Period" (CDC Document about tuberculosis in the period between WWI and WWII)
https://medcoeckapwstorprd01.blob.core.usgovcloudapi.net/pfw-images/dbimages/TB%20-%20chapter%2005-mark%20final.pdf

Chapter 7. Nothing But the Truth — 31
p. 32 Health Care and Medicine in Gainsboro in the early 1900s
https://www.hmdb.org/m.asp?m=142999

p. 33 Biography of Colonel Randall's childhood friend Carroll Swain,
From Cotton to Silk: African American Railroad Workers
https://fromcottontosilk.wordpress.com/bios/carroll-swain/

Chapter 8. Living Life to the Fullest — 35
p. 35 "fill the unforgiving minute with sixty seconds worth of distance run"
Excerpt from Rudyard Kipling poem "If: A Father's Advice to His Son"
https://www.newamericanjournal.net/2023/02/rudyard-kiplings-if-a-fathers-advice-to-his-son/

p. 35 Cannady Farm, site of Roanoke's first aviation landing strips, becomes Roanoke's airport
https://www.flyroa.com/history

Chapter 9. Reversing Roles — 39
p. 39-41 History of Hotel Roanoke
https://www.hotelroanoke.com/southwest_va_hotel/

p. 39-40 Biography of Colonel Randall's childhood friend Carroll Swain,
From Cotton to Silk: African American Railroad Workers
https://fromcottontosilk.wordpress.com/bios/carroll-swain/

Chapter 10 The Sound of Silence — 43
p. 44 *Stop Silicosis* (Film produced in 1938 by the US Dept. of Commerce)
https://archive.org/details/StopSilicosis

Chapter 11 Picking up the Pieces 47

pp. 47-48, 51 Lucy Addison High School
https://en.wikipedia.org/wiki/Lucy_Addison_High_School#:~:text=Lucy%20Addison%20
High%20School's%20first,1929%20during%20the%20Great%20Depression

pp. 47 Timeline for the life of Lucy Addison. Encyclopedia Virginia. Virginia Humanities.
https://encyclopediavirginia.org/entries/addison-lucy-1861-1937/

pp. 50-52 WWII Timeline, Duke University Libraries, Digital Collections
https://blogs.library.duke.edu/digital-collections/adaccess/timeline/wwii-timeline/

Chapter 12 Starting Anew 53

p. 54 "America's Black Air Pioneers, 1900-1939" Major Robert J. Jackeman. Student Report. Air Command & Staff College. April 1988.
https://apps.dtic.mil/sti/tr/pdf/ADA210437.pdf

pp. 54-55 "When the Color Line Ended," Herman S. Wolk. Air Force Magazine. July 1998. Army Chief of Staff, General George C. Marshall's stance on integrated military and Tuskegee
https://www.airandspaceforces.com/PDF/MagazineArchive/Documents/1998/July%20
1998/0798integrate.pdf

p. 55 Eleanor Roosevelt and the Tuskegee Airmen
https://www.fdrlibrary.org/tuskegee

p. 55 "Memorandum for the Chief of Staff regarding Employment of Negro Man Power in War, November 10, 1925; President's Official Files 4245-G: Office of Production Management: Commission on Fair Employment Practices: War Department, 1943: Archives of the President. Franklin D. Roosevelt Library, http://www.fdrlibrary.marist.edu

p. 55 The Army War College Studies Black Soldiers. American Social History Project/Center for Media and Learning. The Graduate Center at City University of New York.
https://shec.ashp.cuny.edu/items/show/808#:~:text=The%20cranial%20cavity%20of%20
the,leadership%2C%20and%20cannot%20accept%20responsibility.

p. 55 Georgia Aviation Hall of Fame: Major General Frank O'Driscoll Hunter
https://www.gaaviationhalloffame.com/hall-of-fame/?no_cache=1&tx_provider-search_providersearchfe%5Bprovider%5D=3387&tx_providersearch_providersearch-fe%5Baction%5D=show&tx_providersearch_idersearchfe%5Bcontroller%5D=Provider&cHash=d901d613259d70da93b673b05ef6f5d0

p. 55 New York Times digitized /archived obituary for Major General Hunter
https://www.nytimes.com/1982/06/27/obituaries/maj-gen-frank-hunter-dies-commanded-force-in-europe.html

p. 55 Freeman Field Mutiny
https://airandspace.si.edu/stories/editorial/mutiny-freeman-field-tuskegee-airmen-trial-part-2

p. 55 Freeman Field Mutiny
https://en.wikipedia.org/wiki/Freeman_Field_mutiny

p. 55 Freeman Field Mutiny. WWII Museum, New Orleans
https://www.nationalww2museum.org/war/articles/freeman-field-mutiny

p. 56 "Black Airmen turn racism, bigotry into opportunity." Randy Roughton, Air Force News Service, published February 4, 2014 Link—af.mil. U.S. AIR FORCE
https://www.offutt.af.mil/News/Article-Display/Article/659679/training-at-tuskegee-turning-dreams-into-reality/

p. 56 Colonel Randall's official discharge certificate from the military following World War II, which he kept in his files. The 2143rd Army Air Force Base Unit, Squadron A was Colonel Randall's unit at Tuskegee. He also kept his "Enlisted Record and Report of Separation and Honorable discharge. He received a World War II Victory ribbon.

Army of the United States, Honorable Discharge.
This is to certify that James E.P. Randall Squadron A, 2143rd Army Air Force Base Unit, Army of the United States, Honorably Discharged from the military service of the United States of America. This certificate is awarded as a testimonial of Honest and Faithful Service to this country.
Given at: Separation Center, Fort George G. Meade, Maryland. Date:22 February 1946
Signed: Richard C O'Connell, Lt. Col. AGD

Another official letter, which was given to WWII veterans following WWII, was from President Harry S. Truman. Colonel Randall kept the following letter—with seal of the President of the United States prominently displayed on the letterhead—in his file.

JAMES E. P. RANDALL

To you who answered the call of your country and served in its Armed Forces to bring about the total defeat of the enemy, I extend the heartfelt thanks of a grateful Nation. As one of the Nation's finest, you undertook the most severe tasks one can be called upon to perform. Because you demonstrated the fortitude, resourcefulness and calm judgment necessary to carry out that task, we now look to you for leadership and example in further exalting our country in peace.

Harry S. Truman
The White House

Chapter 13 Whirlwind — 57

pp. 57-58 (The official letter acknowledging that Colonel Randall separated from the military and then joined the Army Reserves in order to be eligible for pilot training when he completed 2 years of college. He kept the letter for his files.)

Feb. 22, 1946
Subject: Appreciation

WAR DEPARTMENT, The Adjutant General's Office, Washington 25, D.C.
To Pvt. James E.P. Randall, 126-7th Ave N.W., Roanoke, Virginia

1. It is desired to express to you the appreciation of the War Department for your continued service to National Defense through enlistment in the Enlisted Reserve Corps. Your aid and that of other veterans who, like you, are displaying an active interest by enlisting in the Reserve will be invaluable in building and maintaining a sound and effective postwar Army.

2. AR 150-5 and the other Army Regulations governing the Enlisted Reserve Corps will be revised to conform with such statutes as may be enacted to govern the postwar Army. Revised regulations and other information concerning the Enlisted Reserve Corps will be made available in the future.
BY ORDER OF THE SECRETARY OF WAR:
Edward F. Witsell, Major General, Acting The Adjutant General

pp. 58-59. Hampton University
https://home.hamptonu.edu/about/history

Chapter 14 Riding the Rails to Flight School 61

p. 61. Mosher, Willard C (1982) "Railway Postal Service-Revisited." The 470 Railroad Club (March 1982)

pp. 61-62 "Mail-on-the-Fly: Mail by Rail," Smithsonian National Postal Museum
https://postalmuseum.si.edu/exhibition/mail-by-rail/mail-on-the-fly

pp. 61-62 White, John H. (1978). *The American Railroad Passenger Car*. Baltimore, MD: Johns Hopkins University Press. ISBN 0801819652. OCLC 27981 188.

p. 64 Boeing: Historical Snapshot: T-6 Trainer
https://www.boeing.com/content/dam/boeing/boeingdotcom/history/pdf/Boeing_Products.pdf

p. 64 *Air and Space Forces Magazine*
https://www.airandspaceforces.com/weapons-platforms/t-6/

Chapter 15 Wings and A Wedding 67

pp. 67-68 F-51 Mustang mission to protect bombers in the Ploiesti oil field attacks in WWII
https://www.nationalww2museum.org/war/articles/over-cauldron-ploesti-american-air-war-romania

pp. 67-68 https://secure.boeingimages.com/archive/P-51D-Mustang-Fuselage-Wing-Join-2F3XC5FSGEC.html

p. 67-68 Mustang!
https://www.airandspaceforces.com/article/0364mustang/

p. 68 Portraits in Oversight:
Harry Truman and the Investigation of Waste, Fraud, and Abuse in WWII
https://levin-center.org/harry-truman-and-the-investigation-of-waste-fraud-abuse-in-world-war-ii/

Chapter 16 Logistics   71
p. 73 History of Perrin AFB Before and After WWI
https://perrinafbhistoricalmuseum.org/our-history/

Chapter 17 International Students in the Deep South   77
pp. 78 History of Craig AFB in Selma, Alabama.
https://www.selmatimesjournal.com/2019/09/20/from-its-earliest-days-craig-field-a-force-for-change-in-selma/

p, 78 1950 census records for Selma, Alabama
https://www2.census.gov/library/publications/decennial/1950/pc-02/pc-2-11.pdf (population of Selma, Alabama 1950 census. Listed under the county: Dallas. Specific population number listed as 22,629.)

pp.78-79 Lons-La-Saunier, France
https://en.wikipedia.org/wiki/Lons-le-Saunier

pp. 78-79 Poissy, France
https://www.britannica.com/place/Poissy

Chapter 18 From Combat in Korea to Diapers in Dover   81
pp. 81-83 F-51s in Korea, 1950
https://militaryhistory.fandom.com/wiki/USAF_units_and_aircraft_of_the_Korean_War

p. 83 Modern South Korean Air Power: The Republic of Korea Air Force Today
https://www.airuniversity.af.edu/Aether-ASOR/Book-Reviews/Article/3391609/modern-south-korean-air-power-the-republic-of-korea-air-force-today/

p. 83 USAF Organizations in Korea 1950-1953
https://www.dafhistory.af.mil/Portals/16/documents/Timelines/Korea/USAFOrganizationsin-Korea.pdf?ver=2016-08-30-151054-960

p. 83 Map of Korean Theater
Korean Theatre map, National Museum of the United States Air Force. 050428-F-1234P-002.JPG (download permitted)
https://www.nationalmuseum.af.mil/Upcoming/Photos/igphoto/2000573072/

p. 83 The difference between "P" and "F" designations for the Mustang. F-51 refers to the Mustang as a fighter plane; P-51 referred to "pursuit" as the designation. At Craig AFB, the Mustang was referred to as a P-51. Mustangs in Korea during the war were F-51s.

p. 84 The arrival of the 1737th Ferrying Squadron at Dover AFB
https://amcmuseum.org/history/the-flying-history-of-the-1607th-air-transport-wing-h/

Chapter 19 Icarus   89
pp.93-94 (To locate Randall's crash on the chart, list 531217 to indicate the year/month/day of the accident)
https://www.aviationarchaeology.com/listpages/airforce/asp/AF_Monthly_1953.asp

Chapter 20 The Pull of Gravity   97
pp.98-99. "Headquarters 3626th Training Group (Interceptor)Tyndall Air Force Base, Florida. Final Statement. Summary of Flying Training Evaluation of Proficiency." Official report in Colonel Randall's files dated 9 April 1954, issued following his successful completion of the course at Tyndall AFB, Florida.

p. 100 Colonel Randall retained Brigadier General B.E. Allen's 8 December 1955 letter noting his outstanding record in his files. Note: The letter uses the designation 1708th Ferrying Wing. Colonel Randall's squadron is listed as the 1737th Ferry Squadron. The terms "Ferry" and "Ferrying" seemed to be used interchangeably in designations of units. Also, Keflavik-Reykjavik is the name of the airport-city in Iceland, which was a ferrying destination.

pp.102-103 *Training Report. Capt. James E.P. Randall. Headquarters Air Command and Staff College Course: Squadron Officer (SOS) School, Class 56-A. From 9 Jan 56 to 13 April at Air University, Maxwell AFB, Montgomery, Alabama.* [Record in Colonel Randall's files of his performance in comparison to his peers.] As of 1959, SOS, Air Command and Staff College and Air War College became separate entities, but when Jim attended SOS in 1956, it was under Air Command and Staff College. One of the courses at SOS, at the time, was "Commander and Staff." The similarity in titles may be a cause for some confusion.

Chapter 21 A New Start in The West   105
p. 106 Personal conversations with Maxine Pogreba, who lived in Boulder, Colorado, regarding her husband, Dean "Pogie" Pogreba. Passages regarding Colonel Pogreba's WWII experiences are from her book.

Pogie 105 Missing in Action. Maxine Pogreba, Bev Pogreba. Independently published 2019. p. 107 After Colonel Randall had served effectively as the Base Ops officer at Nellis AFB, he had the chance to fly with Jacob "Shorty" Manch as his instructor. Tragically, Manch died in a crash one month later on March 24th, 1958. While Manch was airborne with a student, the aircraft "flamed out" over a residential area of Las Vegas. Manch instructed the student pilot to parachute to safety, but he remained with the plane to reach an area beyond the populace before it crashed.

During WWII, Manch was among the first pilots, members of Doolittle Raiders, to launch off an aircraft carrier to attack Tokyo, Japan, on 18 April 1942, in retribution for the Japanese attack on Pearl Harbor. Lt. Colonel Jacob Earl "Shorty" Manch is buried at Arlington.

p. 107 Burdette, Linda. Virginia Aviation History Project. "A Hero Among Heroes: Virginia's Shorty Manch."
https://www.vahsonline.com/pdf/A-Hero-among-Heroes-Virginias-Shorty-Manch.pdf

p. 107 LTC Jacob Earl "Shorty" Manch. 1918-1958. Arlington National Cemetery
https://www.findagrave.com/memorial/31298895/jacob-earl-manch

p. 107 Doolittle Raid. National Museum of the United States Air Force
https://www.nationalmuseum.af.mil/Visit/Museum-Exhibits/Fact-Sheets/Display/Article/196211/doolittle-raid/

Chapter 22 Life in Post-World War II Europe   109
pp. 109-110 Etain AB, France
https://military-history.fandom.com/wiki/Étain-Rouvres_Air_Base

p. 109 History of the Nevada Test Site (now named the Nevada National Security Site)
https://ahf.nuclearmuseum.org/ahf/location/nevada-test-site/

p. 109 Zone Rouge in France, post-World War I
https://www.warhistoryonline.com/world-war-i/zone-rouge.html
p. 109 Jacobs, Frank. "You Can Still Die From WWI Dangers in France's Red Zone." Atlas Obscura, April 26, 2024.
https://www.atlasobscura.com/articles/red-zones-in-france

p. 109 Red Zone
https://education.nationalgeographic.org/resource/red-zone/

p. 109 The Battle at Verdun, World War I
https://www.britannica.com/event/World-War-I/Major-developments-in-1916

p. 109 General de Gaulle Impacts US decisions about Etain AB
https://military-history.fandom.com/wiki/Étain-Rouvres_Air_Base

p. 111 Colonel Randall referred to the Belgian French that his hosts' children spoke as Belgique.

pp. 114-115 "The Years of Wheelus." Walter J. Boyne. "Air & Space Forces Magazine," January 1, 2008.
https://www.airandspaceforces.com/article/0108wheelus/

pp. 114-115 Wheelus Air Base
https://en.wikipedia.org/wiki/Wheelus_Air_Base

pp. 115, 117 "When the Wall went up: Britain and the Berlin Crisis, 1961." Dr. Richard Smith. 28 July 2021. (Written by a British historian, this is a synopsis of the circumstances leading to the Berlin Wall and the Cuban Missile Crisis in 1961.)
https://history.blog.gov.uk/2021/07/28/when-the-wall-went-up-britain-and-the-berlin-crisis-1961/

p. 117 *New York Times* coverage of the Cuban Missile Crisis (archived)
https://archive.nytimes.com/www.nytimes.com/books/97/07/27/reviews/crisis-23.html

p.118 General Lucius D. Clay Oral History Interview—7/1/1964
https://static.jfklibrary.org/kf3146m07eq840hn777a441xi38b81wy.pdf?odc=20231115182256-0500

Chapter 23 Showdown In South Carolina   123

p. 126 Equalization Schools: South Carolina's History of Unequal Education. Lowcountry Digital History Initiative. Lowcountry Digital Library College of Charleston.
https://ldhi.library.cofc.edu/exhibits/show/equalization-schools/public-schools-desegregate

p. 127 June 11, 1963: From George Wallace to John Kennedy, A Momentous Day for Civil Rights. Morgan Whitaker. NBC News. June 11, 2023.
https://www.nbcnews.com/id/wbna52172836

pp. 127-129 Owens, R.G. (2016) *G.I. Joe V. JIM CROW: Legal Battles Over Off-Base School Segregation On Military Children In The American South, 1962-1964* (Doctoral dissertation).
https://scholarcommons.sc.edu/etd/3434

p. 129 Background information about General Lawrence F. Tanberg
https://www.af.mil/DesktopModules/ArticleCS/Print.aspx?PortalId=1&ModuleId=858&Article=105414

p. 130 The Assassination of President John Fitzgerald Kennedy
https://en.wikipedia.org/wiki/Assassination_of_John_F._Kennedy

p. 131 Commander of Shaw AFB
https://www.airuniversity.af.edu/Portals/10/ASPJ/journals/1964_Vol15_No1-6/1964_Vol15_No6.pdf

p. 131 Organization of the US Air Force, 1964
https://media.defense.gov/2013/Jul/09/2001329950/-1/-1/0/AFD-130709-033.pdf

Chapter 24 On a Wing and a Prayer   133

pp. 135 562nd TAC Fighter Squadron. McConnell Air Force Base, Kansas.
https://en.wikipedia.org/wiki/McConnell_Air_Force_Base

pp. 135-136 McConnell AFB 835th Air Division Commander Maj Gen Edward McGough III
https://www.af.mil/About-Us/Biographies/Display/Article/106254/major-general-edward-a-mcgough-iii/

pp. 135-136 Bio of Major Gen Edward McGough III (835th Air Division Commander at McConnell) Gen. McGough was likely the commander in the photo on page 138. There were three changes of command that year, and General McGough arrived in the summer prior to Colonel Randall's training/soloing in the F-105 and left a few months later for his combat tour flying out of Thailand as part of "Rolling Thunder" to combat missions for North Vietnam.

https://www.legacy.com/us/obituaries/legacyremembers/edward-mcgough-obituary?id=8639697

pp. 138-139 835th Air Division at McConnell until November 1965
https://en.wikipedia.org/wiki/835th_Air_Division

pp. 138,139 355th Wing (ACC) at McConnell, 1964. Air Force Historical Research Agency
https://www.dafhistory.af.mil/About-Us/Fact-Sheets/Display/Article/432175/355-wing-acc

pp. 138-139 388th Tactical Fighter Wing Commander (p. 209 on document)
https://apps.dtic.mil/sti/tr/pdf/ADA154181.pdf
   This was a period of flux. The 388th TAC Fighter Wing fell under 12th Air Force and the 562nd TAC Fighter Squadron was one of four squadrons (560, 561, 562, 563) that fell under the 388th TAC Fighter Wing at McConnell AFB from October 1962 to 8 February 1964. Colonel Olin E. Gilbert was listed as the Squadron Commander from 1 October 1963 to 8 February 1964. The 23rd TAC Fighter Wing replaced the 388th TAC Fighter Wing in February 1964. Then the 388th TAC Fighter Wing replaced the 6234th TAC Fighter Wing in Thailand in 1966. The 388th Fighter Wing is listed as "not manned" from February 1964 until 14 March 1966.
   Colonel Olin E. Gilbert was replaced by Colonel Edwin B. Edwards in 8 February 1964, and Edwards was replaced by Colonel Deward E. Bower in 17 August 1964. Bower served until 12 July 1965. Colonel Randall arrived at McConnell AFB in June 1964.

pp. 138-143 Over a 3-year period, Colonel Randall's biographer taped interviews with him at his home each Tuesday. The sessions often ran as long as 4 hours. Consequently, the biographer would have him recount major stories frequently. This procedure led to a thorough explanation of his remarkable experience of being shot down over the outskirts of Hanoi, North Vietnam, on October 13, 1965.

pp. 144-147 Phillips, Dave. "Tales of Colorado Springs Vietnam War Vet's Lost Helmet Spans Globe, Decades." *The Gazette*. Colorado Springs, Colorado. July 21, 2013.
 8d https://gazette.com/news/tale-of-colorado-springs-vietnam-war-vets-lost-helmet-spans-globe-decades/article_6baf07a8-c837-50ad-93-a97944a709ae.html
(Article in the Colorado Springs *Gazette* that was written by Dave Phillips, who soon thereafter was hired by the *New York Times*. Phillips won the Pulitzer Prize for his articles about the military during his tenure at the *Gazette*)

p. 147 Colonel (ret.) Samuel White—USAF Academy graduate and a Director of the Red Tails Academy who served as a reader and consultant about Colonel Randall's biography—explained that the term "anti-gravity suit," used by Colonel Randall, is now referred to as a Zero-suit, G-suit, Zero-G suit, anti-G suit, etc. It a flight suit designed for pilots to reduce the impact of "pulling Gs" when fighter pilots experience high levels of acceleration force (Gs) during flight.
https://usafals-afe.net/wp-content/uploads/2014/02/The-Anti-G-Suit.pdf

p. 147 A "Mae-West" is a vest-like life preserver. When inflated it gives the upper body the buxom appearance of 1920s and 1930s film and stage actress Mae West.

Chapter 25 Encore at Nellis   151

p. 152 Nellis AFB TAC Fighter Weapons Center
https://www.nellis.af.mil/About/Fact-Sheets/Display/Article/284150/us-air-force-warfare-center/

pp. 152-153 Nellis Fighter Weapons Center/Major General Taylor
https://en.wikipedia.org/wiki/United_States_Air_Force_Warfare_Center
(Note: General Robert G. Taylor was Brigadier General Taylor when he became head of the TAC Fighter Weapons Center in 1966. He was still Brigadier General Taylor in captioned photo on p. 162.

p. 152-153 Major units assigned: 4525th Fighter Weapons Wing. 1 Sept. 1966 to 15 Oct. 1969.
https://en.wikipedia.org/wiki/Nellis_Air_Force_Base

p. 152-153 Nellis Air Force Base History, Units, USAF TAC Fighter Weapons Center
https://military-history.fandom.com/wiki/Nellis_Air_Force_Base

pp.152-154 On several occasions between, June 2017 and 2019, Jim related a detailed account of the fatal accident that General R.G. "Zack" Taylor ordered him to investigate to hypothesize the cause. He never veered from his account of exactly what happened. Although in his 90s, his memory was remarkable.

pp. 157-159 Stamped on the back of a General Dynamics photo of Colonel Randall with a General Dynamics engineer is the company's synopsis of the problem with the radar in the F-111, which Colonel Randall alerted them about; their follow-through proved him right.
As an F-111 test pilot at Nellis AFB Lieutenant Colonel Randall was the Ops Officer for

Operational and Suitability Testing of the F-111 from 1966-1971. Randall regularly performed maneuvers that would ordinarily be considered "derring do" but were necessary to constantly evaluate the F-111's capabilities and possible drawbacks. In this photo taken at Edwards AFB, California, Randall met with a young general Dynamics engineer to discuss a recent test flight, Flying over the sand dunes of Death Valley at very low levels—where the shadow of the aircraft on the ground was nearly the size of the plane indicating it was VERY low altitude, perhaps 100 feet above ground—the radar did not register accurately. Randall deduced that this was due to the polarization of the radar as a result of the density of the sand. (General Dynamics Fort Worth Division, Edwards AFB, March 20, 1967)

p. 157 Colonel Samuel White, USAF Academy graduate and Director of the Red Tails Academy, served as a reader and consultant about Colonel Randall's biography. He explained that the coined term "Wizzo" refers to the WSO or Weapons Systems Officer who accompanies the F-111 pilot on flights.

p. 160 "List of Accidents and Incidents. 1967-1969" The conclusions for each of the following accidents with which Jim was involved are listed by investigative teams as:

1967 January First General Dynamics F-111A first ever loss occurs when pre-production F-111A /c/n A1-09, lands short of the runway at Edwards AFB, CA due to improper wing sweep setting. The crew of 2 is uninjured but when the pilot Major Herbert [Foster] Brightwell goes around to unfasten the WSO Colonel Donovan McCance, he stands in a pool of JP-4, which subsequently ignites killing him. NOTE: More information about Foster Brightwell can be found in "Together We Served."

1968 September 23 General Dynamics F-111A crashes and is destroyed due to control system failure at Nellis AFB, Nevada. Crew ejected safely.

1969 May 29 A USAF General Dynamics F-111 on a training flight out of Nellis AFB, Nevada, crashes due to wind deficient windshield bulged down from the top of the canopy bow and instantly crazed. Tactical Air Command replaces 50 F-111 windshields in 1969 and 93 in 1970.

pp. 161-162 "The F-111—-A Pilot's Report." Senator Howard W. Cannon. Published in the magazine *Data*. September 1968. Article written by Senator Howard W. Cannon following his flight in the F-111A with Colonel James E.P. Randall as the pilot/instructor. It is a thorough overview of the aircraft with an explanation of the F-111s' unique emergency ejection system. Copy of the report in Colonel Randall's files has no designation about the publisher or magazine in which it appeared.

p. 162 The caption under the photo of Colonel Randall guiding Senator Cannon through a simulator session has the date—October 28, 1967—stamped on the back. It is the original official photo that Colonel Randall had in his personal collection and is the correct date.

p. 162 Note: In the captioned photo of Senator Howard Cannon, Lt. Colonel Randall, and General Robert G. Taylor, General Taylor was still Brigadier General Taylor at the time. He became Major General Robert G. Taylor effective March 15, 1968.

pp. 163, 166   Pages in Colonel Randall's files from "Colonel Tests AF's Hottest Combat Jet" *Ebony* magazine. May 1968 issue.

p. 163 Artist Roy LaGrone, former Tuskegee Airman who painted Colonel Randall as an F-111 pilot in 1968 on Nellis flight line.
https://www.af.mil/News/Article-Display/Article/114179/exhibit-features-work-of-tuskegee-airman-turned-artist/

p. 163 Artist Roy LaGrone
https://www.exploepinebluff.com/posts/the-art-of-tuskegee-airman-roy-lagrone

pp. 166-167 474th TAC Fighter Wing
https://en.wikipedia.org/wiki/474th_Tactical_Fighter_Wing
Photo: Colonel Chester Lumley Van Etten was the Nellis 474th TAC Fighter Wing Commander while Colonel Randall was stationed there, and so their interactions were almost daily. Colonel Randall deeply respected him and appreciated Van Etten pinning the shiny eagles of a new colonel on him. Colonel Van Etten had a distinguished and remarkable career, which bears recognition. His exchange with General Patton was a surprising story.

pp.166-167 Colonel Chester Lumley Van Etten
https://www.legacy.com/us/obituaries/nytimes/name/chester-van-etten-obituary?id=25185606

Chapter 26 Return to Thailand 169
p.171 The Mariana Trench

https://www.scientificamerican.com/article/the-mariana-trench-is-7-miles-deep-whats-down-there/

Chapter 27 The Librarian 175

p. 179 Photos with captions that capture the intensity of PACAF Jungle Training.
https://archive.ec47.com/survival.htm

pp. 180-181 Mather Academy. 1887-1983. South Carolina Encyclopedia.
https://www.scencyclopedia.org/sce/entries/mather-academy/
Essie, her 6 sisters, and her brother Richard all attended Mather Academy for the 11th and 12th grades since their small hometown of McBee only provided classes from "primer" to 10th grade. It was expensive because students who lived at a distance from Camden, SC, lived in dorms on campus during the school year.

Chapter 28 Crossroads at Nakon Phanom 183

p. 185 Sapper attacks in Thailand in 1970s
https://www.historynet.com/sapper-attack-the-elite-north-vietnamese-units/

p. 185 https://apps.dtic.mil/sti/tr/pdf/ADA586196.pdf
A previously classified document that covers the jungle forces in Thailand, Laos, and areas that Colonel Randall was involved with regarding his secret mission in Thailand.

Chapter 29 Honoring a Leap of Faith 189

p, 189 History of Eglin AFB
https:eglin.af.mil/Portals/56/documents/history/AFD-141104-075.pdf

pp. 190-191 History of Air Defense Command's Chidlaw Building in Colorado Springs, Colorado
https://www.wikiwand.com/en/articles/Chidlaw_Building
pp. 190-191 North American Aerospace Defense Command History, Colorado Springs, Colorado
https://www.norad.mil/About-NORAD/NORAD-History/

pp. 190-191 The Chidlaw Building.
https://military-history.fandom.com/wiki/Chidlaw_Building

p. 195 "Air Force's General Daniel "Chappie" James, Jr. Rose to 4-Star Excellence." Katie Lange. *DOD News*. February 2022.

https://www.defense.gov/News/Feature-Stories/Story/Article/2930686/air-forces-daniel-chappie-james-jr-rose-to-4-star-excellence/

Chapter 30 Taking Command 199
pp. 200-201 History of Eglin AFB, Panama City, Florida.
https://www.eglin.af.mil/Portals/56/documents/history/AFD-141104-075.pdf

Chapter 31 Piecing Together the Puzzle 207
p. 211 Jim was a colonel worthy of consideration of making general, but he did not receive that promotion; he became an "iron eagle" like his good friend Colonel (ret.) Van Etten, and he retired as a colonel after serving in 3 major wars—World War II, Korea, and Vietnam. He was accorded a special military retirement ceremony, which was hosted by Deputy Commander for Air Defense Tactical Air Command, Major General John L. Piotrowski, on Wednesday, March 5, 1980, in Colonel Randall's honor.

Chapter 32 The Rest of The Story 215
pp. 213-215 Moncrief Army Hospital, Fort Jackson, SC
https://moncrief.tricare.mil/About-Us/Our-History#:~:text=Moncrief%20Army%20Health%20Clinic%20History&text=Dedicated%20in%201972%20as%20Moncrief,quality%20and%20comprehensive%20medical%20care

p. 215 Fort Jackson: Historic Army Post
https://www.gatewaytothearmy.org/history

Chapter 33 The Colors of Patriotism 221
p. 223 Tuskegee Airmen Congressional Gold Medal
https://www.searchablemuseum.com/tuskegee-airmen-congressional-gold-medal/
pp. 228-230 Articles in the Colorado Springs *Gazette* and other news services about the return of Colonel's Randall's helmet after nearly half a century.
https://www.warhistoryonline.com/war-articles/after-decades-a-pilot-is-reunited-with-his-helmet-abandoned-after-being-shot-down-invietnam.html

pp. 228-230 Phillips, Dave. "Tales of Colorado Springs Vietnam War Vet's Lost Helmet Spans Globe, Decades." *The Gazette*. Colorado Springs, Colorado. July 21, 2013.
8d https://gazette.com/news/tale-of-colorado-springs-vietnam-war-vets-lost-helmet-spans-globe-decades/article_6baf07a8-c837-50ad-93-a97944a709ae.html

p. 230 Veterans in Blue
https://www.veterans-in-blue.af.mil/Veterans/VetLib/Article/745443/james-randall/

p. 230 CAF Rise Above. James E.P. Randall. July 12, 2023.
https://cafriseabove.org/james-randall/

pp. 230-231 "Convention Highlights. Thursday, August 1, 2013" Tuskegee Airmen Inc. 42nd National Convention. July 31-August 3, 2013. (Flyer among Colonel Randall's memorabilia.)

pp. 230-231 August 2013 Email communication between Dominique Eluere and Colonel Randall:

On Aug 9, 2013 at 5:04 AM, J E Randall wrote:

Dear Dominique,

These past two months have been the most exciting and emotional days of my life. During my thirty plus years of service to my country I received many awards and decorations, but none to match the pleasure I had upon the presentation of my helmet. Words cannot express how much I appreciate what you and Paco have done to ensure that the helmet would be returned to the rightful owner or his family. I am certainly grateful that the good Lord has kept me around long enough so that I could be the one to receive it.

There are still some good people in this world and you and Paco are tops in my book as being among the great ones. I have often thought the helmet could have been bought by anyone and retained as a war time trophy. However, you put forth the time and effort over the years to locate the individual whose name and organization appeared on the helmet. I know you are aware of how deeply my appreciation goes out to you. I really did enjoy the video that Paco showed of you at the convention.

When I was a flight instructor in Alabama, flying the F-51, three of my four students were from France. About twelve years ago my wife and I were invited to a class reunion in France. She and I attended and we had a most enjoyable week spent with my former students.

My helmet will be placed in a glass case and in a very conspicuous spot in my home. Best regards to you and I do hope our paths will cross one day.

Sincerely, James E. Randall

From: D Eleure Thu, Aug 08 2013 08:29
Subject: Re: Helmet Returned
To: J E Randall, James. James Randall, Colonel

There are indeed no reasons to thank me. I just did what I thought was right. And so did Paco Greg. I feel good knowing your helmet is back to you. This is my reward and it's more than enough.

I wish all the best. God bless you.
Dominque Eluere

Chapter 34 Righteous Resolutions 233

pp. 234-235 Information about Colonel Randall and the Shaw Fourteen's legal case is from Chapter 6 of the PhD dissertation of Dr. Randall George Owens, U.S. Air Forces Central Command theater security cooperation directorate country desk officer.

pp. 234-235 Owens, R.G. (2016) *G.I. Joe V. JIM CROW: Legal Battles Over Off-Base School Segregation On Military Children In The American South, 1962-1964* (Doctoral dissertation).

p. 237 Comments from Colonel Derek O'Malley, Dr. Randall Owens, and Colonel (ret.) James Randall printed in—
"History, achievements of Tuskegee Airman and the 'Shaw Fourteen' Airmen Celebrated." Capt. Neil B. Samson. 20th Fighter Wing Public Affairs. February 22, 2019.
https://www.shaw.af.mil/News/Article-Display/Article/1765171/history-achievements-of-tuskegee-airman-and-the-shaw-fourteen-airmen-celebrated/

p. 238 Colonel James E. P. Randall obituary, 1926-2019
https://obits.gazette.com/us/obituaries/gazette/name/james-randall-obituary?id=8459669
p. 238 "…slip the surly bonds of earth" is a reference from the poem "High Flight" by John Gillespie Magee, Jr., a fighter pilot in the Royal Canadian Air Force.

Biographer Kathleen Esmiol joined Colonel Randall, his wife Essie, daughter Roberta and her husband Mack Rollins, and Mark Dickerson, President of the Hubert "Hook" Jones Chapter of the Tuskegee Airmen in Colorado Springs, in the Randalls' home to photograph Colonel Randall's participation in the ceremony via video conference transmission.

The most extensive and significant aspects of this biography were gained through the 16 two-hour taped interviews of Colonel James Randall recorded by Biographer Kathleen F. Esmiol. Also, Colonel Randall entrusted his flight records to her, one of a fighter pilot's most treasured possessions...the documentation of every military flight he took, the date, base of departure, destination. return flight, hours of flight, etc. The flight records became a working outline for Colonel Randall's biography.

When will the conscience grow so tender that we will act
to prevent human misery than avenge it.
Eleanor Roosevelt

ABOUT THE AUTHOR

Kathleen Esmiol, recognized by Florida State University as a Distinguished Alumna, received her Master's in Gifted Education from the University of Colorado, Colorado Springs (UCCS). During her 25 years as an educator in the Academy District in Colorado Springs, Kathleen delighted in making history come alive for students by working with them to write and produce six plays and an opera. Prentice-Hall honored Kathleen as the 1996 Team Teacher of the West, and Disney selected her as the 2001 Middle School Humanities Teacher of the Year. Kathleen's dedication to researching and preserving important stories in history led her to study the Holocaust in Poland and Israel with WWII Jewish ghetto fighter Vladka Mead, and she spent a short stint in Blagoveshchensk, Russia, teaching English and American studies for the U.S. State Department. Her book, *Everybody Welcome: A Memoir of Fannie Mae Duncan and the Cotton Club*, received the Golden Quill award.

www.ingramcontent.com/pod-product-compliance
Lightning Source LLC
Chambersburg PA
CBHW041247240426
43669CB00027B/2996